Around the Kitchen Table

Elizabeth Colleen Jenkins

Copyright © 2011 Elizabeth Colleen Jenkins

All rights reserved.

ISBN:10 0615571859
ISBN-13: 978-0-615-57185-0

• DEDICATION

To my father who taught me to believe in myself; my mother who never lost faith in me; and to my wonderful family.

ACKNOWLEDGMENTS

I would like to thank my family who made this possible.

CHAPTER ONE

"We're going to have to move this in two sections, Newton." Jake said panting as he and his son tried to move the heavy oak table. It separated in the middle. They each took an end and had to stand it up on its end to get it out of the door to make a new home and new memories at the farm house that Newton had just purchased for him and his family on Shelbyville Highway on the outskirts of Murfreesboro, Tennessee.

The farm house was just down the highway from Jake's. The year was 1946.

"Come on Newton, on the count of three we'll put it on the back of the truck." Jake said as he was breathing heavily. Newton nodded in agreement. After they placed half of the kitchen table on the truck they turned towards the house. Jake never lacked in conversation. He was a tall, well-built man, who worked under contract for the U.S. Postal Service. He had a well-trimmed silver mustache, which matched the thinning hair on his distinctly shaped head.

"You know, Newton, this table belonged to my dad. I can remember eating many a meal on it. It has brought me many a good memories. I hope and pray it will do the same for you. You take care of this table. 'Member to pass it down to family. It's all about family, son."

Newton once again nodded in agreement. "I will, dad."

He was more muscular than his dad. He had played football for his high school and college. They had similar features in the face, except Newton's hair was a dark brown. His eyes were a pale blue, while Jake's were the color of cocoa. Newton wore round wire-rimmed glasses with lenses that were about an inch thick, this hid his one cross-eye, somewhat. Jake also wore round wire-rimmed glasses.

They entered the back of the house. Jake walked around what was left of the table half. "Newton, you lift in the front, and I'll take the back."

"O.K., dad." Newton responded.

His mind drifted off to the house he just purchased. He was excited and scared about getting his own place. He had helped his dad and mom out financially, but now he would be own his on place. He purchased the house and 250 acres for $45,000.00. He remembered when he told Roxie, his wife.

The first words out of her mouth were, "How we ever going to pay for this, Newton?"

"We will." Newton told her assuredly. They had three children. It was time for them to move. They were all piled up in a two-bedroom house with his mother and father, his sister and her husband, and their two kids—a total of eleven people in one house.

"Newton." Jake said, which jolted him back into reality. "Let's get a move on." They lifted the table onto the back of the 1940s Ford pickup. They then got into the front and headed towards Newton's new homestead. They pulled onto the gravel driveway which led to the wrought-iron fence that surrounded the white-wooded farm house.

They decided to take the table through the front door, since the door that led to the kitchen had to be entered through the doorless two-car garage, and four steep concrete steps had to be climbed before one could enter into the kitchen.

Roxie was in the kitchen wiping down the counter with ammonia and water. She heard Jake and Newton enter the living room, come through the dining room, and then they were in the kitchen with half of the table. She pointed to the middle of the kitchen and said, "Set it right here, that will be good." They sat it down breathing heavily. Newton pulled out a handkerchief and wiped his forehead.

Percy came running into the kitchen, and hollered to his sisters. "The table's here." They came running into the kitchen. Jake and Newton headed back out to the truck to retrieve the other half of the table. Percy ran out to the front yard and yelled, "I want to help."

Percy was nine years old at the time. He was a little chunky, one would think he was a little overweight, but he surprised many with his stamina and ability around the farm. He could out lift anyone when it came to hay-hauling time. He had light, brown, wavy hair and light brown eyes. His high cheekbones and long nose showed his Cherokee blood that he inherited from his mother.

Jake looked down at Percy, smiled and said, "Come on you can help me with my end."

Percy lifted when Jake did, but was surprised at how heavy the table was. They had to turn it sideways to get it through the gate of the wrought-iron fence. They walked the sidewalk, and then set it down before they took it up the four steps that led to the front porch. Once up the steps they set it down on the front porch to take a break before they carried it through the house to the kitchen. The front door was already open from the previous trip.

They had to once again turn the table sideways to get it through the front door and kept it that way because from the dining room into the kitchen was the same size doorway. They entered the kitchen. Percy was breathing hard, but he was proud of what he had done. Jake and Newton set the table half down and aligned it with the other table half. They then slid the table together until the grooves and points snapped into place. The two leaves that extended the table were still in the back of the truck.

Roxie walked around the table gliding her hand across the smooth worn wood. There were specks of the color of charcoal dotted all in the deep honey-colored table top and legs. 'The table would do fine,' she thought to herself.

Newton, Jake, Percy, and Roxie stood around it and gazed at it. Roxie ran into the dining room and picked up an oak chair. She carried it into the kitchen and sat it on the side closest to the stove. This would become her permanent place at the table. Newton followed suit and got his chair. He placed his at the head of the table to Roxie's left. Percy got his chair and placed it next to his dad's left. Jake went and got two chairs. He placed one next to Percy, which would be for his sister, Joy. The other one he placed on the other end of the table facing John, this would be for the other sister, Ann, who was the oldest of the children. Jake took the seat at the other end of the table facing Newton.

The four legs of the table were sturdy. They looked like Roman columns at least 12 inches in diameter. They could bear the weight of the two extra leaves, which would extend the table by more than two feet. The table top was at least four inches thick, and around the edges of the table was an overhang that had deep grooves lined in four rows.

Roxie got up from her chair and headed towards the refrigerator. "Ya'll must be hungry. Let me see what we got in the 'frigerator." She said as she opened the door and peered inside the refrigerator.

She spotted what she was looking for the fried chicken that was made by Lelia, Newton's mom. She grabbed the platter and placed it on the table. Roxie had dark brown hair and eyes the color of chocolate. She had high cheekbones and thin lips. She was a tall, full-figured woman and strong, both physically and mentally. She had already bore three children. The two girls were born at the hospital, while she had to have Percy at home. She didn't have time to make it to the hospital. He was born breach and weighed 12 pounds. She had survived living at Jake and Lelia's home along with the rest of the Prater clan that lived there. She was happy to have a home she could finally call her own.

    She opened the kitchen cabinet door and grabbed four plates. The girls would eat later. They were playing outside at the time. She set the plates on the table. She then placed four napkins down. She had made some iced-tea earlier, which was sweet and had lemons floating at the top of the tea pitcher. She found four glasses on the counter in the corner. She hadn't decided in which cabinet to put them in yet. She placed the glasses on the table and poured the sweet iced-tea into them.

    Roxie took her place at the table, and the men started for the chicken. "Leila sure can fry up some good chicken." Jake said as he was chewing the piece he had just put in his mouth.

    Everyone nodded in agreement. They all had a mouth full of chicken. Roxie kept running her hand on the table. She still couldn't believe they had their own place. Newton looked at her and winked. Percy blushed when he saw this interchange between his parents. He wasn't used to seeing his dad act so out of character. He was embarrassed, but really didn't know why. All he knew was his dad was more serious.

****

As the years went by twins were born to Newton and Roxie. They weren't exactly planned, but the table accommodated them. Jake died not long after they moved into their house on Shelbyville Highway. Leila moved in with them because she couldn't get along with her daughter's husband, Herbert. She left the house to them. She set her a bed up in the big hall that faced the only bathroom in the house. She lived there and ate at the kitchen table until she died.

Ann left the house to go to the University of Tennessee in Knoxville. She came back, married, and set up her house in the town of Murfreesboro. Roxie was proud because she married a lawyer, and he would later become a city councilman. They had two girls, Sissy and Samantha. Ann looked more like her dad than any of the other four children of Newton and Roxie. She had his blue eyes. They were a clear, crystal blue. Her hair was really a dark blond, but she liked to lighten it. She was the only one who least changed over the years.

Joy left the house when she married Leo. He was a very popular boy in high school, but drank too excess. They had two children, a girl and a boy, Tricia and Michael. Joy favored her mother, Roxie, except she had darker hair than her, in fact anyone in the family. It was almost a black, but not quite. Her eyes were the color of a deep, rich, semi-sweet chocolate. She ended up divorcing Leo and married her present husband Tim. Out of all of the five children, Percy is the only one who stayed married to the same

person. Percy grew up and joined the Air National Guard when he graduated from high school. He got a job at AVCO, a factory that specialized in airplane parts. While working at AVCO, he went to Middle Tennessee State University and got his degree in Agriculture and Business. He met his present wife, at the local Dairy Dip. He had lost his weight and had become quiet handsome. He stood six-foot and one-inch tall and weighed in at about 180 pounds. He looked like Paul Newman, except Percy had brown eyes instead of blue.
****

    Percy pulled up to the Dairy Dip and spotted Linda. He placed his order of a hamburger and French fries. "It'll be a few minutes she told him," as she turned around to place the order with the cook. Percy said in a low voice, "What's your name?"

    Linda tried to ignore him, but Percy was persistent. He repeated the question a little louder, "What's your name?" She blushed around her cheeks and said, "Linda."

    "My name is Percy," he replied.

    "What kind of name is that?" she asked.

    "I don't know. All I know I was named after my granddad. His name was Percy Lansdan Prater. We called him Jake though."

    "Oh," she said as she eyed him up and down. "Where do you work?"

    "I work at AVCO. In fact, I'm fixing to go into work after I eat. I'm working the swing shift tonight." He said as he noticed her soft brown hair, and her eyes the color of a California sky. "Can I call you sometime?" It came out of his mouth before he could stop it. He figured he had messed up by be being too forward.

She looked at him dead straight in the eyes to determine if he was serious or not. She thought to herself, "What's the harm, he probably won't call anyway," but deep down she hoped he would. She tore off an order form and wrote her number down on the back of it. She slid it to him. He took it and stuck it in his pocket.

"Order's up." She heard the cook say. She turned and got Percy's order. She gave it to him and asked if he needed anything else. He said no.

"I've got to get to work, thanks." Percy said. "I'll call you in the next couple of days."

"O.K." Linda said. She didn't want to seem too anxious.

This was the beginning of a forty-two year relationship and still counting. The year was 1960, and she was a senior in high school at the time. Percy was six years her senior. He did end up calling her.

Their courtship lasted three months. They were married on August 6, 1960, three months after Linda graduated from high school. Their first child, a daughter, Eliza was born, on September 8, 1961. Percy couldn't even hold her because he had gotten rabbit fever from hunting. The second child, Luke, was born on November 20, 1963. Back then they kept women in the hospital longer after giving birth

to a child, more so than they do today. President John F. Kennedy was assassinated during that time and that's all that was on television.
****

    Janice Prater, the oldest of the twins, had the biggest wedding of the family--twelve bridesmaids and twelve groomsmen. She met and married Randy Hutch. He had a bad stuttering problem. She worked and worked with him until he could talk without stuttering. She fell in love, and they married not long after she graduated from high school. Randy didn't live far from the Prater farm. His dad had a huge farm on Kimbro Road. They moved into an old house at the end of the farm. It took years for them to save enough money to tear down the house and build a brand new one. They had one child, Randy, Jr. Janice also favored her mother. Her hair was a little lighter than her mother's, and her eyes were a light walnut brown. She was a big-busted woman, which she inherited that trait from Roxie. She was big-boned and had a small waist. Eventually they divorced and she remarried.

    Joe, Janice's twin, and the youngest of the family, married Linda. She was a big-boned and tall woman. She also had a big mouth. Joe loved to drink. They had one child, Abigal. Joe would later marry two more times. The more he married the worst the women got. Joe had the same coloring of his sister, Janice. He was swayed back and bow-legged. The legs' trait he got from his father, Newton.

****

    This family cried, laughed, and celebrated around the kitchen table. This family was formed around the kitchen table. The family grew in leaps and bounds. If the table could talk, it would have many stories to tell. So here are the many secrets of this kitchen table, which was a staple in this family.

CHAPTER TWO

Eliza had become seven years old. Roxie and her had been grocery shopping. She was spending the day with her grandmother, which she loved to do. Eliza helped her grandmother put the groceries away. Her brother Luke was outside looking at the big goldfish in the watering trough beside the white barn that stood behind the house.

The barn had been built many years back. Eliza liked to go through the barn because one could find all kinds of stuff to haul home. Roxie put the staple of Country Club vanilla ice cream in the freezer. Dessert was always served at every meal and when Roxie didn't prepare a dessert, vanilla ice cream with Hershey's chocolate syrup was always available.

"Eliza get me that roaster down there in that cabinet." Roxie said as she was pointing to the bottom cabinet where Eliza was standing.

Eliza opened up the cabinet door and pulled out what looked like a roaster. It sounded like it would be big. "Is this what you're talking about?"

"Sure is, put it on the counter." She ordered. With five grown children and six grandchildren at the time she had to become a tough old bird. Roxie began to unwrap the big roast. She slapped it into the roaster. "Get me those potatoes on the table, and bring them here."

Eliza lifted the heavy bag of potatoes and handed them to her grandmother. She stood at the other side of her grandmother and watched as she pulled out a sharp knife out the drawer. She began to peel the potatoes.

"Can I help?" Eliza asked expecting to here a no.

"Get a knife, help yourself." Roxie replied.

Eliza excitedly walked to the drawer and pulled her smaller sharp knife out. She grabbed a potato and began peeling, but she was much slower. Her grandmother had already peeled three potatoes by the time Eliza had finished one.

Roxie looked down at Eliza smiled and said, "Don't worry when I first started peeling 'taters I was about your age. I moved mighty slow didn't think I would ever get the hang of it, but if you peel enough of them you'll get faster believe me."

This made Eliza feel better because she felt slow indeed. "What are we making grandmamma?"

"Pot roast with potatoes, carrots, onions and some cornbread," she said proudly like she was cooking for royalty.

They finished with the potatoes. Roxie rinsed them off and placed them around the roast. She went to the oven and set it on 350 degrees.

"Now what did I do with those carrots?" She asked herself.

Eliza looked around the room and spotted them sticking out from under the brown paper grocery bag labeled A & P. "I'll get them," Eliza said.

They finished peeling the carrots, and Roxie cut up them up.. She placed all of this around the roast, put the top on the roaster and then set it in the oven.

She washed her hands, and Eliza wanting to copy her grandmamma did exactly the same. She reached for her book of circle the words she had purchased at the grocery store. She went over the kitchen table and sat down with it. She remembered she needed an ink pen.

Eliza was heading toward the table to sit next to Roxie when she said, "Get me a pen out of that drawer over there, honey."

Eliza got the pen and brought it with her to the table. She sat down right next to Roxie and watched her as she circled words that she had found out of the jumble of letters.

The table had a leaf added to it when Newton and Roxie's children had gotten bigger. The table was a little wobbly, but still sturdy. It had watched the children grow up. The table had seen the children run under it, play under it, hide under it, trying to crawl on it, and of course they ate on it. The children were also known to pop in frequently, usually right around supper time to eat. They brought their grandchildren.

Eliza was looking at the words her grandmother was circling. She studied the list of words to be found. She looked at the scrambled letters. She was trying to find a word. She ran her eyes up and down the rows of letters and diagonally.

"Grandmamma, I found a word, look." Eliza pointed to the word "tramp."

"Yep, sure is," Roxie said as she gLuckd up at the list of words and saw that tramp was on the list.

"Grandmamma, how long have you lived here?" Eliza asked.

Roxie stopped concentrating for a moment and thought, "oh , about 25 years I guess. It'll be 25 years this March come to think of it."

"I like to write you know." Eliza said hoping Roxie would become interested.

"Really, I always liked math myself."

"I don't like math; it's boring." Eliza replied as she made an ugly face.

"I like numbers. All the things you can do with numbers--adding, subtracting, multiplying, and dividing. I would have liked to become an accountant. In fact, I went to at Middle Tenneessee State University, well, it was a small college then."

"You did." Eliza was entranced.

"Well for about a year until I married your granddaddy. I took me a couple of math courses, you know."

"Really, what about English or History," Eliza asked trying to get the subject back onto herself.

"History was interesting enough, but English just bored me to tears with all that reading and writing." Her grandmamma said missing the entire boat.

****

Roxie worked for the U.S. Postal Service at this time. She carried mail on a rural route. She had built up enough leave that she was able to take off about every Friday. She didn't get this job until Janice and Joe were old enough to fend for themselves, up until then she had stayed home. This was also about the time that Newton had a nervous breakdown. He was Roxie's substitute driver when she wanted to take a day off.
****

The year was 1955 and Roxie had come home from grocery shopping. She found Newton in bed crying and not able to get out of bed.

"What's wrong Newton?"

"I can't do it anymore, Roxie. I'm going to sell the pool hall. I'm going to sell the cattle, too. I can't handle it. I don't know what's wrong with me. I feel like I'm going crazy. I can't even make it to town without feeling like I'm going to die or go crazy one."

Newton was almost 50 years old. He would be fifty in one year.

"You just need to rest. You've been putting in too many hours at that pool hall anyway. How much do you think we can get for it?" She looked at Newton. He looked pale and drawn. He couldn't stop crying. She was worried, but she wasn't going to let him know it. He had always provided for the family. He had a feed mill, a dairy farm, and now a pool hall. They never wanted for anything. He was worn out physically, mentally, and emotionally. If he didn't stop, he wasn't going to make it.

"Holden said he would give me $15,000.00 for it."

"Why don't you do it, Newton." Roxie said as her mind was racing. "We've got enough money in the bank. The house and farm are paid for. I'll get a job. You can take a break. Joe and Percy can help with the cattle. We don't have to sell them right now. That will be income coming in."

Newton stayed in bed until supper time. He drug himself to the kitchen table. He sat at his usual spot, the head of the table. Roxie had the food set out on the table. She had cooked all of Newton's favorites--fried corn, fresh tomatoes, roast and potatoes and cornbread and iced tea to wash it down.

Percy was sitting at the table in his spot next to his dad. He was worn out from taking 12 hours at school throughout the week and working 40 hours a week at AVCO. Janice sat next to Percy, and Joe sat at the opposite of the table facing his dad.

Percy noticed it was quieter than usual. He looked at his dad. His face looked swollen, especially around his eyes. His mother was fidgety.

"Newton, here you go." Roxie said as she loaded his plate up with cornbread, fried corn, couple of slices of tomato and a big helping of roast. Newton sat there in a daze. He looked down at his food.

Roxie fixed her plate, as she took a helping she would hand the platter of food to Percy. He would then hand it to Janice, and Janice to Joe.

When Joe had filled his plate Roxie said, "Let's say grace."

Everyone bowed their head as Roxie lead the prayer. Percy thought this was unusual since his dad usually lead the prayer. "Dear Lord, thank you for the food we are about to eat, which will nourish our bodies. We are grateful that everyone made it home this evening safe. Thank you for the many blessings you have given us. Amen."

Everyone at the table followed with an "Amen," except for Newton. He slowly put the fried corn in his mouth and chewed. He didn't want to hurt Roxie's feelings after all of the trouble she went to cook the meal. He was so tired. He just wanted to lay down in the bed and hide under the covers. He felt like such a failure.

"How's school today, Percy?" Roxie asked trying to break the silence in the room. "It was pretty interesting." He answered with a mouth full of food.

"Janice what about you?" Roxie asked.

"Well, Mrs. Pittard gave me homework tonight, yuk." Janice and Joe were both nine years old and in fourth grade. "It's due back tomorrow."

"What kind of homework." Roxie prodded.

"I got to read a chapter in my reading book." Janice explained.

"What about you Joe?" Roxie asked looking down at Joe, expecting anything but the truth coming from his mouth.

"I ain't got no homework, mama." He'd rather lie than tell the truth. When he did try to tell the truth it was always stretched to the limit. "Mrs. Smotherman didn't give us any reading to do."

Roxie responded, "Did she give you anything else to do?" She always had to pull the truth out of Joe like catching a fighting 15-pound catfish.

"We got a spelling test tomorrow." He knew he had slipped up. She had him dead to rights.

"Well, I guess after supper you better be studying for that spelling test."

Janice stuck her tongue out at Joe and made a face. Joe stuck his tongue out at her and then kicked her. They were both still eating and pestered each other throughout the remaining of the meal.

Roxie turned to Newton, "How's everything?"

"Fine," he mumbled. He scooted his chair back, stumbled, and then headed back to the den.

Percy knew something was wrong with his dad because he didn't finish his meal. He looked at his mother until eye contact was made with her. She was holding a fork full of fried corn and said, "We'll talk after supper."

When Joe and Janice finished, they headed to the front bedroom to do their homework. Roxie exhaled long and hard. Percy sat at the table giving his mother time to collect her thoughts.

"Your dad's had a breakdown. I'm worried about him, Percy. He's not going to be able to work anymore."

"What do you mean a breakdown?"

"I came home from shopping, and he was in the bed crying saying he couldn't do it anymore. I believe he can't do it anymore. I think it's a combination of everything. His mother just dying, working all of them long hours at the pool hall, running the dairy farm, and you can't help him like you used to. You being in college and working. You know Joe isn't half the worker you were at his age."

"Are you going to be alright?" Percy asked with concern. Percy was born more mature than the rest of the kids. Newton and Roxie both knew this. Of all the kids, they worried about him the least. They knew he would make it. Percy worked hard on the dairy farm and the pool hall when he was younger. He saved at least half of his money at the time. When he was younger he saved 75% of it.

"Yeah, I'll be alright. I'm just worried about your father. What are we going to do? If Janice and Joe want to go to college, I don't know how we are going to pay for it.? Percy promise me if they want to go to college you'll make sure they can go."

"I will." He replied and took on the responsibility. From that point on he took ten percent of his paycheck and put it in a savings account for his brother and sister's college fund.

He thought, 'What the heck, if they don't go to college then I'll have it for my family.'
****

"Grandmother, you know I'm going to write a book about the family." Eliza said looking up at her grandmother for a reply.

"That ought to be one book, I say." Roxie said.

Eliza, who had been named after both her grandmother's, noticed that there was an undertone of hoping she wouldn't find out everything about the family. Eliza took the hint and didn't mention writing a book again, but she did find another word.

"Look Grandmamma, there's a word, it's 'begin.' She was proud that she had found another word for her grandmother.

"Sure enough, there it is." Roxie said and she circled the 'begin.'

She picked up her booklet and set it on the counter. "I guess we better get the table set. It's almost 5:00. Percy and your mom will be here anytime to pick you up. I'm sure they'll stay to eat."

This had always been the way it was. If Roxie kept the grandkids for the day it was a given that when mom and dad came to pick them up they would show up around supper time. Roxie headed for the cabinet and grabbed six plates.

She turned and handed them to Eliza, "Here set these on the table, while I check on the roast to see how it's coming along."

Roxie opened the oven door the heat came pouring out. Eliza could feel the heat hit her legs as she went around the table and set the plates down. "Which drawer did you moved the knives and forks to, grandmamma?"

"Right over there by the refrigerator, honey. I thought it would be more convenient by the bowls and ice cream." She replied as she pulled the roaster out of the oven.

She pulled the top off of it and poked at the roast. "Just about right, I guess I better get the cornbread mixed up."

Roxie grabbed a bowl and began to throw in some cornmeal that she had gotten out of the canister with her hand. "Get me an egg, honey." Eliza got an egg out of the refrigerator door and handed it to Roxie, who cracked it into the bowl. Roxie then poured some oil in the bowl.

"Get me the milk, will you honey."

Eliza went back to the refrigerator and got the milk. She handed it to her grandmother.

"Thanks, honey." Roxie had already put the iron skillet in the oven with oil in it so it would be nice and hot. She finished mixing the cornbread. Roxie pulled out the skillet and poured the batter into the hot skillet. Eliza heard it sizzle as the batter hit the oil.

"How do you make cornbread grandmamma?"

Roxie wiped her hands on the apron she had put on. "Well, whatever you do don't follow the recipe on the cornmeal package. It doesn't come out right. It took me about ten times of making it before I knew what kind of consistency would turn out just right. I don't know the measurements exactly. I just know how to throw in the cornmeal by the feel of it in my hand."

Eliza didn't really understand the 'feel by my hand' bit, but she knew her grandmother didn't use measuring cups like her mother did. She just threw the ingredients in the bowl and started mixing.

Luke came running into the kitchen. His shirt was soaking wet. "I almost caught one of those fish in the trough."

"Looks like you almost fell in the trough. How were you trying to catch it?" Roxie asked as she looked at him up and down.

"With my hands, it slipped out of 'em though." Luke replied looking a little disappointed.

"You need to go upstairs and change your clothes. We'll be eating as soon as your granddad and mom and dad get here."

Luke headed up the stairs to change.

Eliza heard the front screen door open. She ran through the dining room until she reached her mom and dad. "Hey, mama and daddy, me and grandmother cooked roast, potatoes, carrots, and cornbread for supper."

"You did?" Her mother said looking down at Eliza. She was ready to pick up Eliza and Luke. She missed them, but she and Percy had been looking at the construction of their new house. They also had been shopping for new furniture.

The house was going to be at the end of the Prater' farm. Percy had paid his dad for the land, which was three acres. His dad couldn't farm it anymore. He was getting up in age. "Hey, honey,"

Percy said to Eliza, "so you been helping your grandmamma cook?"

"Yeah, doesn't it smell good."

"Yeah, it does, where's your brother?" He asked as he was in the kitchen by now.

"Oh, he's upstairs changing clothes. He got wet trying to catch one of those fish out of the trough." Eliza replied as she rolled her eyes in her head like she was too big for such things.

The back door opened and it was Newton. He had a golf bag on his shoulder. His hair was gray and slicked back. He had black-rimmed glasses on now. The golf course was just down the street from where they lived.

"Hey, Newton, we are just about to eat." Roxie said and she was wiping her hands on the apron. "How's the house coming?" She turned and asked Percy and Linda. Luke came running down the stairs.

"They're almost finished with it. They have to paint the inside and do a little trim work. I'd say we'd be moving in about one month." Percy replied as he took a bite of roast that was sitting on a platter now on the table.

Everyone started taking their place at the table. Newton had come back in the kitchen from putting up his golf bag and washing his hands. He sat at the head of the table. Roxie sat in her spot to Newton's right. Percy sat to Newton's left, always by his dad. Linda sat next to Percy. Eliza and Luke sat at the other end of the table.   Newton always took first helpings. Roxie made sure of that. Percy then helped himself. The food was then passed to Linda, the kids and to Roxie. Everyone drank iced tea.

"So you think the house will be finished in about one month.?" Roxie repeated to make sure Newton heard. Newton peered over his thick glasses and looked for a reply from Percy.

"Yeah, I think so."

"Now you let me know when you'll be moving so I can fix some food for ya'll. Ya'll come over here and eat after you move all of the stuff in your house. Your not going to feel like cooking Linda." Roxie said with assured experience on the subject.

"O.K." Percy said. "I've already asked Joe to help us move. Randall said he would help too.
"Linda's already been packing. Isn't that right honey?"

Linda nodded in agreement. Her mouth was full of roast and potatoes. She chewed fast and swallowed hard. She didn't believe in talking with food in one's mouth. "You don't realize how much stuff you have until you start packing."

Roxie was nodding, "Yeah, I remember when me and Newton moved into this place. We didn't think we would ever fill it up. It was so much space. It didn't take any time to fill it up."

CHAPTER THREE

The house on Barfield Lane was finished and moving day had arrived. Everyone had gathered at Newton and Roxie's for breakfast.

"Joe go get me one of those table leaf's out of the den closet." Roxie said as she slapped cooked sausages on the paper-lined plate.

"I think everyone's here mama." Percy said with excitement. He was ready to eat breakfast and get moved into his new home.

Joe was carrying the leaf.

"I think your right Percy, help your brother put that leaf in the table." Roxie said as she was still cooking sausages. Newton was mixing eggs up in a bowl. He was working on the second carton eggs.

"Newton you finished with those eggs yet." Roxie asked, while she was eyeing Percy and Joe putting the leaf in the table. Newton scooted the eggs over to Roxie. She poured them into the frying pan. She then put the toast that lay on the cookie sheet into the oven.

"Come on everybody, breakfast is ready." Roxie yelled loud enough for everyone in the house and out of the house to hear.

The table was set for nine people. Newton and Roxie took their normal positions at the kitchen table. Joe and Luke sat at the other end of the table. Percy, Linda, and Randy sat at the left of Newton. Eliza and Baxter sat to Roxie's right.

"How many more loads you think we are looking at Percy?" Joe asked as he was putting grape jelly on his toast and stuffing a sausage into his mouth.

"We'll we all got trucks we're using. I'd say two to three more loads." Percy said with eggs in his mouth.

Eliza was excited and scared. She had her own room. She was also already tired from packing the one load into the trucks. Eliza and Luke were in charge of the boxes that weren't too heavy and getting them to the truck and handing them to one of the men.

"What do you think about having your own room, Eliza?" Roxie said looking down at her.

Eliza looked up at Roxie and said excitedly, "I can't wait. I don't have to share my room with anyone." She said as she was looking at Luke and rolling her eyes. "I've got me a poster board with a lady bug on it. I'm going to put all the things that are special to me on it."

"Uh-um." Roxie murmured as she smiled at Percy and Linda. "Things sure have changed I can remember sharing a room with my sister until I married." Roxie retorted.

"Until you got married?" Eliza couldn't believe it. How did she stand it?

****

She readjusted her headband, which kept sliding forward because her hair was too thick. She hated her hair. It was thick, wavy and dark blonde. When it grew it grew out as well as long.

Whenever she went to the grocery store with her mother all of the old ladies would say, "I wish I had hair like that."

Eliza would just cringe inside. She wanted straight hair, but the best straightener wouldn't even do. She remembered hearing someone say you could iron your hair with wax paper. She ran inside when she got home from school and turned the iron on full blast. She got the wax paper out of the kitchen drawer her mother kept it in and ran upstairs to the sewing room where she had already turned the iron on. She held the wax paper up to her hair and put some in it and folded it over. With the other hand she held the iron to the wax paper and had it there for about 15 seconds.

"What in the world are you doing?" Linda ran into the sewing room. She had just come up the stairs to change into something more comfortable after being off work when she looked into the sewing room. She couldn't believe what she saw. She knew her daughter didn't like her hair, but this was crazy.

"I'm trying to iron my hair, mama. They say at school you can do it and it would come out straight." Eliza said shocked to see her mother so upset.

"You'll burn your hair is what you'll do. Only blacks can do that, honey. Their hair won't burn if you put an iron to it, and anyway it's a different kind of iron." Linda wasn't too sure about the information she was sharing with Eliza, but she was hoping this would stop her from putting an iron to her hair. It was scaring her.

"Mama, I hate my hair. I want it straight like all of the other girls."

"Your hair is fine honey. Do you know how many people would give their right eye tooth to have hair with as much curl and body as yours?" Her mama asked her for the thousandth time.

Eliza gave up and put the iron down. She had heard this many times from her mother. She knew her mother believed it, but Eliza didn't believe it.
****

Roxie was still finishing her reply when Eliza's mind drifted back to the breakfast meal. "...come to think of it I have never had my own room." Eliza couldn't believe it, not ever having your own room.

"I hadn't never had my own room either," said Linda, who was finishing her breakfast. "I shared a room with my brother, Larry, until Steve and Diane were born. Then Diane and I shared a room until I got married, and I'm still sharing a room."

Everyone went around the table sharing if they ever had their own room. Eliza listened as each one shared if they had ever had their own room. They all had either shared a room with a brother or sister until they got married. She felt very lucky to have her own room, her own space, her own territory.

"Things sure are different today. Everybody thinks they got to have their own room." Roxie said closing the room conversation.

"Uh-um," Newton mumbled with a mouth full of eggs. Everyone looked at him since he didn't usually have anything to say at any meal time. In fact, ever since his breakdown he spoke less than before, which wasn't that much to begin with.

Joe was picking at Luke at the end of the table. Luke was starting to get perturbed with him. Joe wasn't much more mature than Luke, but he was much older. Luke was eight years old, and Joe was twenty-four years old. "Stop it," Luke finally blurted out loudly as Joe was rubbing his hand on top of Luke's head.

"S-o-r-r-y," said Joe as he realized everyone had stopped eating and talking to look at him and Luke. Roxie gave Joe a disapproving look.

"Well, ya'll about ready," said Percy excitedly.

"Yeah, just a minute, let me finishing eating this sausage, and I'll be ready." Joe said.

"Baxter and I are going to head on over there. Joe, you go with Randall. Linda, you got the kids right?" Percy said as he was standing up and pushing his chair in at the kitchen table and looking around at everyone.

"Percy, what time do you think you'll be finished so I can I have supper ready?" Roxie said looking up at him.

"I'd say around six, if it's earlier then I'll give you a call. You know we have our phone already set up. It's the same number it was at Rose Avenue, 893-2703." Percy answered.

Percy and Baxter were the first to pull into the gravel driveway of their permanent residence on 697 Barfield Road followed by Linda, Eliza and Luke. About five minutes later Randy and Joe arrived with their truck load of furniture.

Percy and Baxter had already moved the king-sized bed into Percy and Linda's brand-new bedroom. The bedroom suite Percy had made while they lived on Rose Avenue. It was made of deep cherry. Percy worked meticulously on the suite, which consisted of a chest of drawers and a dresser with a marble top. The marble he had gotten from Newton's sister, Ruth, on a deal he made with her.
****

Everyone in the family thought Ruth would be an old maid because she waited until later in life to get married. Herbert came along and as Percy said, "Lelia couldn't wait to push Herbert under the supper table. After Herbert and Ruth got married she was trying to think of ways to pull him out from under the supper table."

After Newton and Roxie moved out and Jake died Lelia was getting tired of Herbert's attitude. "I can't stand that Herbert, Newton, he's no good, doesn't treat Ruth right. Ruth's made her bed. I'm going to make sure she's taking care of, but I'm not going to sit around and watch them two." Roxie was at the kitchen table with Newton and Lelia.

"Newton let me talk to you a minute." Roxie motioned for him to come into the dining room.

He followed Roxie into the other room. "What do you think, Newton? Think we should offer to let her move in with us? You know we stayed with them before we got this place. We got plenty of room." Roxie was saying, as Newton was nodding in agreement.

"I agree." Newton said, which stopped Roxie. It was agreed they would move Newton's mother, Lelia, in over the weekend.

They went back into the kitchen and found Lelia sitting at the kitchen table. Newton sat down at his usual place and looked at his mother, who was sitting to his left. "Mama, if you want to, you can move in with us. We can set you up a dresser and a bed in the room in front of the bathroom."

Lelia said, "I don't want to put you out none. It'll be too much on ya'll, especially you Roxie."

"No, it won't. You're not happy over there. Life's too short to be miserable, you know."

"Yeah, we'll that's true. If I stay over there much longer somebody's going get their feelings hurt, and I'm afraid it won't be me."

"Mama, come on now, just move in. It's no trouble. We'll move you in this weekend."

Everyone was quiet at the table while Lelia was deciding. "Well, alright then. Now, Roxie I'm going to help you as much as I can."

Lelia's father died leaving her several pieces of marble. They stuck it out in the barn not thinking it was worth much. Percy heard about the marble. He went over to visit Ruth.

"I tell you what Ruth I'll clean out that barn if you give me two pieces of that marble." Percy's mind was always able to turn nothing into something.

"What do you want with it? You can have it as far as I'm concerned. I have no use for it." Ruth replied.

Percy still cleaned the barn out for her since Herbert wasn't ever going to get around to it, and it was beginning to look like an eye sore to drivers on Shelbyville Highway. He took the marble and was able to make a living room table and a dresser. The marble was placed on top of each. When the rest of the family heard that he had gotten the marble from Aunt Ruth they weren't too happy.

****

Randy and Joe brought the four-poster bed in the house. "Hey, Percy where do you want this bed to go." Joe said as he was holding his end of the both the headboard and footboard of the bed.

"Bring it up here," Percy was shouting from the end of the steps. "It's going into Eliza's room."

Joe and Randall hauled the bed up to the bedroom and set it up. The drawers had to be taken out of the dresser because it was so heavy. The bedroom suite was a rich, dark cherry. The wood had aged for several decades before Percy had even made the furniture. He made a queen-sized four-poster bed, a chest of drawers, and dresser with an oval mirror.
****

"Now, Ann I'm letting you use this until I get married. You and Tom can get a lot of use out of it." Percy told Ann the day she was leaving for Florida on her honeymoon. She had told Percy she didn't know what they were going to do for a bedroom suite since they didn't have one.

"Oh, Percy that is so sweet. I promise I'll give it back to you when you get married. This suite is something that should stay in your family."
****

"Mom, we are going to be over there in about 30 minutes." Percy said to Roxie on his brand new phone that was installed on his desk that he had made for the space that was in the den.

"We'll be waiting on you." She replied out of breath from cooking up a storm all day long.

Newton could see the caravan pulling up the long gravel driveway. "They're here Roxie."

Roxie began setting the hot food out on the table--fried corn, fresh cut green beans, steaming cornbread, fried chicken, and new potatoes. Percy was the first one to enter through the kitchen door. He was soaking wet with sweat.

"Come on sit down. You look worn out. Here's a glass of tea." Roxie said as she was setting the tea in front of Percy.

Percy lifted up the glass and drank it all; it seemed like in one big gulp. Roxie instinctively filled it back up with tea after she filled everyone else's glass with tea first. Everyone else was coming through the kitchen door and took their places at the table.

"Ya'll look like one worn out bunch. I'll beat you're hungry. You'll eat this and sleep like a baby." Roxie was talking to the whole crowd.

Eliza and Luke couldn't decide whether sleeping or eating was more important. Eating won the contest once the fried chicken was passed in front of them.

"Well did you get it all moved in." Roxie asked waiting on an answer from someone.

"Yeah, the house on Rose Avenue is empty." Linda replied. She was the only one who didn't have a mouth full of food at the time. "I'll need to go over there tomorrow and clean it up so we can get our deposit back."

"I didn't think we were going to get it all in the house today, but we did. Getting those bedroom suites up the stairs was the worst part." Percy added when he finished swallowing his chicken.

"Have you got the beds set up yet." Roxie asked.

"Yeah, we did that when we took the bedroom furniture upstairs. Then Linda went ahead and got the sheets and bedspreads on so we can sleep tonight."

"Linda do you know where the towels and washrags are?" Percy asked looking at Linda.

"There's a set in each bathroom."

"Good, I'm taking a long hot bath when I get home."

"Me too," said Linda.

"Me, too," said Eliza.

"Me, too," chimed in Luke.

"Well, me, too," said Joe. Everyone laughed, but not long because it wore them out even more.

"Now, Joe, Baxter and Randy, I'd like to give you a little something for helping me out. I couldn't have done it without ya'll." Percy said as he reached for his wallet.

"I don't want anything. You helped me move Percy." Baxter said.

"Don't worry about it, Percy, remember when you helped me and Janice move." Randy said.

Joe really wanted the money, but didn't want to seem greedy so he said, "I don't want any money, you helped me and Linda move." He finally said, but it hurt coming out of his mouth. Joe wanted everyone to like him. He didn't want anyone mad at him just like Newton.

CHAPTER FOUR

Shoog was licking her fingers at the kitchen sink. She had been there all day long helping Roxie prepare the Thanksgiving dinner. The kitchen table was full of scrumptious food.

"Shoog, let's start the rolls, Joe and Linda just pulled up the driveway. I think everybody's here now."

Shoog wiped her hands on the apron wrapped around her waist that looked like two dishtowels that had been sewn together. Shoog was always there on the holidays. Roxie cooked a feast at the Thanksgiving and Christmas dinners. She insisted on doing it herself. The only help she would accept was from Shoog because they paid her. Now, Shoog had been in the family since Newton was a little boy.

When Jake passed away he gave Shoog's father five acres of land. Shoog's father helped Jake farm his land. Jake built him a house on his own land, so he would always be on hand for work. When Shoog's father died he left the house and five acres to Shoog and her family, since she was really the only one that amounted to anything.

Shoog had a house full of kids, and she supported them by doing housework for white folks. She wasn't but four feet nine inches tall. She was black as a piece of coal, and her eyes were dark brown with red in the whites of them. She always wore white. Shoog didn't either believe in deodarant or didn't know about it because when she got to helping Roxie she would start stinking to high heaven. By the time dinner was over her apron and top of her uniform was stained with gravy, grease, and anything else she had her hands into.

Shoog got the rolls she had been working on all day and stuck them in the hot oven to bake. The kitchen was warm and smelled delicious with all of the dishes Roxie and Shoog had prepared. Before Shoog would set anything on the kitchen table she would sample it. If it wasn't to her liking she would work on it by throwing more salt and pepper into it then taste it again until it was to her satisfaction. The way Shoog sampled the dishes was she would stick her index finger into the dish and then lick her finger. She never washed her hands in between the lickings.

"Shoog you make the best rolls in the world," Percy came up to her and bent down to give her a hug.

"Oh, go on now, Percy. My is that Eliza. You've grown and look at that Luke. Percy you got some fine looking kids."

"I know." Percy said as he was taking a piece of turkey off the platter that was sitting on the table.

"When's dinner going be ready? I'm starving, daddy." Luke said as he looked up at his dad.

"They're getting it on the table right now. It looks like it will be any minute now." Percy said as he was sticking a piece of country ham in his mouth.

"Hey, momma," Joe came around the table to where Roxie stood and gave her a big hug. Linda, his wife, gave Percy a big hug and then to Linda, Percy's wife.

Eliza loved Thanksgiving dinner's out at grandmother and granddaddy's house. She loved the smell of the house, the love in the house, and the food on the table. Everyone was happy and safe when they got to Newton and Roxie's house.

Ann and Tom were already primed for the occasion. They had been drinking since noon. It was Thanksgiving. Ann and Tom were in a marriage for their children, well Ann was. Ann had decided that she would stay married to Tom until their two girls got out of high school and graduated from college. Tom made a good living as an attorney. He averaged a 100,000.00 a year, and Ann wanted her girls to have the best of everything.

****

Ann and Tom were married after they both graduated from college. Tom drank heavily. One might call him an alcoholic. He also made moves on any woman who was standing by when he happened to get the notion in him. Some of the women obliged and some didn't. Ann found out about this.

Tom got drunk one night and went over Joy's house, Ann's sister, banging on her door. "Let me in, let me in."

Joy thinking something might be wrong with Ann opened the door.

She was greeted with Tom saying in his drunken stupor. "I've been wanting some of you since the first time I saw you."

"Tom you're out of your head. You need to go home."

"No, what I need is you." He started moving toward her and tried to back her up against the wall. Joy being sober and having a little more agility than Tom, headed toward the left.

Tom was right with her. "Come on baby, you know you want some of me."

"Tom why don't you just sit down, and I'll fix you a drink." She was lying to him, but thought if he got his mind on drinking it would get his mind off of her.

"That sounds good to me. Fix you one, too, honey. We've got a long night ahead of us."

Joy scrambled into her kitchen and picked up the phone receiver that was hanging on the wall. She started dialing Percy's number, and making noise by opening and closing the cabinet doors. His phone began ringing. She heard someone pickup the other end of the phone.

"Percy, Percy," Joy said in a whisper.

"No, this is Linda."

"Is Percy there?"

"Yeah, just a minute." She hurried to get Percy she had heard this frantic sound in Joy's voice before. "It's your sister, Joy, on the phone. She sounds upset."

Percy walked fast to the phone. "Joy, what's going on?"

"Percy, you've got to come over here. Tom's over here drunk and trying to get into my pant that damn no for good drunk. Ann ought to just divorce his sick ass."

"I'll be over there."

Percy looked over at Linda. "I got to go over to Joy's house. It seems Tom's over there trying to get Joy. He's drunk, of course."

"You be careful Percy." Linda said to Percy as he headed out the door.

Joy found an old whiskey bottle under the sink. It had just enough in it to make a drink for Tom. She opened the refrigerator door to see if she had some coke, luckily she did.

"Hey baby, what about my drink?" Tom was yelling from the living room.

"I'm fixing it right now. I had to find some whiskey." Joy said as she was mixing his drink. She was trying to think of something to stall Tom. She found some nuts in the cabinet and got them out.

She came into the living room. "Here we go a nice drink. I thought you might like some nuts, too."

Tom was stretched out on the couch. He had one foot on the floor and the other one on the couch. He was sitting halfway up the end of the couch. The foot that was on the floor looked like he was using it to steady his body. Joy walked over to him with the drink and nuts.

"Thanks, Joy." Tom said as he took a big gulp and then belched.

Joy thought how replusive. There he was slouched out on her couch. All she could see was his big belly, slitted blood-shot eyes, and his tomato-shaped head. 'What ever did Ann see in him?' she thought. 'He's one gross looking man. If he wasn't my sister's husband, I think I would but a baseball bat to his head.'

Tom had one eye barely open and the other one shut. He was beginning to see two of everything, so when he kept one eye shut he just saw one of everything. He took another sip of his drink and looked over at Joy with his one eye. She was looking out the window hoping to see Percy at any minute. He didn't live that far away from her.

"Hey, Joy, come on over hear and sit down with me. You look like you're cold. I'll warm you up." Tom belched again.

Joy had her arms crossed and began pacing the floor trying to think of an excuse. "Not right now, Tom. I need to go to the bathroom." 'That was it,' she thought. 'I'll stay in the bathroom until Percy gets here.'

"Hurry it up, I'm ready to get on with it."

Joy went in the bathroom and locked the door. She climbed on top of the toilet and looked out the bathroom window because she would be able to see Percy pulling up the driveway. It seemed like she was in there forever, but it was only a couple of minutes when she saw the white Chevrolet pull into the drive. She stepped off the toilet and flushed it. She straightened her clothes and headed out of the bathroom. About the time she got into the living room Percy was standing on the front porch getting ready to ring the door bell. Joy opened the door for him.

"Come on in." She said hurriedly to Percy.

Tom turned to see who was at the front door. "Well, look who's here."

Percy asked, "What you doing Tom?"

For the first time, Tom stopped to think why he was over at Joy's house. It was like he had been in a blackout and just come too. He looked around and realized where he was and why he came. He was at a loss of words. He tried to come up with something that made sense.

"Well, uh, um, I was driving and um, well," he was thinking hard. He didn't want to tell Percy that he came by to get into his sister's pants. "I passed by Joy's house, and saw the light on. I thought I might visit with her, and I needed to use the bathroom, didn't want to use a public restroom. You know those can be pretty dirty. Yeah, that's it. I came by to visit Joy and use the bathroom."

"Well, don't you think it's time for you to go on home, Tom." Percy replied with pursed lips.

Tom didn't want to argue with Percy. He had sort of come too and realized the story he gave to Percy was pretty thin. He didn't want to push his luck. "Yeah, I think I'd better get on home, Ann's probably wondering where I am."

He got up from the couch and stumbled forward. The room was spinning. He put his hand on the wall to stop it.

Joy feeling courageous now that big brother was there to protect her couldn't keep from saying, "Well, Tom you never did use the bathroom. That's the whole reason you came by wasn't it?"

Tom headed towards the bathroom like a whipped dog. He stumbled and finally made it in the bathroom and closed the door. He fumbled for his zipper and finally found it. He began to relieve himself. He thought he would never stop. He shook it and stuck it back in his pants. He looked down and realized he pissed all around the toilet, very little made it in. The rest of the urine was all on the tile floor. He flushed and headed out into the living room.

He met Percy and Joy who stopped talking when he entered the living room. "Well, folks, I'm going home."

"Do you need me to follow you, Tom?" Percy asked to make sure he made it home and that he wouldn't come back over to Joy's.

"No, no, I can make it." Tom assured Percy. "Oh, yeah, Joy I think I got a little piss on your floor, sorry."

Joy's eyes glared at Tom, but he didn't notice. Percy did. She thought, 'First he comes over here and tries to get in my pants and married to my sister. Then he pisses on my floor.'

Tom slowly walked out the front door. He got into his new black Lincoln and headed towards his house, where Ann and his two daughters were waiting on him.

"Percy do you think we should tell, Ann?"

"I don't think so, she knows how he is when he's drinking. She hasn't chosen to do anything about it up to this point. She probably won't now. I'm sure she has her reasons for staying with him. The Lincoln being one of them, girls taken care of financially, she can do what she wants, he's usually too drunk to care. He doesn't physically hurt her. He does go to work."

"You're probably right. I hope he doesn't go home and blab his big mouth to her." Joy said knowing how drunks can be.

Percy stayed with her until he felt Tom had enough time to get home, or get the notion out of his head that he would come back and visit Joy. Percy sat in the chair that was by the window so he could keep an eye out of the window while he listened to his sister go on about Tom.

"I know one thing. He's got some balls to come over here and pester me like that. When he was in college and they caught him peeking through the women's restroom. They should have kicked him out then, but money talks you know. Ann thought it was just a phase he was going through. Well, damn the man is 36 years old how long is this phase gonna' last?"

This brought back memories of her failed marriage. Joy had divorced her husband, Leo. He was class president, a charmer, and swept Joy off her feet. Leo had thick, wavy, blondish-red hair and stood six foot tall. He was thin, but muscular. He had a grin that was irresistible. She ended up pregnant with her first child. Joy was still in high school at the time, a junior. Newton and Roxie decided to send her to a girls' school in Nashville for pregnant girls so she wouldn't miss any of her education. After Tricia was born Joy didn't have the energy to go to school and raise a child. When Tricia was about six months old, Joy and Leo married.

The marriage was rocky from the beginning. Leo drank heavily and the more he drank the more abusive he got. Leo didn't like the responsibility of having a child and trying to make ends meet financially. Leo's dad owned a garage where cars were worked on. Leo worked for his dad and hated it. Joy stayed home with Tricia and hated it.

After Percy and Linda were married, Linda found out quickly how volatile Joy and Leo's marriage was. The phone rang at the triplex on Maney Avenue they were living in when they first married.

Percy picked it up, "Hello."

"Percy, Percy, you there?" Joy asked in a whisper.

"Yeah," he replied.

"You got to come over right now. Leo's tearing the house up. Tricia's crying. Leo's swinging a broom at me. I got myself locked in the bathroom. God, I hope he doesn't cut the telephone wire like he did last time."

"I'll be over. Just stay in the bathroom."

"You don't have to worry. I'm staying put."

"I'm heading to Leo's and Joy's. He's drunk again. I don't know when I'll be back." Percy said to Linda as he was putting his jacket on.

By this time Joy and Leo had another child, Michael. Tricia was six years old and Michael was three years old. Joy stayed with Leo because she didn't think she could go back home. She really didn't want to go back home. It would be too much for her mother and dad. Tricia was hiding behind the couch with a knife in her hand. She didn't know what she was going to do with it, but she knew her dad wasn't going to hurt her or her mother any more.

"Joy where the hell are you?" Leo yelled. "Get you ass out here. I want to talk to you."

Tricia was shaking behind the couch. She hoped he had forgotten about her for now. There was dead silence. There was no answer from Joy. Michael was sleeping in the back bedroom. Joy wondered how Michael slept through the chaos, but he always did.

"Joy, I said where the hell are you?" He repeated.

There wasn't a reply. There was knock on the door and then the doorbell rang.

Percy was standing on the front porch, again. He had done this many times. He never told Joy she ought to leave him. He knew she was doing the best she could. She wasn't working. Leo made sure she didn't get job. He wanted her home taking care of the kids, while he worked, drank, and caroused around the town.

Percy kept knocking on the front door. He knew Leo would eventually stagger to the front door.

Leo finally made it to the front door. He realized it was Percy and tried to straighten himself up. It was a fatal attempt.

"Hey, Percy, what do you want?" Leo had lowered his tone a great deal.

"Well, Joy called me and said she was afraid you were going to hurt yourself."

"She did." Leo said shocked that Joy actually cared he might get hurt. They had a hate and sometimes love relationship.

Percy said this to protect his sister. He didn't want Leo getting any more angry than he already was. He came on through the front door. He noticed broken glass on the living room floor and in the kitchen. He walked into the den and noticed Tricia's black hair behind the couch. He could see the silver blade to the knife she was holding.

Percy motioned for her to give him the knife. Tricia felt safe knowing her uncle was at her house. It wasn't the first time, and it wouldn't be the last. She hesitated, and Percy nodded his headed in agreement that it would be alright for her to hand him the knife.

He whispered, "Go own back to your room. It's alright. You'll be o.k."

Tears were running down Tricia's face. She hated when her daddy got drunk. In fact, she hated her daddy. She ran back to her room. She got in her bed and covered her head with her covers. She wished this would all just go away. She was scared.

Percy looked at Leo who was trying not to act drunk. He was leaned against the kitchen counter because if he stood on his own he was afraid he would fall down. Joy had come out of the bathroom and was standing in the hallway.

"Leo, why don't you just go on and lay down. You look like you're about to fall asleep." Percy had a way of convincing people what he said was a good idea. Percy thought if he was sleeping he wouldn't be bothering Joy anymore.

"You know," Leo burped. "I am a little tired." Leo realized he was drunk. From where he stood in the kitchen he could see the living room and den, there was broken glass everywhere. 'I've done it again.' Leo thought. 'I've done enough damage. I'm going to have hell to pay tomorrow. I wonder what I did.'

"Excuse me." Leo said as he was running back to the bathroom. He ran past Joy, who was still in the hallway. He barely made it to the toilet and threw up. He didn't think he was ever going to quit, but finally it subsided.

He came out of the bathroom. "I'm going to bed. I'll talk to ya'll later. Percy, nice to see ya." Leo staggered back to their bedroom they very rarely shared because Joy couldn't stand Leo when he was drunk, which was most of the time lately.

Percy and Joy had moved to the den. They both lit up cigarettes. "What am I going to do Percy? I can't keep living like this. I've tried talking to Leo when he's sober. He always promises he's going to stop drinking, but he never does."

"You know mom and dad are making the house note, so really the house is yours." Percy said trying to get Joy to think of her options.

CHAPTER FIVE

    Tim, Joy's second husband, was walking around the kitchen table taking a piece of country ham and stuffing it into his mouth, which he washed down with a can of beer. Tim had a peculiar laugh about him. He had married Joy about two years ago in Newton and Roxie's house.
    Percy told Joy on several occasions, "He's the best thing that ever happened to you Joy."
    It made Joy mad because she knew he was right. When they got married Tim took over all financial aspects of their marriage. This made Newton and Roxie very happy because they didn't have to keep paying on the house any longer. In fact, they didn't have to give Joy any more money.
    Joy ended up getting a job with the federal government working for a federal court judge. She was his deputy clerk. Tim worked for the Food and Drug Administration. Tim put a stop to Tricia and Michael playing with the children across the street. This was good for the children because the oldest child, Pamela and Tricia's friend, ended up overdosing on heroin. The middle child, Sissy and a friend of Michael's, got hooked on drugs and still is. The youngest child, Jimmy, also a friend of

Michael's, did so many drugs he doesn't even know half the time whom he is.

"Shoog, how have you been doing?" Tim asked while he was chewing his country ham.

"All right," she replied.

"That's good. This is some good country ham." He wasn't talking to anyone in particular.

"Tim, you been working hard?" Percy asked Tim.

They began moving toward the dining room.

"We had to shut down this grocery store in Alabama. You should have seen it. It was infested with rats and bugs. They were serving fresh meat out of there. It's a wonder someone didn't get sick from buying meat at that place."

"Really."

"Oh yeah, it was a mom and pop store. They didn't need to be in business. We had already given them a warning. When we went by there the other day it was even worse. They have 30 days to get the store in compliance, or they will be shut down for good."

"Uh-um." Percy couldn't get a word in for Tim talking about the store they had to shut down.

Percy was moving around, and Tim was still talking. Percy noticed Randy and Jan had moved over towards them.

"You look like your going to drop anytime now." Percy said to Jan. She was just six months pregnant and had already gained 50 pounds.

"Yeah, don't I." She replied sarcastically and rolled her eyes. "I'm miserable. God, I wished I would drop right now."

Percy laughed. He thought it was funny seeing Jan so miserable. He never would forget the Christmas when Jan was thirteen years old, and Newton and Roxie had gotten her a wrist watch for Christmas. She didn't like it, and she threw it clear across the living room then went over to it and stomped on it. Percy and Linda couldn't believe it.

Percy thought at that time, 'Ungrateful bitch, mom worked her ass off to get her that watch. It was fourteen carat gold, and she stomps on it. I would stomp on her. She's got a lose screw somewhere in her head.'

He kept walking through the crowd in the house. 'I hope Jan has a child just like she was.'

"Hey, Randy, how is it going?" Percy asked.

"Al-right," Randy replied, but his alright was drug out.

"How's farming coming along?"

"We had a good year." Randy worked on his dad's farm. Randy was a man of few words. He didn't talk that much because he used to stutter. He also loved to drink his beer, which relaxed him enough where he could speak in public.

Joe was married to Linda. Everyone called her Linda#2 because she was the second Linda in the family. They lived in a trailer, which faced the Shelbyville Highway. Joe worked for Budweiser, and Linda worked for the federal government. They were always broke. They had Percy come over on several occasions and plan a budget for them. They never stuck to it.

Linda was loud and a big woman. Newton and Roxie tolerated her. Linda was also very opinionated, which wasn't very much appreciated by the family. Jan and Randy went over to play cards with them. Jan told Linda she had big brown cow eyes. Linda was pissed at Jan for over a year about this.

Joe walked up to Percy, "How's the banking business?"

"It's o.k."

Both of them had a Jack and Coke. Percy was sipping his, and Joe was guzzling his.

"Everyone dinner's ready." Roxie hollered and her voice was heard throughout the house. "I've asked Tim to say the blessing."

Everyone bowed their head in unison. Tim began with the prayer, "Dear Heavenly Father, we are thankful for the food we are about to eat, for everyone arriving safely to this house, and for the family gathering. Amen."

"Amen." Everyone said.

Newton was always the first to go around the kitchen table.

****

Percy watched as his dad went around the table. He remembered back to the year 1946 when his dad's old Ford got stuck on the railroad tracks. Ann, Joy, and Percy were in the back of the car, while Newton and Roxie were up front. The car stalled on the tracks. Next thing Percy remembers is hearing the train whistle blowing down the tracks. The train was heading right for them.

"Newton, you got to get this car off the track." Roxie was screaming.

Newton was turning the key, but to no avail.

The train was coming closer and closer. Roxie yelled. "Come on kids let's get out of the car. You're going to get yourself killed Newton."

They piled out of the car and got off the railroad track. Newton was still in the car trying to start it. The train was real close by now. The motor turned over and Newton floored it. He got on the other side of the railroad tracks. Roxie breathed a sigh of relief.

****

"Now, Newton you just help yourself." Roxie said to him. She babied him, and he let her. In fact, deep down he really liked it.

Newton walked slowly around the kitchen table and filled his plate with sweet potatoes, country ham, turkey and dressing, homemade rolls, fried corn, cranberry sauce, lima beans, green beans, and macaroni and cheese.

He walked into the dining room and sat at the head of the oval table. Shoog brought him a glass of sweet iced tea. He nodded to her and said, "Thank ya."

As the dishes were emptying Shoog was refilling them with more food from the pots and pans on the stove. The men and women of the family went around the table and filled their plates. The children were big enough now to fill their own plates.

Tables were scattered throughout the house. The adults, which meant Roxie and Newton, and the brothers and sisters, and their wives' and husband's sat at the dining room table. The grandchildren, friends of Newton and Roxie's, Newton's sister Ruth and her family, sat at the card tables that were in the den, hall and living room.

Everyone stuffed their faces until they couldn't be stuffed any longer. Most people brought their plates into the kitchen and sat it on the counter. Shoog was there to scrape the plate into the trash can she had sitting beside the kitchen sink. All of the food was still on the table.

The desserts were sitting on another table along with smaller plates. There was jam cake, coconut cake, pecan pie, chess pie, and fudge. This was all washed down with Roxie's boiled custard made from scratch, which was topped off with whipped cream. Newton and Roxie always put a little Jack in their boiled custard, as well as the other adults. This was the only liquor they drank throughout the year, except at Christmas.

Shoog stayed in the kitchen and scraped plates and licked her fingers. The family helped themselves to the desserts. The children ran through the house. The women came in the kitchen and began cleaning the kitchen table and washing dishes. It was always the same each year.

"The men just sit in there and get to do nothing." Jan would say.

"It's always been like that don't you know, honey." Roxie would reply.

The rest of the women would nod in agreement. None dared ask the men to help in the kitchen. Some were afraid they would say no. Others didn't want them in the kitchen. Others thought it wasn't a man's place to be in the kitchen--it was a woman's place. There was the old woman role in the kitchen and then the changing woman role in the kitchen.

 Roxie would never dream of asking Newton to help her cook in the kitchen, but he did help dry the dishes when it was just him and her. She didn't like him washing dishes because he always missed spots on the plates. Roxie was a woman ahead of her time, but she didn't think of herself that way.

 She went to two years of college before she married Newton. She learned to drive a car when most women depended on their husband's or brother's to drive them around town during her time. She bore five children, cooked, cleaned, sewed, and had a rural postal route. She was a die-hard Republican when Murfreesboro was made up of a majority of Democrats. She was the only woman to go the Republican convention. It wasn't heard of in those days.

 By this time all of the women in the family held jobs, but they were still expected to clean the house, do the laundry, go grocery shopping. and take care of the children. They were in a new time and new era. It was the late sixties, when free love and drugs were on one side, and war, responsibilities, and family were on the other.

 "Maybe when our girls are grown their husbands will help them a lot more." Ann said.

 "Yeah, right." Joy said. "It will be a cold day in hell."

 The men in the family made more money than the women. They thought of themselves as the breadwinners. In fact, most of the money the men made went to pay all of the bills. The money the women made went on luxury items, a second car, clothes for the children, or a bigger house.

After the dining room table was cleared off, two leaves were taken out of it and whoever wanted to could play poker. It was for money and fun. The more they drank, the longer the game got. Others sat at the card tables and played canasta and caught up on each others' family.

The children played in the front bedroom. They loved to play beat the clock. Usually the oldest child told one of the younger children to do something in 30 seconds. If the child didn't do it, they lost. Another favorite game was dare. They would each dare, double dare, triple dare, and so on until someone would usually give in and try to do the dare.

The kids came running out of the bedroom through the living room, the dining room, the kitchen, and then up the stairs where there was a pool table. Roxie, who was playing Rook with Newton and their postal friends, Bess and Margaret, was facing the bedroom. They were sitting at a card table that had been set up in front of the fireplace in the living room. She could see the mess.

"Well, I know the kids are having fun cause the room is a total mess. If it was straight in there I would know either they had been up to something or wasn't having any fun." Roxie wasn't talking to anyone at the table in particular just anyone who would listen.

Linda headed into the front bedroom to see the damage the kids had done. She began picking up the coats and putting them back on the bed. The curtains were half hanging down. The bedspread was on the floor. All of the trinkets had been moved around.

"Linda just leave that room alone. I'll straighten it up tomorrow. I won't have anything to do. Anyway them kids will be back in there to mess it up once they get finished doing whatever their doing upstairs." Roxie hollered from the living room as she played a red one. She went back to playing the game. "The messier the room is the more fun they've had."

Linda stopped picking up the bedroom and went back into the dining room to play another hand of canasta with Linda, Joe's wife, Eliza and Tricia. Eliza was proud that she had learned how to play canasta and felt grown up playing with two grown women and her cousin, who was three years her senior. Tricia and Eliza were already close because before Joy got married to Tim she would always come over with Tricia and Michael to Percy and Linda's house. The grown-ups would talk in the kitchen, while the kids played Twister upstairs in Luke's bedroom.

When Tim and Joy got married Eliza went over to their house and spent the night with Tricia. They would stay up all night and talk about boys and eat junk food. The next day Joy would take them to work with her. They would sit in court and listen to the cases. Eliza loved this. She was intrigued by the whole scene. She never wanted to leave the courtroom. She could have stayed there all day. Tricia and Eliza would then go to downtown Nashville and shop at the major department stores. They would come back and have lunch with Joy. They would then go back into the courtroom until it was time for Joy to get off of work.

The poker game was roaring. They were playing five card stud on this round. Percy was the dealer.

"How many do you want, Jan?"

"Give me three."

"Tim?"

"I'll take two."

"Joe?"

"I'll take one."

"What about you, Joy?"

"I guess give me three."

"I'll take two." Percy said to the crowd.

Everyone showed their hand. Jan had a pair of deuces. Tim showed his hand slowly, one card at a time, it was a pair of nines. Joe had an ace, king, queen, jack of spades followed by a three of hearts. Joy showed a mixture of hearts and diamonds, but it didn't make anything. Percy showed three eights.

"Look at that." Jan said loudly.

"Percy you've had all of the luck tonight." Tim said disappointedly.

Percy scooted all of the chips his way. He had made five dollars off that hand.

"I'm calling it a night, folks." Percy said as he began cashing in his chips. Everyone else began counting in theirs too. Percy didn't lose any money. He had gained about twenty dollars. Tim lost ten dollars. Jan lost five dollars. Joe gain about two dollars. Joy won about three dollars.

Every family gathered up its children and said the usual goodbyes. The kitchen table had the chairs put back around it. The table held dishes covered up with aluminum foil. The rest of the food was in the refrigerator.

CHAPTER SIX

Christmas Eve had arrived, and everyone was heading over to Newton and Roxie's house. The first to arrive were Percy and Linda with Eliza and Luke. They parked in front of the wrought-iron fence along with the rest of Prater clan. Eliza and Luke ran up the sidewalk and up the four-steps and through the front door. The aroma of Christmas hit their noses-- turkey and dressing, fried corn, green beans, country ham, cranberry sauce, homemade rolls, sweet potatoes, mashed potatoes, macaroni and cheese, pies, cakes, and boiled custard

The Christmas tree Percy had cut for Newton and Roxie was a live cedar that stood 11 feet tall, since the ceiling in the living room climbed to 12 feet. There had to be room for the star at the top of the tree. The tree came off their farm. It was decorated with the big colored bulbs, icicles, and ornaments that Roxie had made herself. A light was at the base of the tree, which turned a disc of four different colors. This light hit the tree just right. It would go from yellow to red to blue to green. Eliza was mesmerized with it.

Percy and Linda came through the front door and put the Christmas gifts under the tree. All of the children brought gifts for Newton and Roxie. The family had gotten so big that they decided to draw names between the children and grandchildren. No one knew whose name they got until Christmas Eve.

The children looked forward to when the presents were open.

About the time Percy, Linda, Eliza, and Luke got their coats off they were put in the front bedroom, Joy, Ken, Tricia and Michael walked through the front door loaded down with Christmas gifts. The rest of the family slowly dwindled into the warm house. The gas fireplace emitted beautiful flames and heat in the living room and den.

Shoog had been there all day long with Roxie preparing the Christmas Eve dinner. The kitchen was the warmest room in the house. Her starched white outfit was already dirty with food stains. She looked shorter than usual to the grandchildren because they were growing taller, and Shoog was staying the same height. Percy walked in and saw Shoog licking her fingers. She was testing the giblet gravy.

"How's it coming along, Shoog?"

"Mighty fine, the gravy is done."

"Here Shoog put this in the gravy boat." Roxie said as she passed the gravy boat to her. They had worked together so long together they had this down to a fine art by now the family just stayed out of their way. By the time the gravy boat was being filled meant this was the last detail to be done before dinner was officially being served.

The usual blessing was said. Newton went first, followed by the kids, the men, the women and Percy last. Everyone was enjoying their dinner.

"I know who has Michael's name." Luke said with a gleam in his eye.

Michael asked, "Who has my name, Luke, who?"

"I'm not telling, you." He began to laugh thinking this was funny.

"You don't know who has Michael's name Luke. You're just saying that to get him all worked up." Eliza said as she put some turkey and dressing in her mouth.

"No, I really do. I helped mama bye the present." Luke blurted out.

"Great." Eliza said because half the fun at Christmas was trying to guess who had your name. So when Luke blurted this out he was able to deduce either Eliza or Luke had his name more than likey Luke since he went with his mama and helped her get the present.

All the kids hurried through their dinner and especially Newton. He was just as bad as the kids because he secretly wanted to open his presents. Roxie just wanted to rest. She wasn't feeling up to par. He stomach was still hurting. She told herself she would make an appointment with the doctor after Christmas because the pain was becoming almost unbearable. The worst part was when she had to have a bowel movement it was excruciating pain.

Everyone had gathered in the living room Newton and Roxie were sitting in front of the fireplace in their designated chairs. Eliza and Michael were the official hander out of presents. It was a given that Newton and Roxie would first get about six presents first before anyone else would get theirs so they could start opening their presents, and then Eliza and Michael would pass out the remaining presents.

All the presents were handed out. Eliza opened her present from Samantha it was a beautiful purse, "Thank you, Samantha."

"Your welcome," Samantha hollered clear across the room even though she didn't have a hand in the purchase of the purse. She took all the credit, plus it was good manners.

Luke was walking through all the paper with a big black trash bag and collecting trash. This was his official job. When he got to Michael he said. "I told I knew who had your name."

"Yes, you did Luke, thanks, I really appreciate the present."

"You're welcome I helped mama pick it out myself. I told you so."

Newton and Roxie were surrounded by opened presents. Roxie was in dire pain and had to excuse herself, but not without thanking everyone for her present. She felt like this was as good as time as any to slip away and go to the bathroom while everyone was busy with their newly opened presents. She would be left in peace and maybe could relax and take her time. It was absolutely unbearable.

Newton stood up and began handing out his present to the grandchildren it was a crisp $20 dollar bill. It remained $20 until the day he died. He didn't take into account the state of the economy or inflation.

Eliza said, "thank you granddaddy," and kissed him on the cheek.

Michael also kissed his grandfather on the head and thanked his grandfather. The rest of the grandchildren just thanked their grandfather or well most of them did. The ones that thought of to thank him—teenagers.

Shoog and the women congregated in the kitchen later joined by Roxie who had a little relief but was worn out by the ordeal. They once again talked about how life was unfair. How they had to prepare the food and work, plus clean it up, while all the men had to do was really work.

"There's always two sides to every story and then there's the truth." Roxie chimed in on the men verses women issue.

"That's what my mama always says." Linda said in shock because she couldn't believe she actually heard someone else say the saying beside her own mother.

"Well, I'm sure men have their side too is all I'm saying." Roxie said. She folded up the dish towel like that closed the subject. "How about some canasta ladies?"

Eliza and her mother were partners and Tricia and Linda number 2 were partners. They played for a couple of hours until the score was 450 to 475. Eliza and her mother were 450, and Eliza wanted to win in the worst way. The poker game was getting rowdy also. This would be the last hand of the night for both tables the excitement was almost unbearable. Eliza bid her hand carefully and close. Her mother did the same. In the end they squeaked out a win by ten points. It didn't matter by how many points all that mattered was they won, and it ended a perfect Christmas Eve. Now she could go home and wonder what would be waiting under the Christmas tree for her the next morning when she got up.

     All the games ended. Everyone said their goodbyes. Roxie and Newton retired to the bed. Roxie was never so happy to get in bed in her life it was like an oasis in the desert of her life. She knew she would be making an appointment with the doctor as soon as possible with no delay now and no excuses.

CHAPTER SEVEN

"Look, I found them." Luke was pointing to the *Pecan Sandies* he found in the hall tree under some sweaters.

Tricia, Eliza, and Michael were waiting for Luke to open the cookies. It was a ritual when they spent the night at Newton and Roxie's, someone, usually Luke, would hunt down the cookies Newton hid them when he knew they would be there. Newton had a sweet tooth just as bad if not worse than his grandchildren.

Luke did the honors of opening the package. Everyone took two cookies. He closed the package back up. They all giggled and ate their cookies knowing they had out foxed their granddad once again.

"I wonder why he always hides his cookies. It doesn't make any sense." Tricia said with her mouth full of cookies.

"Cause he doesn't want us eating his cookies, that's why." Eliza replied.

"We better get those cookies back before granddaddy knows they're missing." Michael said as he finished his second cookie.

They all ran down the stairs which came into the kitchen. Newton and Roxie were sitting in the den watching *Lawrence Welk*. They all sat around the kitchen table deciding who would take the cookies back. This was going to be a difficult task since the hall was right in front of the den, and their grandparents were in there watching television.

"You do it." Eliza said to her brother.

"I'm the one that got them. You do it." He retorted back to his sister.

"No, I'll get caught. I just know it. What about you Michael?" Eliza queried him.

He stood there for a few seconds and grabbed the cookies from Luke and ran back to the hall. He was grateful the hall was dark. He opened the bottom of the hall tree and stuck the cookies under the clothes that were in there.

"What are you doing in there Michael?" Roxie yelled from the den.

"I, I was looking for some, uh, my coat."

"Your coat?" She asked with suspicion.

"Yeah, I want to make sure it's here so when I have to get up in the morning to deliver newspapers. I'll know where it's at." He thought of the best story on such short notice.

"Oh, o.k." She decided to drop it. The *Lawrence Welk* show began playing a song she really enjoyed.

"Grandmamma, is it alright if we get some ice cream?" Michael asked as she walked into the den.

"Sure, honey, go ahead. Just make sure and put the bowls in the sink when ya'll get finished."

Tricia, Eliza, and Luke had moved their way into the dining room and were eaves dropping when they heard they could have some ice cream. They all ran into the kitchen. Tricia got the *Polar Pak* vanilla ice cream out of the freezer. Luke had beat her to the *Hershey's* chocolate syrup. Eliza was getting the bowls when Michael walked into the kitchen.

"Grandmamma said we could have some ice cream." He looked around and saw his sister and cousins already getting everything ready. Michael got the spoons out and set them around the kitchen table.

Eliza set the bowls out on the table, and Luke the chocolate syrup. Tricia had already put the ice cream on the table. Everyone filled their bowls up and poured chocolate syrup on their ice cream. Eliza was sitting where Roxie usually sat. Luke was sitting where Newton sat. Tricia was sitting across from Eliza and Michael across from Luke.

Tricia got up and put the ice cream back in the freezer. Michael was making a mixture of his ice cream and chocolate syrup. It was a smooth creamy light brown texture. The way he always liked.

"What time do you have to get up in the morning, Michael?" Eliza asked as she put a mouth full of ice cream in her mouth.

"I'm going to have to get up around 4 a.m."

"Four o'clock in the morning!" She exclaimed with disbelief.

"No four o'clock in the afternoon. Yes, four in the morning that's why it's a morning paper." Michael said rolling his eyes.

"Whose going to take you to get the papers?"

"Tricia, she can drive now. She's going to drive me around to deliver them just this once because my bike is locked up in the garage, and mom and dad won't be back from Crossville until tomorrow afternoon.

"Well, ya'll mise well stay up. Hey let's all stay up."

"Yeah," chimed in Luke.

With that they all looked around at each other and decided they would all stay up late. They put their bowls and spoons in the sink and ran up the stairs. There were two queen-sized four-poster beds in the room. It was a huge upstairs with two beds and two chest of drawers. One window looked out the driveway, and the other window looked out the back yard.

Tricia and Eliza had already made claim to the bed that was closest to the front window. The guys took the other bed. There was a long closet in the big room that covered the whole length of the room. The girls went in there to change into their pajamas.

"Turn that light back on." Eliza yelled to her brother. He had turned it off just as she was getting her pants off.

"Come on Luke." Tricia yelled.

"It's not me. I didn't do it." He said innocently.

"Well who did it then a ghost?" Eliza asked as she had gotten off her pants by now and was putting on her nightgown.

"Yeah, maybe it was a ghost." He decided to turn on the light.

Eliza shot out of the closest and hit her brother in his arm.

"Ouch, that hurt." He said rubbing his arm.

"Well, quit doing that. It's not funny." She said with a little menace in her voice.

"Hey, you know what we brought?" Michael got everyone's attention.

"What?" Luke asked.

"The twister game."

"Let's play!" Eliza said with excitement.

"O.K. but let's do something different. We all have to wear socks. That will make it harder for us to stay in the spot." Michael said as he was laying the game out on the floor.

"Yeah, let's do that." Tricia said.

Everyone put their socks on, and got on the game. "Ooh, you got left hand green, Eliza."

"Great this ought to be fun." She had her left foot on blue and right on red. Her right hand was on yellow. She took her left hand off the blue and heading towards the green. In order to do this she was going to have to go over her brother.

"You're hurting me. Get off of me!" He shouted.

"Oh, you're o.k. Just be still so I don't fall." When Luke heard this statement he pretending like he had to cough. When he was coughing it lifted up his back, which made Eliza lose her baLuke. She fell and when she did her brother went with her. She made sure of that. If she was going down, he was too.

Tricia and Michael were holding their own, but it was getting shaky. Luke turned the spinner it landed on right hand red. It was Tricia's turn. She tried with all her might to make it without falling but to no avail. It was final, Michael was the winner of that game.

"Let's play another." Luke said with excitement. It was already getting around 10:00 p.m., but they all remembered they were going to stay up all night.

"O.K., let's." Tricia said.

They began the game. Michael was the first to get knocked out this round, followed by Luke. Only Tricia and Eliza were left.

"Come on Michael spin it. My legs and arms are killing me." Eliza said with exasperation.

"Oh, are they now? Wait just a minute. Luke do you want to spin this time?" He asked trying to stall for time.

Luke caught on quick. "Well, I don't know." He hesitated for what seemed like five minutes to Eliza. "Naw, you go ahead."

"Well, O.K." Michael said slowly.

"Come on Michael!" Tricia yelled.

This jolted Michael into a spin. It landed on blue right foot. It was Eliza's turn. She thought to herself. 'This is going to be tricky. I'm going to win this game.' She took her right foot off the red circle and leaned her leg over Tricia's and barely landed her right toe on the blue circle, but she made it. If some part of the foot was on the circle it counted. She breathed deeply.

"Right hand yellow." Michael yelled out to Tricia.

Tricia leaned backwards to get her hand or finger on the nearest yellow circle, but it wasn't going to happen. She fell.

"I won! I won!" Eliza said excitedly.

"Yeah, yeah, we know." Luke said sarcastically to his sister.

"You're just mad cause you didn't win." She retored.

"What do you want to do now?" Michael said.

"Hey, what are ya'll doing up there?" Roxie had opened the door that lead to the upstairs bedroom. She had heard the thumping downstairs while they were playing Twister. It was 11:00 p.m. by now. "Ya'll need to be getting in the bed. Michael and Tricia ya'll got to get up early in the morning and deliver those papers. Now get with it."

With those words the decision was made what they were going to do next. Tricia and Eliza crawled into bed, and Michael and Luke crawled into their bed. It wasn't long before Michael and Luke were fast asleep.

"Hey, Tricia you care if I go with ya'll? I've never been on a paper route before?"

"No, I don't care."

The silence filled the room as everyone slept in the room.

Eliza woke up to the smell of sausage cooking. It filled the upstairs. She sat up in the bed and looked around. Tricia and Michael were gone. Luke was still sleeping in the bed but was moving around. The room was filled with sunlight.

Eliza got out of the bed and went in to the closet to put her clothes on. The light was still on from where Tricia and Michael had been earlier putting on their clothes. Eliza went down the stairs and opened the door that led into the kitchen. Newton was sitting at the head of the table drinking black coffee. Roxie was standing in front of the stove frying sausage.

"How'd you sleep?" She questioned Eliza.

"Pretty good," Eliza replied back sleepily.

"Michael and Tricia ought to be back in about 30 minutes. Breakfast will be ready by then. Put these plates around the table."

Eliza lifted up the stack of plates and set them on the table. She then laid each plate around the kitchen table. Newton would sit at the head of course. Roxie in her usual spot closest to the stove. Tricia and Eliza would sit to Newton's left, and Michael and Luke would sit directly across from Newton. She went automatically to the silverware drawer and got out forks and knives. She laid them next to the plates.

Newton had already gotten the glasses out and put them on the table. He got the butter and jelly out of the refrigerator. He got a cookie sheet and laid it on the counter close to Roxie. He opened the loaf of bread and filled the cookie sheet with bread until the pieces were hanging off the sides. Newton then got a dozen eggs out of the refrigerator and began cracking them in a bowl for Roxie.

Eliza was sitting at her designated seat when Michael and Tricia walked through the kitchen door. The cold air swept through the kitchen and under Eliza's feet. She shuttered. They were dragging their feet. Eliza looked at Tricia and Michael and both of them had dark circles under their eyes, and their hair was messed up.

"Did you get all the papers delivered?" Roxie asked as she was pouring the eggs into the skillet she had just fried the sausage in. She left enough grease in the pan to fry the eggs and give it flavor as she always said.

"Yeah." Michael said rubbing his eyes.

"You and Tricia eat a good breakfast and then go up to bed and rest." She knew better than to say go to sleep because they would fight that idea. She did know once they had a full belly and laid down they would be fast asleep.

Luke came down the stairs and sat in his chair. Roxie was putting the eggs on the table and toast on everyone's plate. Newton had poured milk for everyone. Everyone was fixing their plates.

"I guess I fell asleep Michael. I really wanted to go to deliver newspapers with you." Luke said to Michael as he just took a gulp of milk.

"You didn't miss anything. I just threw the newspapers out the door and onto people's lawns." Michael was yawning.

"I wanted to go too." Eliza chimed in.

Patricia was buttering her toast. "Like Michael said you didn't miss anything."

"Grandmamma is it o.k. for me to go out to the barn when I get finished eating?" Eliza asked hoping for an affirmative.

"Sure, honey."

She couldn't wait to go. "I'm going too." Luke added.

"That's fine." Roxie said as she was putting jelly on her toast. "Newton do you think I cooked this sausages long enough?"

"Taste's alright to me." Newton spoke in his few words that got the point across.

"Yeah, grandmamma it's all good." Tricia said with the other grandchildren nodding in agreement.

Breakfast was over. Tricia and Michael went upstairs to lie down. Eliza and Luke took all of the plates off the table and put them on the counter. Newton was already putting water in the sink along with dishwashing detergent. The suds were filling the sink.

"Grandmamma do you need us to do anything else?" Eliza asked hoping the answer would be no.

"No, honey, you go ahead." She had already taken her place as dishwasher, and Newton was the rinser and dryer.

Eliza ran outside to the brisk cold air. It hit her face, and she was now at another level of alertness. Luke was right behind her. "I'll race you to the barn." Luke said with a grin on his face.

"O.K." Eliza would pacify him.

"Now, when I say three we'll go. One, two, and" Luke took off. "three."

Eliza wasn't mad. She half expected it from her brother. He was always in competition with her, and she never understood why. She took off running and decided she would let him win this one. Luke was already at the barn entrance when Eliza arrived.

"Let's go up into the loft." Luke said to Eliza hoping the answer would be yes.

"O.K."

They climbed the stairs into the loft. The back of the barn had an opening as well as the front. They walked over to the edge of the back barn opening and stood right on the edge looking out. They could see fields full of corn and cotton. The scent of hay filled Eliza's nostrils. Eliza and Lukee sat on a bale of hay that they had helped put into the barn. They sat there in a peaceful moment their bellies full with breakfast. The sun was hitting their feet and warmed them. Eliza looked around the loft and noticed hay was all around the edges.

"Look, did you see that?" Eliza said with excitement.

"What?"

"It looked like a big mouse!" Eliza exclaimed.

"It was probably a rat." Luke said like it was nothing.

"A rat. They don't bite do they?" Eliza asked in a worried tone.

"No. I don't think so only if you're trying to bother them. Except that time I heard about a hoard of rats that attacked this blonde headed girl who was sitting on a bale of hay." He said and began to laugh.

"Oh, be quiet." She said relaxing a bit.

"Got ya." He replied still laughing.

Eliza remained cool on the outside, but her inside was churning with fear. She couldn't let her brother know she was scared. She watched the rat go underneath the hay in the corner.

"Boo," Luke said laughing as he watched his sister jerk. She slapped him on the arm. He slapped her back.

"Come on let's go downstairs." Eliza said wanting to leave the rat behind.

Luke made it to the stairs first. "Ha, ha, ha, ha, ha, I beat you."

"I don't care."

They stopped at the entrance of the barn. The names Newton, Percy, and Joe were spray painted in black on three boards. Eliza wondered who painted it and why. She wondered when it was done. She decided she would ask her dad when they picked her up.

Eliza and Luke headed down the middle of the barn which had stalls on the right hand side and a trough on the left. The barn was used now mainly for storage and to keep hay for the beef cattle. The dairy cattle had been gone for about 15 years.

    The dairy barn, which was to the right of the barn, hadn't been used in years. Spider webs stretched across the stalls. Eliza opened the first door she came too. It had a little trough in it, which had once been used by an animal. It was now filled with big burlap feed sacks that had been soaked in medicine for the beef cattle. Percy would stretch a rope across an entrance into a field. He would hang the burlap sacks from the rope. The cattle would walk under the sacks, and this would keep the insects away.

    The second stall was filled with five-gallon buckets, sacks of feed, and sacks of seed to be sowed in the front fields at Newton's. Percy had taken over running the farm for Newton. He leased it from his dad and ran beef cattle on it. Percy did this mainly to give his mom and dad some extra income and to keep the farm from running down. If he didn't do it, then Newton would have to pay someone to do it. The rest of the family didn't take too much interest in the farm. They had all gotten away from the farm and were now in the city. They couldn't wait to get away. Time changes people's hearts and attitudes.

    The trough on the left had been filled with chicks that Eliza had gotten from 4-H. Percy had set up a pen for the chicks. Eliza remembered the cold night she walked into the barn and saw the yellow chicks. They had heat lamps shining on them so they wouldn't freeze to death. Inside the pen were about

50 chicks, all chirping for their mama who wasn't coming back. Round silver containers filled with water were set in two corners. The other two corners were filled with feed for the chicks.

"Now when they get bigger you can put them in the red barn close to the house." Percy said as Eliza looked down at the chickens.

It was about two months, and they were ready to be moved to the red barn. Eliza walked from her house to the red barn every morning and evening to feed and water the chickens. It wasn't long before eggs were being laid. Eliza sold the eggs to anyone who would buy them. The money was put in a jar in the pantry and when more chicken feed was to be bought that money was used.

"Come on let's go to the watering trough and see how many goldfish are in there." Luke said running to the trough. Eliza followed behind him.

Eliza looked down into the trough. She could see three goldfish. Last time she saw only two. They were pretty big for goldfish. Luke was sticking his hands in the icy water trying to catch one.

"Leave the fish alone, Luke."

Eliza wondered what the fish ate. She did know that Newton walked out to the pond daily and threw in bread crumbs or any leftovers for the fish. If the fish didn't eat it, then whatever else was living in the trough the fish would eat that. Eliza ran her finger gently across the top of the water. One of the fish followed her finger. The warm sun was hitting her back, and it reflected on the goldfish. It glimmered a beautiful color of gold and orange.

Luke had moved to the other side of the trough. He was facing his sister. "I wonder if any of them fish are pregnant?"

"I don't know. I guess we'll find out around spring time." Now Eliza didn't know anything about the gestation period for a goldfish, but she assumed it was the same as a cow. If the goldfish was pregnant, it would be having babies in the spring.

"Ha, ha, gotcha." Luke splashed water in his sister's face.

Eliza returned the favor to him. Before long they were both cold and wet. Eliza started around the trough to get a hold of her brother. He ran off. She began the chase. They ended up on the other side of the barn. They both stopped and looked up at the feed trough on a trolley. It had at one time went into the silo and was filled with feed. The trough was then pushed out of the silo along the trolley. The trolley ran the length of the side of the barn. When the barn was in its heyday the trough was filled daily, especially in the winter, the feed was hauled from the trough on the trolley to the trough at cow level. Whoever pushed the trolley would empty it with buckets into the troughs. This was the newest invention since sliced bread and made life much easier for the Prater farm.

"I wish we had a grownup here." Luke said looking up at the trolley.

It was a great form of entertainment. The last time it was used was when Uncle Joe had come by to get some corn from his mother. Eliza and Luke took turns sitting in the trolley, and Uncle Joe would push them down the track until it ended.

"Yeah, me too." Eliza replied reading Luke's mind. She wouldn't mind a ride in the trolley.

They walked out into the front of the barn. Eliza looked up at the sky which was full of white streaks against a cornflower blue sky. The warm air from her body hitting the cold air made a cloud that followed her around. The day seemed lazy. It was a day she didn't have to think about school. A day to explore, a day to do what she wanted to do.

Eliza and her brother headed over to the deserted milk barn. Eliza peeked through the frosted windows into the barn. It looked like it was being used as a storage shed. It was full of equipment she didn't recognize and equipment she did. She was peering into the room where the cows were milked every morning. There were milking machines standing still in the barn waiting to be used again and looking quite lonely. Eventually, the machines were sold at a cheap price to another dairy farmer.

Eliza and Luke pushed on a door until it opened up. They walked in Eliza looking around. She wondered what it was like when it was in full operation. She stood their and wondered why all of the cows were sold. She figured it was because Newton had just gotten too old to run the operation, and Percy and Joe had families and careers of their own and couldn't help.

CHAPTER EIGHT

Church was over, and Eliza was thrilled. They were going to Newton and Roxie's. Eliza was thirteen by this time and was liking her hair better. Luke was eleven, Tricia was sixteen and Michael was fourteen. Percy pulled the Chevrolet into the long gravel driveway that was lined with maples. There were eight maples on each side of the driveway. The maples had been planted by Newton when they had first moved into the house. Eliza had heard the story many times from her father.

"Dad, planted those trees, and I can remember him watering those trees every day. He carried buckets of water and watered those trees. A five-gallon bucket per tree." Her dad said reminscenting.

Eliza looked at how much the trees had grown in thirty years. The trunks were at least two feet around, and they stood guard over the driveway. She loved their color at this time. They had turned a marigold color, and the leaves were still hanging onto their branches. They hadn't fallen. It was a beautiful sight. She took a deep breath and smelled the fresh, crisp air, which meant Fall and then Winter.

Eliza looked over the seat and saw Joy's car. 'Alright, Tricia and Michael are here. We'll be able to play.' Newton and Roxie were sitting in their appointed rockers on the brick-red front porch. Joy was sitting beside Roxie. Michael and Tricia were sitting on the other side of the porch with their feet dangling off of it.

The car stopped, and Eliza and Luke jumped out. "Hey, Tricia. Hey, Michael." Eliza said excitedly. She and her brother ran over to them, while Percy and Linda walked up the sidewalk and each pulled a rocker close to Newton and Roxie. Percy sat beside Newton, and Linda sat beside Percy. All four kids were sitting on the porch hanging their feet over it trying to decide what to do.

"I heard this recipe on T.V." Roxie was saying to anyone who would listen. "It's pecan tarts. It's a simple recipe. I made a batch of them. They're sitting on the kitchen table. They're pretty good, if I do say so myself. Ya'll need to try one."

With that statement the grandkids knew what they would do next. They ran into the kitchen and sat around the kitchen table. The pecan tarts were sitting on a big, thick plate with a yellow band surrounding it. Each grandchild took a pecan tart.

"These are good, grandmamma." Luke said as Roxie walked into the kitchen followed by the rest of the crew.

"Now, ya'll need to save some for us."

"O.K." Tricia said as she was chewing her first bite.

Roxie made a pot of coffee. The kids finished their pecan tarts and headed out the kitchen door to play outside. Next, the adults took their seats around the kitchen table. Roxie put five coffee cups around the percolator. Everyone fixed their own cup and took their seat around the table. Newton had already put saucers on the table for everyone. Percy was the first to get seated. He took a pecan tart and took a bite. He was pleasantly surprised.

"Mama, these are pretty good." He said gratefully. She had been on the angel food cake, strawberries, and ice cream kick. Roxie had a habit of making a dessert. If everyone liked it, she would make it all of the time. This could go on for months. The angel food cake last six month, and before that it was chess pies. Prior to that it was sugar cookies. He was glad for a change. No one ever wanted to tell her that variety is the spice of life.

Everyone looked at each other and grinned. They were all grateful they didn't have to eat angel food cake. This was always a topic of discussion behind Roxie's back of how she could stretch a dessert out for months. Eliza remembered her dad talking about Roxie and her meatloaf. Now there wasn't much Roxie couldn't cook according to Percy, but meatloaf wasn't one of them.

"Mama would cook meatloaf one night. It was so thick, full of oatmeal. She'd slap it on your plate. All you could do was just sit there and look at it, and hope it would go away. The next night she'd fix spaghetti, and she would have cut up that damned meatloaf and call them meatballs. It was nasty."

Linda didn't ever cook meatloaf for Percy's supper because he had a permanent meatloaf block phobia.

"How's everything at the branch?" Roxie was addressing Percy as he was finishing his pecan tart.

"I'm having to train a new assistant manager. I wish they would decide who they wanted as an assistant."

Percy worked at the bank in Murfreesboro that had been in the town since 1903. It was the longest running bank in the town. It would later be bought out by another bank. Percy was the manager at the West Main Branch at the time. He would later become a vice president and then over security, which entailed embezzlement, fraud, bad checks, and so on. He found his niche when he went into security.

"Well, who is it? Is it someone we know?" Roxie asked.

"No, I don't think you know him. He's one of these new kids that thinks they know everything. He's name is Wayne Jennings."

"Oh, is he that red-headed boy that was in there Friday?" She queried.

"Yeah, that was him. He's friendly enough. It's just going to take some work on smoothing him out. Probably as soon as I get him trained they'll put him at another branch." Percy sighed.

West Main Branch was the busiest branch in Murfreesboro. Percy had become the trainer of manager's. He would train them and then they would go to another branch to be manager. He had started at the bank as a teller, but moved up quickly due to dependability, a good attitude, and smarts.

"You know Mildred and Bess retired from the Post Office. This is going to be their last month."Roxie said changing the subject. "I'm working one more year and I'm retiring."

She would be 65 years old and was looking forward to her retirement. She could work in the garden. She would be able to do anything she wanted to do.

****

"Let's get in the car." Michael said to everyone. They all looked at each other and decided it was the right thing to do. It was grandmother's old beat up postal car. Tricia sat at the driver's seat, and Eliza sat in the passenger seat. Luke and Michael were sitting in the back seat. Tricia put the car in reverse, and the garage being on a slight decline began to roll down the hill into the field.

"This is neat." Luke said looking out the window he had just rolled down.

"Yeah." Eliza said as she was looking out the back window. "Tricia, stop the car, stop the car! We're headed right towards the black pot." The black pot was cast iron, and Eliza knew when the car hit it the car would be torn up.

Tricia tried to get the gear back into first, but was not successful. The car kept rolling towards the black pot. Tricia was trying harder.

"I can't get it in first gear!" She was only used to driving automatic cars, not stick shifts.
****

Eliza had practiced driving Percy's truck in the corn field. He usually put it in gear for her. She would then shift gears from first to fourth and then to reverse, but she was afraid to get over to the driver's seat with the car still rolling. She did this until she had it down pretty good. Eliza first learned to drive a truck in Newton and Roxie's front fields. Hay had to be cut, bailed, and hauled in the fall and spring. She was ten years old when she first was given the job of driving the truck to haul hay. Percy put it in the lowest gear possible.

"Now, honey, you need to just barely keep your foot on the pedal. We just need to have the truck moving at a slow pace. No sudden stops. If that happens, then all the hay will fall off the truck. O.K.?" He explained to her where she could understand.

"O.K., daddy." It was a little rocky at first. She jolted the truck when she took her foot off the gas and then put it back on suddenly.

"Watch it down there." Luke yelled.

At hay hauling time it was a given that Luke and Percy would haul hay. Newton would watch from the front porch. They always needed at least two more helpers. Catty-corner across from Newton and Roxie's farm lived Two Bales. He saw the hay being bailed and came over to talk with Percy, who was leaning against his two-ton flatbed truck.

"Hey, are you Mr. Jenkins?" He said as he stood in front of Percy. He was a chubby, chocolate-colored brown boy. He had big round eyes, which were wide open as he looked up at Percy.

"I am." He looked down at the boy, who couldn't of been no more than eleven years old. The boy stood only 4'11".

"You looking for help hauling hay? I saw you bailing it. I figured you needed help." The boy began questioning.

"Yeah, I might be. Can you haul hay?" Percy asked him.

"Mr. Prater, I can haul two bales at a time." With short sales pitch he got the job.

When he said he could haul two bales at a time they began calling him Two Bales. He maybe just maybe could have loaded two bales of straw at a time, but two bales of hay was out of the question. Percy knew it was. He had years of practice, and, after a while, would get worn out hauling two bales at a time. Two Bales kept up with Luke. Percy fed all of his helpers and paid them at that time three cents a bale.

"I tell you what I think it was mistake offering to feed these boys. They sure can eat." He was feeding Two Bales, Luke, and cousin Neil.

****

"Eliza, you and Michael need to run to the house and get somebody to help me stop this car!" Tricia was yelling by this time.

She had elected them two because they could run the fastest. Eliza and Michael hopped out of the rolling car. They hit the ground in a dead run. They ran up the stairs into the kitchen. Eliza made it first. She was panting hard from the run. Michael followed panting just as hard.

"What is it, Eliza?" Percy asked afraid of the answer.

"The car. . . .it's rolling. . ." She was pointing to the field. "The black pot. . ." She was still trying to catch her breath.

Joe had come by for a visit and looked Percy in the eyes. They jumped to their feet and headed out the door. They looked, and the car had about 100 feet before it hit the black pot. Luke was in the backseat yelling and waving his arms out the window.

Joe and Percy ran as hard as they could. As soon as they got in ear shot of Tricia. Percy yelled for her to scoot over. Joe grabbed the handle of the driver's door and jumped in. He put his foot on the brake and clutch at the same time. The car stopped. Ten more feet and it would have hit the black pot. Percy opened the door on the passengers' side and got in.

"What were ya'll thinking?" He said looking at Tricia and Luke.

"We just got in and were pretending like we were driving. I guess I knocked it out of gear, and it started rolling. I couldn't stop it." Tricia said looking down at her lap. All one could see was her thick, curly black hair.

"Yeah, daddy, she couldn't stop it." Luke chimed in.

Joe put the car in first gear and headed back towards the open garage where the car had been originally. Percy looked up and saw the whole crew was standing in the driveway. Michael and Eliza were getting an ear full.

"What were you thinking getting into the car in the first place? Someone could have gotten hurt." Linda said looking at Eliza almost eye to eye. Eliza was 5'2", and her mother was 5'3".

"We just got in the car to pretend to drive. The car started rolling. I don't know why," came Eliza's quick response to her mother.

The car was almost to the garage by now. They all scooted out of the way so Joe could get the vehicle into the garage. Tricia and Luke were the first to get out, followed by Joe and Percy.

"Is everyone o.k.?" Roxie asked.

"Yeah, everyone's fine. I think they got a little scare in them." Percy replied. "I don't think they'll be getting into the car anymore."

"No harm done. Let's get back in the house, now." Roxie said as she headed up the steps into the kitchen.

The adults took their seats back at the table. The kids ran upstairs to play.

"You said you were retiring in a year?" Percy asked as he took another pecan tart. He was glad with the dessert change. "These sure are good."

"That's right. I plan on it. Oh, my stomach, excuse me." She ran to the bathroom.

"I was getting worn out with that angel food cake. I wonder how long the pecan tart dessert will last?" Joe said to everyone at the table when Roxie got up to leave.

Newton looked over his glasses at Joe with a disapproving look. Joe took the hint and didn't say another word about the angel food cake or the pecan tarts. Roxie made them for the next three months until December came around. She then came upon a recipe for fruit cake cookies. It didn't have the heavy, thick goopy taste of fruit cake. In fact, the cookies were light and delicious with just enough fruit not to overwhelm the cookie.

Roxie made it back into the kitchen. She sat down slowly. Her stomach hurt all over, but she wasn't going to tell anyone. She didn't want to worry anybody.

"Let's play some *Rook*." Joy said.

"That sounds like a good idea. We got time for one game. Who wants to play?" Percy asked looking at everyone around the table.

It was decided that Joe, Newton, Joy, and Percy would play a game of *Rook*. Linda and Roxie stayed in the kitchen. Percy and Joy got the card table and set it up in the usual spot in front of the fireplace in the living room. He went back into the kitchen and noticed his mother was pale looking.

"Mama, you sure you don't want to play?"

"No, go ahead. I'm just going to sit here and relax."

Percy could feel his mother was keeping something from him, but didn't push it. It wasn't like her to not play a game of cards, especially *Rook*. She looked tired and worn out. This wasn't like Roxie either. She was the type that stayed busy from the time she woke up, 5:00 a.m., until the time she went to bed, 10:30 p.m.

"If you change your mind just let me know." Percy said with a little concern in his voice.

"I will," was Roxie's short reply because she was so tired.

Tricia, Eliza, Michael, and Luke came roaring down the stairs.

"Grandmamma, can we have some more pecan tarts?" Luke blurted out before he was even in the kitchen.

"Sure, help yourself."

Roxie and Linda were still sitting at the table. Luke took Newton's seat. Linda was sitting to his left, and Eliza sat next to her mom. Michael sat at the other end of the table. Tricia set next to her grandmamma.

"When are we going to draw names for Christmas, grandmamma?" Tricia asked as she finished her pecan tart.

"At Thanksgiving like we always do, that's if I'm still living." Roxie said as her eyes locked on Eliza's.

Eliza had a keen sense about her. She didn't like that statement at all. Her grandmamma was acting like she was dying, and that was something she didn't even want to contemplate. Eliza never really thought about death since no one in her immediate family had died. She hadn't really had to deal with it.

She thought to herself. 'I don't want grandmamma to die. I'll miss her. What about Thanksgiving? What about Christmas? I'll never see her again.' She wouldn't think about it anymore. She would pretend her grandmother didn't make that statement.

Linda said, "Don't talk like that. You'll be around here for a long time."

The living room was full of action. Newton was winning at *Rook*. He was chewing on his cigar as he gathered up the kitty. He and Joe had 100 points to win the game, and they would be out. Percy, Joy, and Joe were all smoking their cigarettes, eating Charlie Chips, and drinking iced tea. It didn't matter how cold it got outside Roxie always had iced tea, and no matter how hot it got she always had coffee.

"I don't believe it." Joy looked at Percy as Newton laid down the red one. They knew they were beaten.

"Some people have all the luck." Percy said. "We're beat."

Newton replied back in an usual short response for him. "I'd rather be lucky than rich."

Newton enjoyed the glory. He loved playing any kind of games that required skill and excelled at all games he attempted. He loved *Canasta, Rook,* and *Checkers.*

Percy always said he didn't see anyone who could beat his dad at *Checkers.* "Well we better go. It's getting to be late. We got to get the kids fed and off to bed."

Linda walked into the living room. After years of marriage it was like they could read each other's minds. She was ready to go.

Percy looked up at her and said, "Are you about ready to go, Hon?" He always called her Hon, short for Honey.

Linda shook her head yes. Everyone started heading out the front door telling Newton and Roxie goodbye.

The days were shorter, and the sun began setting early. It was 4:30 p.m., and the sky looked a deep pink with streaks of orange as the sun was shining its final rays. Percy, Linda, Eliza, and Luke were packed in the car as it headed down the driveway. Percy pulled the car out onto Shelbyville Highway.

"How do you think mother looked?" Percy asked taking a glance at Linda hoping for a good reply.

"I think she looked a little tired."

"Do you really? I did too. I think she looks weak. Maybe she's just coming down with a cold or something." Percy was talking more to himself trying to figure it out.

"Yeah, maybe. I think she should retire now. She's got enough time in to retire. She needs to take a break, ever since I've known her she's been working." Linda wanted to make him feel better because she just felt something wasn't with right Roxie. She could feel it in her gut.

"You're right. She raised us kids then she went to work at the post office. She's bound to need a break. It's not like they don't have the money. They could live comfortably." Percy agreed with Linda. He didn't want to say anything, but he was worried about his mother.

The rest of the short ride was silent. By the time they pulled into their driveway there was a thin streak of orange left in the nighttime sky.

CHAPTER NINE

The grandkids grew up and didn't need to be around Newton and Roxie. They had their own lives to live. They still showed up on Thanksgiving and Christmas and other special occasions. Roxie retired from the postal service along with Newton. Roxie still planted a garden big enough to feed the town of Murfreesboro even though it was just her and Newton in the house. She froze vegetables all summer long to last them through the fall, winter, and spring. What she didn't freeze or eat, she gave away to friends, neighbors and family. On the weekends Newton and Roxie played cards with their friends, or their sons' and daughters'.

Percy and Luke saw Newton and Roxie almost on a daily basis. They were running the farm. Eliza helped around the farm when life wasn't taken her to more exciting places. Of all the children Percy and his family saw Newton and Roxie the most. They still came by for dinners. Percy had a strong family ethic, which was instilled by his mother and father. If they were blood family, it was taught you stood by them no matter what, no matter how crazy, or how much trouble they happened to get into—it was through thick or thin.

Percy and Luke walked into the kitchen, and Roxie was sitting at the table. Percy could tell she was in pain. "What's wrong mama?"

"Oh, nothing my stomach is hurting a little." She tried to play it off as something insignificant.

"What do you mean a little?" Percy prodded her for more information.

"It just hurts, that's all." Roxie said a little defensively. Roxie hated going to doctors. She hated the waiting. She hated spending the money. Worst of all she hated bad news.

"What's going on mama? I know you haven't been feeling good for some time." He had noticed she had really looked tired the last couple of months. Her skin coloring was changing to a sallow pale instead of the healthy rosy light tan.

"I'm just passing a little blood when I go to the bathroom that's all. It's probably hemorrhoids." She tried for nonchalant this time.

"Do you mean when you have a bowel movement?" He tried not to sound concerned this time because he knew his mother would clam up tighter than an oyster shell on the subject.

"Yeah," she didn't tell him she was passing blood in her urine as well.

"Well, is it every time?" It was trying to pull teeth to get an answer out of her. He had to ask her direct questions.

Roxie didn't want to answer the question. To answer it meant to admit something was wrong with her, and she didn't want to do that. She looked down at her cup of coffee. "Well, not every time."

Percy knew good and well she was lying at this point. His mother was what held the family together. He knew she didn't want to admit that she might be mortal, and worse of all she didn't want to go to the doctor. He poured him a cup of coffee and told Luke to go to see Newton. He was trying to decide whether to say something to her or not. He sat down at his usual spot at the kitchen table and was facing her. He was looking at her square in the eyes. "Have you considered going to see Dr. Hester?"

"It's crossed my mind." She was still a little defensive, but she was having to admit to herself the pain was beginning to be too much for her.

"Well, why don't you make an appointment?" He tried to make it sound like a suggestion.

"I'll do it when I get around to it." This meant the matter was closed.

"Alright," he knew the subject had gone too far.

Luke came back into the kitchen. He went to the refrigerator and looked inside to see if there was anything to eat. He did this every time he came over to his grandmother's. It didn't matter if he had been over there twice in one day, it was a habit. He didn't see anything he wanted and decided to fix him a glass of iced tea. He drank it almost in one gulp. His dad and him had been working hard all day, and he was dying of thirst.

"Well, I guess we'd better go." Percy said to Luke, who put the glass in the sink. "Mama you think about what I said."

"I'll think about it." She was ready for them to leave. All she wanted to do was to lay on the couch and watch the news. Her back and stomach were knotted up. 'Maybe it's gas,' she thought to herself.

With Percy and Luke gone Roxie stood up and went to the kitchen counter. She was almost doubled over in pain. She took a pain reliever and went to the den to join Newton, who was watching the evening news. She laid on the couch and propped her feet up under the end pillow of the pale green velveteen couch. Newton looked at her for a moment. He thought it was odd that Roxie was lying down but decided not to say anything.

Roxie laid on the couch in almost constant pain. It was a dull pain coupled with sharp shooting pains. Roxie knew she needed to go to the bathroom, but dreaded it. The news was over, and she made her way to the bathroom. She thought she was going to kill over in pain before it was finally over. Once her bowel movement was over she felt much better. When she finished she told herself she would call and make an appointment after Christmas. She wanted to enjoy the holidays.

****

It was Christmas Eve, and Newton had gone to get Shoog. Roxie was in the kitchen preparing the dressing. The turkey was in the oven, and the country ham had already been taken out of the lard can ready to be carved when Shoog walked in.

"Shoog, how you doing?" Roxie asked while she was stirring the dressing.

"I'm fine, just fine." She had her spotless white uniform on with the apron that was soon to be covered with stains of all sorts.

"Newton go plug the tree up. The kids will be here before long." She was thoroughly enjoying herself. She had resorted to plunging her hands in the big bowl and mixing the dressing by hand. When she felt it was good and mixed she began pouring it in iron skillets and cake pans. She had it down to an art by now.

Shoog began making the giblet gravy. Her and Roxie had worked together for so long they each knew which duty was theirs to do. The eggs had already been boiled. Shoog was standing over the trash can peeling the eggs. She looked up at Roxie and noticed her coloring was a little off. It was hard to tell with white people because they didn't have any color she thought to herself, but she knew something was different about Roxie.

"You're looking a little peeked, Ms. Prater. You not feeling up to your old self these days?" Shoog tried to brooch the subject.

"Oh, I'm alright, just a little stomach problem." She would hope this reply would close the subject.

"You know what will take care of that don't you?" Shoog didn't expect an answer, "a little castor oil."

Roxie was trying to avoid the subject, so she decided to change it. "You're right." She figured if she agreed with her that would be the end of the subject. "How's the gravy coming?"

Shoog took the hint. "Eggs are chopped and in the pan with the rest of the stuff. Now it's cooking time. I'll get the cranberry sauce on the table."

Roxie was washing her hands and decided to sit down for a few minutes. Her legs and back ached from standing for so long. She had been in the kitchen since early morning. Shoog took a peak at the green beans and fried corn on the stove. She stirred them both and stuck her finger in the fried corn then licked it, the final approval taste test. "Roxie, you make the best fried corn."

"Ain't nothing to it." She said a little weakly.

"I've been in many a houses, and yours is the best by far." Her fried corn was the best, but she knew Roxie wasn't her old self—something was off. She was trying to make her feel better.

Roxie was sitting at the kitchen table with a cup of coffee resting her body. "Oh, the tea. Shoog can you boil me some tea bags?"

"Shore can." Shoog got right to it.

The turkey had cooled enough, and Shoog took to cutting it up. The platter was full. Percy, Linda, Eliza, and Luke came through the back door.

"Mr. Percy," came Shoog's reply as she headed towards Percy.

"Shoog." She went up to him and gave him a big hug. He hugged her back. Shoog then proceeded to hug everyone in the family. Eliza and Linda had their hands full of pans of uncooked homemade rolls. Eliza's rolls had passed the taste test of Shoog and Roxie, so she was appointed the official roll maker. Shoog took the pans and set them on the counter. She pinched Eliza's face and told her how much she had grown. Eliza was now about four inches taller than Shoog.

"Percy can you get that ham out of there and cut it up for us?" Roxie asked. She was worn out, but she wasn't about to admit it.

"Sure." Percy proceeded to lift the ham out of the container. All of the newspaper that surrounded it he stuck back in the container. "Can someone get me a platter?"

Shoog hurried to the counter and got the platter for the country ham. Percy placed the ham on it and made himself a little niche on the kitchen table.

"I need a knife." One was presented to him before he took a seat by Shoog.

He looked at his mom and for the first time realized how old and worn out she looked. "How you feeling mom?"

"I'm alright." Her standard, quick reply, which meant no further discussion.

Percy didn't take the hint. "What about your stomach?" Shoog overheard the conversation.

"I told her what she needed was a good dose of castor oil. You know that will clean anybody out.

If there's still problems after that then you go to the doctor."

Percy laughed, and Roxie made herself laugh. She had already tried that, but all that did was make her hurt more and the commode would be filled with blood.

Joy and her family were next through the back door. They came with wine and beer. Ken had already downed about three on the way from Nashville to Murfreesboro, so he was feeling no pain. Joy was a little tipsy herself. Michael and Tricia went into the living room to talk with Luke and Eliza. Shoog gave her hugs to Joy and Tim. The kids got away before she could hug them. By this time Shoog had worked up quiet an odor.

Roxie finally got up and took the dressing out of the oven and set it on the table, where a spot had been made for it. The rest was put on the counter. The rest of the family had piled into the house. Family was everywhere in the den, the living room, dining room, and kitchen. The men were picking at the turkey and country ham. The women were sitting at the card tables that were set up in the dining room, which after the meal and presents, would be used as canasta tables.

Tim was asked to say the blessing. He hiccupped a couple of times during the thanking of the food and family part. It was an unwritten law that Newton got first dibbs, any adult, or child trying to go first would be pulled back in line. Roxie had catered to Newton's every whim since they were married, but once the break down occurred she went into over catering.

Usually the men talked in the kitchen and drank their wine, beer, or Jack Daniels, while the mother's made sure the kids had a plate of food and then they helped themselves. The kids were all old enough to help themselves, so it was every person for him or herself. Usually the teenagers went next, they were all ravenous and then the wives. Last were the men, and Percy usually went the very last.

Dinner was being eaten, and everyone was complimented who had cooked. Newton was finished and ready for his presents. Everyone brought their plates in the kitchen, while Shoog commenced to washing and cleaning. Roxie and Newton took their usual seats in front of the fireplace, which was lit and emitting a beautiful orange glow. Michael and Eliza had taken the role as the persons who handed out the presents. They knew first to give Newton and Roxie at least four presents by their chairs, and then they could hand out the other presents.

Roxie looked around at her family and was quiet proud. She savored the moment. Ann was married to a successful lawyer. They had two children, one in college studying accounting, the other in high school, who would be a successful woman some day.

Percy was a successful banker, his family well taken care of. Linda worked for the county, and, their children were both still in school. She had no doubt they would be alright. Eliza was going to go to college, and Luke was planning on going to college himself.

Joy worked for a federal judge, and Tim worked for the federal government. Michael was still in high school and would be going to college, and Tricia was presently working on her degree in college.

Jan and Randy seemed to be happy. He was running and maintaining his grandfather's farm, which would someday be his. Jan was working at the bank, Percy worked at. Randy was in middle school.

Joe drank a little too much, but he had a good job at *Coca-Cola*. Amanda was still in middle school. Joe was on his second wife. Roxie could tolerate her. Joe's first wife wasn't good enough for him. She thought to herself, or he wouldn't have left her. She just married him for his future money. She was a gold digger from Nashville.

She bent down to get her first present, and she grimaced in pain. It was a sharp, shooting pain in her stomach and back. She looked around to see if anyone noticed. She evaluated the situation and determined no one did. She took a deep breath and commenced to opening her present. It was given to her by Ann and Tom. It was a beautiful night gown.

By now the scene was full of paper strewn from one end of the living room to the other. Luke had over the years became the trash collector. He had a big trash bag and was stuffing it with opened and torn wrapping paper.

Newton got up from his seat and began handing out the envelopes to the grandchildren. It had the usual twenty dollars stuffed inside it. The grandchildren said their thanks. Eliza and Michael were the only ones who hugged Newton. Newton was not a hugger or a kisser. Eliza kissed him on his cheek.
The older girls and the women began to play canasta, while the men and some of the sisters started to play poker. Tom lost a lot and fast. He was now standing beside the poker players drinking his bloody mary. His speech was slurred. Over the years he had swelled up all over, but especially in his gut, which looked like a balloon ready to pop.

Joe had a beer gut and couldn't scoot his chair up all the way to the table. Joy and Percy had both lost weight and looked the healtiest of the clan. Ann was too thin and drank wine like water. She never was beligerent or seemed drunk. Jan had put on weight. She yo-yoed throughout her life. Right now she was on the low end of her weight.

Roxie watched the bathroom. Everyone was busy, so she made a bee line to the toilet. She tried to walk straight as if nothing was wrong with her, but she was in agony by now. She had hardly eaten anything for dinner. She was in there a good fifteen minutes in total pain and agony. She was looking up at the ceiling telling herself and God.

"God, I'll make a doctor's appointment after Christmas. I promise just let this pain stop." Once she was finished the pain did stop. She hadn't forgotten her promise to herself and God.

CHAPTER TEN

Percy came in through the kitchen. It was a cold, blistery day in January. The wind cut through him like a knife. The aroma of coffee hit his nostrils. Roxie was sitting at the table in her usual spot with her hands wrapped around the coffee cup. Percy went to the coffee pot and fixed him a cup of coffee, heavy on the sugar and cream. He sat down at his usual spot across from Roxie. Newton was back in the den watching the early evening news. Jimmy Carter's smile was plastered all over the television set. Newton didn't vote for him. He always went with the Republicans.

Percy looked across the table at her mother. She looked worn out. He could tell she had lost some weight. Usually at this time of day, she was busy cooking supper, but she was trying to get her strength up for it.

"How you feeling these days?" Percy said looking at his mom straight in the eyes.

"I've had better days. I've made an appointment with Dr. Hester." She quickly looked down at her coffee cup.

It was an admission of defeat. Percy knew it too. For his mother to voluntarily go to the doctor was unheard of. She had to be in dire pain. He could remember when his brother and sister were born. The water broke in the tub, and Newton and him had to heave her up out of the tub, get some clothes on her, and drive her to the doctor's office. She barely got in the doctor's office before she had both of them. She had Percy at home, and he was born breach weighing 13 pounds.

Percy finally answered. "You have. When are you going?"

"Day after tomorrow, I've told Newton it's just a checkup." Roxie said trying to convince herself also it was just a checkup.

Percy knew it wasn't just a checkup. He feared what might be wrong with her. He knew something was wrong with her, but he decided he needed to be more of support to his mother at this moment. "I'm glad you're going. You want me to take you there?"

"No, that's alright. Newton's going to drive me."

They sat in silence for awhile drinking their coffee for about five minutes. "I got three pregnant heifers. They should drop about spring time." Percy said looking for words to say.

"That's good. How's the kids and Linda doing?" She asked grateful the subject had been changed.

"There fine, fine. Eliza is going to start college this fall. Luke moved up a year in high school. He'll be graduating a year early. You know Luke. He wants to be the first in everything." He took another sip of coffee. "Linda likes her job at the Circuit Court Clerk's office."

"That's good." She was proud of Percy and his family.

"You want me to go and pick up something for you and dad to eat?" It was already 5:30, and she hadn't even begun to cook supper. They usually ate around 6:00 p.m.

Roxie wanted to give into the temptation, but pride wouldn't let her. Spending money on going out to eat was a waste of money, especially when there was food at the house to eat. "That's alright."

"Now, mom it wouldn't be any trouble. I can run down to town and pick ya'll some chicken or a hamburger up." He said hoping she would take him up on the offer.

Murfreesboro had grown tremendously over the last thirty years. The only places one used to go out to eat at were mom and pop restaurants. Next, Shoney's came into town and then Dairy Queen. After a few more years the most of the fast food joints arrived.

Roxie really wanted to give in at this point. She was in so much pain from sitting up that it was almost unbearable. She wasn't even hungry, but she had to make sure Newton was fed. Percy realized his mother was torn between cooking a home-cooked meal for Newton, or getting fast food in which Newton would turn his nose up.

"You know how Newton is. He wants a home-cooked meal."

"I tell you what. Linda's always cooking too much for us. You know Eliza works at night half the time, and Luke is running around with his friends. Linda still cooks for four though. I'll call her and see if she's getting close to having dinner ready. We'll bring you a couple of plates over." He felt he had found a compromise with his mother that would work.

Roxie looked down at the table. "I don't want you to go to a bunch of trouble for us."

"No trouble." He was getting close to convincing her.

"Well, don't fix me much to eat. I haven't had much of an appetite lately." She finally consented without saying a definite yes, but she gave the o.k.

Percy got up from the table and poured the left over coffee in the sink. "I'll be back in about twenty minutes."

"Alright, I'll see you then."

Percy left, and Roxie got up from the table and headed for the bathroom. Newton was oblivious. He was engrossed in the news. She had just finished and felt a little better when Percy and Linda came through the back door in the kitchen.

Linda had the crock pot wrapped in a dishtowel to keep the food warm. Roxie came into the kitchen. She sat down at the table. Linda put the crock pot in the middle of the kitchen table. It was full of roast, potatoes, and carrots. She turned the oven on to warm up the rolls. While the rolls were warming she set the table. Roxie looked at the non-stop energy of Linda. She had taken control of the situation.

With the evening news over, Newton came into the kitchen due to hunger pangs. Percy had fixed him another cup of coffee. Linda examined the coffee pot and determined that a fresh pot needed to be made. She hastily poured the old coffee out and had the new coffee brewing in less than a minute. Roxie was getting more tired just looking at her in action. Linda found the napkins and placed them around the plates.

Linda had timed it right, the rolls and coffee were finished at the same time. "Mr. Prater do you want a cup of coffee?"

He was already sitting at the table ready to eat. "Sure."

Linda poured him a cup and brought it to him. "What about you Mrs. Prater?"

"I think I will." She was glad to have some company over for a change. She was feeling a little better since she had gone to the restroom. Maybe she could eat after all she thought to herself. Linda fixed both of them a cup of coffee.

Linda finally sat down with rolls in hand. She passed them to Percy. She lifted the lid off the crock pot, and the delicious aroma filled the room. Percy had told Linda about his conversation with his mother. Everyone's plate was full of roast and vegetables. Newton was still trying to figure out why they came by. His question was soon answered.

"Percy and I were sitting in the kitchen. I said to him why don't we go by your mom and dad's house with this. It'll just go to waste. The kids are always eating out now with their friends."

Roxie helped Linda out. "Well, we sure do appreciate it. I was just sitting at the table trying to figure out what I would cook for supper. This sure is good."

"Thank you. It's easy. You just through it all in the crock pot and turn it on. Throw a couple of cans of soup in there. Crock pots a thing to have if you work and have kids."

"I might need to get me one of those." Roxie would never get one. It was too modern. She cooked over the stove. She was just saying it to be nice to Linda.

After dinner, Linda told Roxie just to sit still, she would do all of the cleaning up. Newton, Roxie, and Percy sat at the table and talked about the upcoming elections. The democrats were running the state, but this didn't deter them at all for voting Republican. They believed in the Republican values-- working hard, taking care of your family, getting an education, and saving money. They didn't depend on Social Security.

"I'm surprised it's lasted as long as it has." Newton said before he took a sip of his fresh-brewed coffee.

"Me either." Roxie said looking at Newton. "Could you imagine how we'd be living if we had to just survive off of Social Security?" She answered the question for him. "That's it, we'd be just surviving."

Now, their house and farm were paid for, but it would still be just enough to get by, and they didn't want to just get by. They wanted to save.

Percy was cleaning his teeth with a toothpick. "In twenty years the Social Security system will be in trouble. By the time Luke and Eliza get old enough to draw it, there probably won't be any left. The government's borrowing from it now. Just wait and see."

"You're probably right." Linda chimed in from the kitchen sink.

Linda finished the dishes and cleaned out her crock pot then sat down at the table. "What do you think about Alexander for governor?"

"I think he might win this election?" Percy said. "He's going all over the state in that red and black flannel shirt. I hope he washes it. God, I bet it stinks." Everyone laughed.

"He's got a good chance." Newton said.

"He's getting my vote, stinking or not." Roxie finally said trying to hide the pain in her side.

"Linda, I guess we better get going."

"I guess you're right." They got up from the kitchen table and began heading for the door.

"Thank you Linda for bringing supper. I was just worn out. Guess I been doing too much lately."

"Your welcome, any time, you know you always cooked for us at least twice a week when the kids were little." Linda said trying to make Roxie feel better.

****

    The day after tomorrow arrived, and Newton drove Roxie to Dr. Hester's. It was a biting to the bone cold day. Snow was forecasted. The high was to be only twenty degrees. Only in Tennessee one day it might be fifty degrees, and the next it could be ten below.

    Newton drove around the town square then down East Main Street ending at the medical center. Dr. Hester's nurse, Sara, a big, burly woman, called Roxie's name. The typical blood pressure was taken along with the weight and temperature. She was then lead into an examination room.

    "What brings you in here today Mrs. Prater?"

    Roxie adjusted her body on the table until she got comfortable. "I've been having a lot of pain in my stomach and lower back. I'm having a hard time having bowel movements. When I do have one it's all bloody. It's probably hemorrhoids."

    The nurse was writing on the chart never looking up. When she finished she said. "You'll need to strip down and put this gown on. Dr. Hester will be in here in a few minutes."

    Dr. Hester wasn't long in coming. He entered the room. "It's been a while since I've seen you Roxie. How you been doing?" He could call her that since they were about the same age. She was the only doctor she had ever been too.

"I'm alright." She lied, or she wouldn't have been at the doctor's office.

"What about Newton?" Dr. Hester asked.

"He's fine." This wasn't a lie.

"I hear you've been having some problems with your bowel movements?" He said looking at his chart.

"That's right." She didn't want to say too much. It was bad enough that she was there.

"Well, lay back on the table. Let's see what's going on here." He poked and prodded all up and down her stomach and abdomen.

"Oh, that hurts!" Roxie about jumped off the table.

"I hate to do this, but I'm going to need to do a rectal and pelvic examination." Dr. Hester left the room to go and get Sara. She was there in a flash.

Dr. Hester proceeded with the examination. He noticed blood in both areas. "Have you been passing blood when you urinate?"

"A little." This was a small fib in Roxie's mind. She told herself it was a little, but in fact it was becoming heavier with each day. She had already gone through menopause.

When he finished his rubber gloves were covered in blood. He knew she would need to see a specialist.

"Roxie I'm going to have Sara here make you an appointment with Dr. Smith, the gastrologist. They'll probably run some tests on you. More than likely they'll do what's called a colonoscopy."

"A what!" She sounded shocked because she didn't like the sound of that word at all.

"It's a test. They run a tube through your rectum with a scope on it to see if you have any polyps."

"I will be asleep during this won't I?" Roxie asked with fear in her voice.

"You sure will. Other than that everything else looks alright. Do you have any questions?" He tried to sound reassuring and calming to her.

"No." She was ready to high-tail it out there.

"Go ahead, get dressed, and Sara will be in here with your appointment. Are you having a lot of pain when you have a bowel movement." He knew she had to be, but wanted to know for sure.

"Most of the time," Roxie finally conceded.

"I'm going to write you a prescription for some valium. That'll knock the edge off." Dr. Hester said hoping that would help her until her appointment with Dr. Smith.

They left, and Roxie proceeded to get dressed. She was barely finished when efficient Sara knocked and walked through the door. "Here's your prescription, get it filled as soon as you leave, don't wait for the pain. You got lucky. You can get into see Dr. Smith tomorrow at 2:00."

"Thank you." Roxie said as she took the prescription from the nurse. She was hoping she would have a couple of days before she had to go back to another doctor.

Roxie went out into the waiting room. Newton was sitting there with keys in hand ready to go. He hated doctor's office's about as much as Roxie did. His thinking was when someone went to the doctor they always came out worse, and if they went to the doctor's office the person was lucky to come out alive.

They got into the car. The snow had started to fall and was sticking to the roads. It had been twenty degrees for the past three days. The schools were already letting out early. The traffic was heavier than normal. Parents picking up children, school buses on the road, and employees trying to get home before it got any worse. It was a good ten minutes before the car warmed up.

Newton finally broke the silence. "What'd the doctor have to say?"

"I've got to go tomorrow to see a Dr. Smith. He's some kind of stomach doctor. They want to run some tests on me. Oh, yeah, by the way, we need to stop by the pharmacist to get this prescription filled. I'll know more tomorrow." Roxie replied with to the point information trying to sound matter of fact like it wasn't anything.

CHAPTER 11

Roxie and Newton got home. She took two valiums as prescribed. She hated taking medicine, but she was hurting from the waist down. If she wanted to get dinner cooked then she had to take the medicine. She made a simple dinner--meatloaf, mashed potatoes, and green beans, which she had frozen over the summer. Also, cornbread the primary staple at her table was provided.

They ate supper in quietness. Roxie noticed the north wind whipping through the crevices of the house. The gas heat had already been turned up when they had gotten home, and the house was just now getting comfortable. It looked bright outside because of the two-inch thick snow that covered the ground. Roxie barely touched her food. She was worried about tomorrow. She hated the thought of going to another doctor, but she had no choice the pain was almost to the unbearable point.

"Newton after supper let's go sit in the living room, turn on the gas fire, and watch the snow."

"Alright," he wondered what had gotten into Roxie her wanting to look at a fire, but he didn't want to deny her request.

She loved looking at fresh fallen snow before any tracks were made in it. Before the salt trucks came out and made it a dirty snow. After the table was cleared off and the dishes cleaned they went into the living room. Roxie began the fire, and they sat for a good hour watching the snow fall. It was peaceful and serene.

"Newton, you remember back in the fifties when the schools let out, and everybody and their cousin showed up out here."

"Yep," he remembered all the cars parked out in the front field in front of the house.

"All the kid's friends were driving out here to play in the fields. They were driving from town to the country." She laughed. "Remember what I did?"

"Sure do."

"I called the county school superintendent, Dr. Howe, and told him he needed to come out to my house and see all the kids out here. If they could make it out here then they could make it to school. I was practically feeding every kid in the county." Now Roxie wouldn't admit it, but she loved every minute of it.

They both laughed. "School resumed the next day. Boy, all those kids were mad at me for awhile. I was tired of feeding them."

They enjoyed the snow for a little while longer and then went to bed.

The next day arrived with another two inches of snow on the ground for a total of four inches. The primary roads had been salted. Roxie woke up in pain. She needed to go to the bathroom, but dreaded it. She knew it would be nothing but anguish and pain. She didn't have an appetite. She took two valiums and waited for them to kick in before she tried to go to the bathroom. She finally relieved herself and then got ready to go to see Dr. Smith. She was ready by noon. She finally ate a bowl of cereal.

When Roxie had just finished Newton came into the kitchen. "You ready to go?"

It was 1:00, but they both believed in being early for appointments. Normally it took about twenty minutes to get to the doctor, but since the snow had hit the night before Newton was allowing 45 minutes with 15 minutes to spare.

Roxie put the bowl in the sink, "Whenever you are."

Newton went outside to start the car so it would warm up. After about five minutes he came back into the kitchen. "Let's go."

Roxie went out and got into the warm, cozy car. They slid down the driveway and made it to Shelbyville Highway. It was a little rough getting onto the highway. The further they got into town the easier the roads had gotten. The roads were a muddy, nasty, brown color, and the bottom of the cars were covered with brown ice.

Once inside the doctor's office Roxie had to fill out all of the necessary paperwork, which she hated to do. She felt insurance companies were nothing but a bunch of thieves. She didn't have to wait long before she heard her name called.

She went through all of the preliminaries again with the blood pressure and weight. The nurse asked Roxie about the symptoms that brought her here. She was told to lie on the table and wait for Dr. Smith.

Dr. Smith came through the door with reader glasses perched on his nose and graying hair. He was quiet handsome Roxie thought to herself. He got right to business. "I see you've been referred to me by Dr. Hester."

"Yes, that's right."

Dr. Smith went over to Roxie, who was lying on the table. "I'm going to feel around. You need to tell me if it hurts."

He began pressing around her abdomen. "That hurts." In fact, she hurt everywhere that he poked around on her stomach. Dr. Smith had the results of the rectal examination.

"Mrs. Prater, I'm going to need to do a colonoscopy on you." Roxie didn't want to hear this, but she figured it would happen so she wasn't in too much shock.

"When," she was hoping she would have a little time to prepare herself for it.

"Let me look at my schedule." He pulled out a pocket calendar and spotted an opening. "I don't have one tomorrow, but I have one the next day. That's probably best anyway because you're going to have to drink some stuff to make you go to the bathroom. This will clean you out and give us a clear picture when we go in. Is Thursday, alright then?"

"Yes. I guess so." Questions started coming to her mind. "What exactly does this do? Am I going to be asleep? Will it hurt?"

Dr. Smith took the comforting role. "Yes, we will put you to sleep. You won't feel a thing. The test is done by a scope. We insert the scope through your rectum. We are looking for polyps. If there are any then we remove them and do a biopsy on them to see if they're cancerous. Once the polyps are removed most of your pain will go away. If we see hemorrhoids we remove those too. You know those can be quiet painful."

"Now, Dr. Smith if you find anything, that say can't be cured, like cancer, I just want you to sew me back up. I don't want you to remove anything." Roxie didn't want to die her last days in chemotherapy and radiation with no hair.

Dr. Smith didn't say anything. He finally spoke up after a moment of silence. "Do you have any more questions?"

"I don't think so."

"No here's your prescription for the laxative. Get that filled and you'll begin drinking the liquid tomorrow around 1:00 p.m. I see you at the doctor's office on Thursday at 7:00 a.m."

"Alright," now she was ready to go.

Roxie was glad to get out of the office. She didn't know what she was going to tell Newton. She didn't want to worry him. She decided she would talk with Percy first. She was sure he would be by later on tonight after he checked the cows.

The cold air hit Roxie's face as they were headed for the car. It was almost dark by now. The sun had peeked out in the afternoon and helped melt a little of the snow, but the roads would be iced over again because the temperature was to be around ten degrees. The car was cold and took a good ten minutes to get warm. They stopped by the pharmacy to pick up Roxie's prescription and were heading home. It began snowing again.

They made it home just as the roads were beginning to turn to ice, and the roads were covered in a thin layer of velvety white. Roxie could see Percy making his rounds in the front field making sure all the cows were accounted for. She figured he would be in shortly. She made it up the steps, through the garage, and into the kitchen.

Newton was headed back into the den when Roxie said, "I'll have supper ready in about 30 minutes."

"Alright," he didn't want to miss the news. He figured Roxie was alright, if not she would tell him so, but he had a gut feeling she wasn't telling him everything. He had been married to her long enough to know when she was ready to talk. Roxie would let you know when she was ready to talk and not before.

Roxie opened the refrigerator door to see what kind of leftovers were in there. After standing there in silence for about a minute she decided they would have leftover vegetables. There was enough fried corn, green beans, and new potatoes for the two of them. She took two pain pills and began taking the containers out of the refrigerator, putting the contents into pans and placing the pans on the stove on low heat. She wouldn't have a microwave. She thought it dried the food out and took the flavor away. She sat down at the kitchen table to rest when she heard the back door open.

Percy came in through the garage and saw his mom sitting at the table. Roxie looked up at him and asked. "All of the cows accounted for?"

"Yeah," he was glad of it too because it meant he didn't have to hunt one down.

"It's going to be another cold night." Roxie said trying to make light conversation.

"Yeah, I know. I had to put out some more hay. I hope I have enough to last till spring." Percy said and thought this each year. He always had more than enough hay. He had so much hay that he usually sold some to the neighboring farmers, who really didn't have enough hay to last through the winter.

"I'm sure you'll have enough. Spring will be here before you know it."

"Well, how did the doctor's visit go today?" Percy asked as he was filling his cup from the truck up with fresh coffee Roxie had brewed when she got home.

"I guess, o.k. This Dr. Smith is wanting to do a colonoscopy on me."

"A what!" Percy said shockingly.

"A colonoscopy," Roxie repeated.

"What's that?" Percy asked as he took a sip of his coffee loaded with sugar and milk.

Roxie looked down at her coffee cup sitting on the table. She took a deep breath and proceeded with the story. "They told me it was some kind of scope they put in my rectum. They look to see if there are any polyps. If there are then they remove them, but I told them if they found anything else just to sew me back up."

Roxie waited for Percy's reply. "So when are you having this done?"

"Day after tomorrow, I've got to be at the doctor's office on Thursday at 7:00 a.m. It's only supposed to take about an hour."

"Have you told dad yet?"

Roxie looked down at the table. Percy knew she hadn't by the way his mother reacted. "No."

"Do you want me to tell him? You know you're going to have to have someone to drive you home." Percy said trying not to sound like he was scolding her.

"I know, but you know how upset he gets about things."

****

Percy sat at the table thinking about when the dog that came from nowhere showed up at Newton and Roxie's house. Newton didn't understand why it kept hanging around the house. What he didn't tell anyone was that he was feeding it scrap food every day.

All the grandkids loved the dog. It was a pretty collie. Everyone called her "Friend." Newton thought of the name. You could hold your hand out, and Friend would hold her paw out and shake hands with you. When Friend got hit by a car on the Shelbyville Highway, Newton and Eliza were the ones who took it the hardest. Newton cried for days, and Eliza followed with a couple of days of crying.

****

Roxie got up from the table to stir the vegetables. She decided they were done and began to set the pans on the table. "Newton." She hollered from the kitchen. Newton turned off the television and came into the kitchen. "Percy." He said as he sat at the head of the table.

"Dad," Percy said as he watched his mother fix her dad's plate as she had done for over 40 years. He let his dad get about halfway finished with his meal and decided it was time to tell his dad. He cleared his throat and lit a cigarette. "Dad, you know mother went to the doctor today?"

"Uh-um," Newton answered with a mouth full of food.

"Well, they want to do a little procedure on her Thursday." Newton stopped eating for a minute and looked at Percy.

Percy took a drag off his cigarette and took another sip of coffee. Newton finally spoke when he swallowed his food. "What kind?"

"It's called a colonoscopy." Then Percy proceeded to explain the procedure to him. He finally ended by saying. "She's having it done Thursday at 7:00 a.m. It only takes about an hour."

Roxie broke into the conversation. "I've got to prepare for it tomorrow. They want me to drink all of this stuff to clean me out. They told me that would be the worst part of it, getting ready for it."

Newton pushed his plate to the middle of the table and drank his coffee. He couldn't decide whether to be worried or not. He figured if Percy said it was just a procedure then it probably wasn't much to worry about. Then his mind drifted to when they would be putting Roxie to sleep. A lot of people didn't wake up, anything could happen. He started sniffling and a tear came out of his eye. He pulled out the handy handkerchief out of his pocket and blew his nose.

"What is it dad?"

"Well, wh-what if she doesn't wake up?"

"Dad, they're just going to lightly sedate her. It's not like putting her in a deep sleep." This answer seemed to satisfy him for the moment.

Percy sat with them a little longer then looked at his watch. It was 6:15. "I need to be going. Linda's probably got supper ready."

CHAPTER 12

Roxie was anxious when she got up. The high today would be 30 degrees. She couldn't wait for this procedure to be over, to be feeling better, and for spring to arrive, so she could plant her garden. The day before had been rough on her physically by her having to drink all the liquid. This caused her to be in the bathroom practically all day in so much pain that the pain killers weren't even helping.

She made it to the bathroom and splashed water on her face to wake herself up. She cleaned her teeth and then went into the kitchen to make

Newton some coffee. She wished she could have a cup, but if she drank it then they might not perform the procedure. She didn't want to have to go through another night like she did last night.

An hour later they were on the way to the doctor's office. Not a word was spoken on the way there. Newton didn't know what to say, neither did Roxie. Newton and Roxie sat in the waiting room, and it wasn't long before Roxie's name was called back. The nurse asked Newton if he would be driving Mrs. Prater home. He told her he would.

"Mrs. Prater, you'll need to strip down to nothing. Put this gown on, make sure it opens up in the back. When you're finished come on out. You can put your clothes in the plastic bag. We'll hold it for you. Use this marker to write your name on the bag."

Roxie took the bag and marker and went into the dressing room. When she had been lead back there she was amazed to see a mini operating room behind the double doors she had just gone through. She had wondered how they were going to do this in the office. She realized there were two parts to the building--the patient part and the procedure part. Roxie came out of the room with her bag. The nurse was waiting on her and took the bag. She led Roxie to her prep room where they would be putting her to sleep.

"Another person will be in here in a few minutes." The nurse said as she left the room. Another nurse entered and took her blood pressure and temperature. When she came in she brought a concoction of liquid in plastic bags hanging on a hook that rolled in with her.

"Now Mrs. Prater I'm going to try to find a vein and then I'm going to give you some medicine that will make you relaxed and sleepy. It might leave a funny taste in your mouth." The nurse strapped the rubber around Roxie's arm, tapping and thumping for a vein. She finally found one and inserted the needle.

"It's going to be two different injections, Mrs. Prater." The nurse said as she filled the syringes up with the medicine. "The first one will be the one that will leave a funny taste in your mouth." She said as she shot the medicine into the IV.

It wasn't five seconds, and the taste hit her mouth. "It tastes like onions."

"Onions, I haven't heard that one before?" The nurse questioned as she injected the second medicinal formula. "Now, you just relax, and we'll be in here in a few minutes."

Roxie laid on the cold table covered up with a sheet and hospital blanket. She was out in fifteen seconds. Three hours later Roxie woke up in a hospital room. She slowly opened her eyes and looked around. She saw Newton sitting to her left side. His head in his hands and he was sniffling. Percy was at the foot of the bed. The girls were by the window in the room. Joe was close to the door. Percy was the first to realize that his mother had woken up.

"Hey, mom." Percy said softly.

"Hey, Percy." Roxie said. Newton jerked his head up and looked at Roxie. He put out his hand to hold hers. She scooted her hand over to his, and he squeezed it. He began crying. She was still groggy. She wondered why she was in the hospital. She moved her other hand, and it touched a bag that seemed to be attached to her abdomen. She had a feeling this wasn't good. She wouldn't have to wonder for long.

Dr. Smith walked into the room with a chart in hand.

"How you doing Mrs. Prater?"

"I guess I'm alright. Why am I in here? What's this bag doing on me?" She said still groggy from the procedure.

Dr. Smith hated this part of his job more than any. "Well, when we got in there Mrs. Prater we ran into some problems."

She waited for him to continue. "You whole colon was full of cancer. I had to do radical surgery. If I left it in there after opening you, it would have spread and you wouldn't have had that much longer. I took the whole colon out. I tried to get all of the cancer out, but I'm going to have to refer you to an oncologist. The bag is permanent. It's where all of your waste will go. You'll have to change the bag daily. I wish I had better news for you."

"You mean I have cancer, Dr. Smith." Roxie said looking under the sheets on the bed and staring at the bag. She was afraid to look at anyone because she knew she would begin to cry. Newton started to cry and got out his handkerchief.

"Yes, I'm afraid so." Dr. Smith said while trying to think of some words of encouragement. "But where I'm sending you is the best. Once, they run some tests, get you going on treatments, there's no telling how long they can extend your life."

"And what if I don't get any treatments?" Roxie asked. All breathing seemed to stop when she asked this question, even Newton stopped sniffling.

"It's not good, Mrs. Prater." He wasn't expecting this question most patients wanted to live. "You would have maybe two months."

"Oh." Roxie didn't know what else to say. "I guess I have no choice then do I?"

"Not if you want to live. You should be getting out of here in about two days. We want to monitor you. I'll get my nurse to make you an appointment with Dr. Yung the oncologist. The nurse will be in here later on to show you how to change the bag."

Roxie was finished with the conversation. She had nothing left to say. She was mad at the moment. She had told him not to do what he did, but he did it anyway. Now she had to live with a bag hanging on her body for the rest of her life, however long that would be. She wanted everyone to leave, and she especially wanted Newton to stop crying. She couldn't think. This was too much, too fast and all at once.

Her mind was racing. 'Would she be able to work her garden this spring? Would she play canasta again? Would she see another Christmas or Thanksgiving? Would she make it to Easter? She wanted to see all of her grandchildren graduate from high school and college. There was so much still left undone, so much living to do.'

Dr. Smith interrupted her train of thought. "Do you have any more questions?"

"No."

"Then I will see you tomorrow."

Once the doctor left all of the girls came over to the bed and hugged their mother. Newton was still holding one of Roxie's hands.

Ann was holding back tears herself. "Mom do you need anything?"

"No, honey," Roxie replied groggily.

"What about one of those puzzle word books you like to work?" Ann wasn't giving up. She wanted to be able to do something for her mother, who had always done for her asking nothing in return.

"Whatever you want to do, honey," Roxie finally said in resignation.

Joy was next in line. She really didn't know what to say. Her mother had done so much for her. She couldn't bear the thought of actually losing her now or ever. She always thought her mother would be around. Now she was faced with her mother's mortality, as well as her own. "If you need anything, anything just let me know." She hugged her tight and kissed her cheek.

"Alright, honey."

Jan came up behind Joy. She bent down and hugged her mother. She couldn't talk. She knew if she did she would cry, so she didn't say anything.

Ann led the girls. "Mom we've got to go, but we'll back tomorrow to see you, alright?"

"I'll see ya'll tomorrow." Roxie said glad some of the room was going to clear out. She wanted to be left alone with her thoughts.

This left Percy and Joe in the room. Joe was ready to leave with the girls, but he hadn't said anything to his mother since she had come too from the surgery. He decided he would leave at the next opportune moment.

"I'm thirsty." Roxie said.

"I'll get you something." Joe said. He needed to get out and smoke a cigarette.

"Would you?" Roxie asked hopefully.

"Sure, what do you want?"

"A coke with lots of ice." This sounded like it would hit the spot to Roxie, so this is what she asked for.

"I'll be back in a few minutes." Joe rushed out the door. He went outside before he went into the cafeteria to smoke a cigarette.

This left Percy, Newton, and Roxie. Percy broke the ice. "How you holding up?"

"I guess as good as I can considering I just found out I have cancer, and I have to wear this stupid bag for the rest of my life."

Percy pulled up a chair and put it on the other side of his mother. He looked her dead straight in the eyes. "Now, you'll get use to the bag, mother. As for the cancer you'll get treatments and be back to yourself in no time."

Roxie wasn't too convinced at the moment, but it sounded good. She was ready to go home. "I hope so." She finally said with little conviction.

Joe finally made it back with the Coke. Roxie drank it down in less than a minute. "Boy, that sure was good, thank you."

"Mother, I need to go back to work." This was all Joe could think of at the moment. It sounded good, so he said it. He was known to stretch the truth, and this was one of those times. It was 6:00 at night. He was working at Budweiser delivering beer. The truth was he had gotten one of his co-workers to handle his deliveries for the day. He just needed to get out of the hospital. He was getting depressed.

"You go on." Roxie said.

"I'll see you tomorrow." Joe said as he headed out the door. He was afraid to hug his mother for fear of breaking down or her breaking down, so he left.

The room was silent. Percy got up from his chair and put it back against the wall. "I guess I better be going too. I'll be back tomorrow. Do you want me to bring anything for you?"

"No, that's alright."

"What about you dad?" Percy asked thinking of his dad, and his needs now.

"No, nothing, I don't need nothing." Newton said shaking his head back and forth, while he was readjusting his handkerchief. All Newton wanted was for Roxie to be better and at home.

His thoughts drifted. 'He didn't want to face her sickness. She had always been the strong one. She was the one who held the family together. He was the weak one. Why couldn't he have cancer? Why couldn't he be the one lying in the hospital bed? It wasn't fair. They haven't had enough time together.'

Percy accepted their answers, and he left to go home to Linda. He wanted to go home, give Linda a big hug, appreciate her, and tell her about his day.

CHAPTER 13

Roxie made it home two days later. She was instructed on how to care for "her bag" as she called it, which she detested. She was glad to be home. Newton had never left her side during the hospital stay. He was ready to sleep in his bed. A warm front had come through, which melted all of the snow and gave everyone a feeling of an early spring.

She had to go to the oncologist on Tuesday and dreaded it. She wouldn't think about that right now. She wanted a good home-cooked meal. "Newton look in the deep freezer and get some corn, butter beans, and a roast."

Newton went out to the back porch and located the vegetables that Roxie had frozen over the summer. He finally found the roast under some chicken. He brought it back into the kitchen and set the packages on the kitchen counter. Roxie was busy making some fresh-brewed coffee. "I want a home-cooked meal that hospital food didn't have enough flavor to suit me."

"Yep," was the only short reply that Newton gave, but it said it all.

"Let's sit at the table and have a cup of coffee. I'm starving. You want some toast and jelly?"

"Sure." Newton thought to himself, well at least she's getting her appetite back, maybe she's getting better. Newton sat at his usual spot. Roxie threw some bread on a cookie sheet and turned the oven on broil. She poured two cups of coffee and set them on the table. She then went back to the oven, took the cookie sheet out, and flipped the bread.

Once the toast was done, Roxie got the stick butter from the counter, and a jar of homemade blackberry jam that Linda had made and given to her, down at the table, and buttered all of the toast.

Newton took his two pieces and put them on a napkin, while Roxie had already taken her two and smothered them with blackberry jam. Roxie had finished eating her toast before Newton even had his covered with the jam.

"Maybe we'll have an early spring this year, I sure hope so." Roxie was feeling much better now that she had eaten and was home.

"Maybe," Newton wasn't much on conversation. He was a much better listener, and he loved to listen to Roxie.

Roxie felt full of energy. She had been laying in that hospital bed for three full days, and she was about to go stir crazy. She was ready to be on her feet, cooking. She didn't feel like she had cancer, except for the bag. She decided she was going to enjoy the rest of the day. Newton and Roxie talked a few more minutes.

Newton got up from the kitchen table picking up his paper towel with the toast crumbs on it and threw it in the garbage can on the way to the den. He took his coffee cup and headed for the den to watch some television.

Roxie sat a few moments longer at the kitchen table, but not long before Percy came through the back door into the kitchen. He helped himself to a cup of coffee and sat down at his usual spot. He took a sip of coffee, lit a cigarette, and took a long drag. He finally spoke, "How you feeling, mom?"

"You know I feel pretty good considering I've had my colon taken out. I really don't feel like I have cancer. The only thing that's different is this bag hanging on me, but I'm sure I'll get used to it. I guess I'll have to get used to it. I don't really have a choice, do I?"

"I guess not." Percy said eyeing his mother. She did look better. He was glad to see her back home.

"I'm cooking a big dinner--roast, fried corn, butter beans, potatoes, and cornbread that hospital food has a lot to be desired. It's just too bland for me. No wonder people die in the hospital. They probably die from starvation."

Percy just listened to his mother, while he drank his coffee, and smoked his cigarette. Roxie finally paused for a moment to take a sip of her coffee.

"Are you in any pain?"

"No, not really. I'm just sore from where they took out my colon."

"Now, don't you go and do too much, mother. You know you just got out of the hospital."

"I won't."

Percy knew this fell on deaf ears. He could tell his mother would be up all day washing clothes, cooking, and cleaning.

"How's dad taking all of this?"

"Well, he's taking it a lot better than I thought he'd be. He's not going around the house crying. You know how sensitive he is."

"Yeah."

"When his mother died he cried for weeks, same with his father. Even when that dog, Friend, died he cried I know for a good week." Roxie said remembering back.

"You're right. I remember that I didn't ever think he was going to stop crying when grandmamma Lily died." Percy recalled.

"You know Percy I might go to that radiologist on Tuesday, and they won't have to do any kind of treatment on me." She took another sip of coffee.

"You could be right." Percy wanted her to be right. He didn't want to have to see his mother suffer.

Percy finished his coffee and smoked another cigarette. His mother got up and put the container of butter beans and fried corn in cold water in the sink, so they would thaw out quicker. Percy got up from the table and headed towards the kitchen door that lead out through the garage. "Now remember mother don't you wear yourself out."

"Don't you worry about me."

Roxie spent the next few hours sweeping the kitchen floor, cleaning the bathroom, and doing two loads of clothes including the sheets. She wanted to sleep on nice clean sheets tonight she told Newton, who was watching television. He did take a break to strip the bed for Roxie and bring the sheets to the back porch where the washer and dryer were.

Roxie then took a long hot bath. She wanted to wash away the surgery and hospital smell. She was in there a good hour because she had to take special care with "the bag." Once her bath was over she put on some clean clothes and went into the kitchen to put the roast and potatoes on.

Roxie made some more fresh-brewed coffee, poured her a cup, and sat at the table drinking it alone. Her mind began to race. She was too young to die. She was only 67 that wasn't old at all. She remembered when she was young and thought anybody over 40 years old was ancient. She wanted to live at least another 10 years, maybe even twenty, but she would be happy with ten. This would give her enough time to see her grandkids graduate from college and some of them hopefully have some kids of their own. She wanted to be a great-grandmother. She was going to beat this thing she told herself.

An hour passed while she sat at the table doing circle word puzzles. After she had finished four puzzles she decided it was time for her to get the fried corn and butter beans going.

Roxie stood at the stove for a good hour. The roast had been put in the oven earlier, and it was filling the kitchen with a heavenly aroma. The sun was setting as she looked out the kitchen window above the sink washing her hands. She admired its beautiful shades of purple, pink, and deep yellow it left across the sky. She thought to herself. 'If I die heaven's got to be a sight to see. God made all of this for us to enjoy. Heaven would be the place to be.'

She went back to the stove turning down the heat on the corn and beans, and then took her seat back at the table deciding to work more puzzles. Newton shuffled into the kitchen to pour him some more coffee and to see how dinner was coming along. He was getting hungry. About the time he got to the coffee pot Roxie said, "ooh."

"What is it Roxie?" Newton said turning to see what was the matter.

"It's nothing just a shooting pain up my stomach that's all. It just caught my breath." Roxie was still in pain but didn't want to show it to Newton for fear he might start crying. She decided she better take some pain medicine. "Newton hand me that medicine on the windowsill, will you?"

He got her bottle of medicine and gave it to her. She took two blue valiums out and swallowed them with her coffee. She just did too much today that was it. She told herself. The back door opened and in bounced Luke and Percy.

Percy went over to the coffee pot while Luke took a seat at the table. "Sure does smell good in here." Percy said sitting down at the table.

"Sure does doesn't it?" Roxie said trying to act like she wasn't in pain.

Percy spotted it right away. He knew his mother had probably been on her feet most of the day, not paying a word of attention to what the doctor told her when she left for her to rest. "How you feeling mother?"

"I'm o.k." She wouldn't look him in the face another good sign she wasn't telling the whole truth.

"After dinner you probably just need to take it easy. You've just been through an operation."

"I think I will. After dinner and once the kitchen's cleaned up I think I'll just lay on the couch."

"I think that's a good idea." Percy said as he lit a cigarette. "Well, we just came in here to see if you needed anything."

"No, we're fine." Roxie spoke for both her and Newton.

Percy stayed long enough to finish his cigarette and then him and Luke left. Roxie wanted to lay on the couch right now because she was hurting all over. 'Maybe once these pain pills kick in I'll feel better. Supper won't be ready for another thirty minutes.' She thought to herself as she sat at the table not moving. Eventually the pain did subside. She was able to enjoy her dinner. Newton helped her with the dishes, which she still insisted on practically washing before she put them in the dishwasher.

She then went into the bedroom and put a night gown on. She did precisely what she said she would do, lay on the couch. She ached all over, but it had been dulled a little by the valiums. She decided to take two more before she went to bed so she could get a good night's sleep, which she didn't have in the hospital. She laid in her comfortable bed and was asleep almost the minute she closed her eyes.

The next few days Roxie didn't do as much as she had done the first day she had gotten home from the hospital. She would do a task and then rest for an hour. Tuesday finally got here, a cold front had swooped down into Tennessee. The temperature wasn't getting above twenty degrees with a north wind of ten to fifteen miles an hour. Later in the week the weather forecasters were predicting temperatures in the fifties. Roxie bundled up and got into the warm car Newton had already started up ten minutes earlier.

The drive was quiet. Neither one talked to the other. Newton was hoping her cancer would be gone, and she wouldn't have to go through chemotherapy. Roxie was hoping for the same. Once inside the doctor's office, Roxie had to fill out pages of paperwork which took a good thirty minutes.

"Roxie Prater." The nurse called out into the waiting room. Roxie got up and followed the nurse back to the scales. She stepped on them and weighed 175 pounds. She had lost ten pounds in a week. The usual preliminaries took place. The nurse put Roxie in a sky blue room and told her Dr. Jung would be with her in a few minutes.

Dr. Jung came through the door. "How you doing Mrs. Prater?" Dr. Jung was a short, older man who at one time had black hair, but was now laced with gray. He was definitely from Asian decent. He seemed jovial. Roxie had a good feeling about him.

She felt he would shoot it too her straight but in a nice way.

"I'm a still a little sore from the operation, but other than that I feel pretty good." This had become her standard response.

"I'm sure you are." He looked at her chart and studied it for a few minutes before he spoke. "Mrs. Prater, I think the best course of action to take is to run some tests to see if the cancer has spread. I can get the nurse to set you up an appointment tomorrow."

Roxie didn't like this at all. She didn't want to go to anymore doctors. All she could think of was how every time someone went to the doctor, including her, they came out worse for it. She decided she didn't have any choice. She would take these tests and make a decision from there.

Dr. Jung left and moments later the nurse entered with a slip of paper. "You're to go to the hospital tomorrow at 10:00 a.m. on the second floor. Plan to be there for about three hours and don't eat or drink anything after midnight. I've already got you an appointment with us the next day at 9:00 a.m. Do you have any questions?"

Roxie shook her head in the negative.

"Well we'll see you day after tomorrow then. You're free to go."

Roxie got off the patient table and headed for the door. She wanted to get out of there and not come back. She was going to be run through a serious of tests like a guinea pig she thought to herself. She made it out to the waiting room and spotted Newton. He got up, and they went out to the car.

When they got into the car and about half way home Newton finally spoke up. "What did the doctor say?"

"I've got to get some tests run on me tomorrow and then go back to see him the next day. I've got to be at the hospital at 10:00 a.m."

"Oh." Newton didn't know how to respond. He could tell by the tone of Roxie's voice that she wasn't happy at all about this. The rest of the trip home was made in silence.

The next day was a series of four tests that Roxie had to endure. When she finally got out she was starving. They had left the hospital and were circling the town square. "Let's get something to eat at the café, I'm starving."

Newton pulled into a parking space and came to a halt. They got out and went into the café. The waitress came over and took their order. It wasn't long before the food came back. Roxie had fried chicken, mashed potatoes, green beans, and fried corn. Newton got roast beef, potatoes, carrots, and cornbread. Roxie inhaled her food. Newton was still eating when the waitress came back over and got Roxie's plate. "Do any of you want a dessert?"

Roxie replied trying to hold back a burp. "I think I'll have me a piece of chess pie."

"What about you sir?"

"Nothing for me."

The pie arrived, and Roxie finished it off about the same time Newton got finished with his meal. "I feel better." Roxie said as she burped under her breath. "That hit the spot."

"Sure did." Newton would rather have Roxie's cooking, but he knew she had been through an ordeal the last couple of days, so he went along. They got up to leave when Percy and Linda came through the door.

"Hey, Mrs. Prater. You having a late lunch like we are?" Linda asked.

"Yeah."

Percy looked at his mom and asked. "Did you just get finished with all your tests?"

"Yeah, I did. I've got to go back to the doctor tomorrow at 9:00. Well, we see ya'll later. I'm exhausted. I think I going to go home and rest till tomorrow."

CHAPTER 14

Roxie was up at 6:00 getting ready for the doctor. She took a shower, made coffee, and was putting out paper towels for the toast when Newton entered the kitchen. She was full of nervous energy. She was hoping Dr. Jung would be telling her the cancer was gone. It had magically disappeared then her thoughts turned to the worst. She could hear the doctor telling her there was no reason for any kind of treatment she was too long gone. She looked up at Newton who was standing beside the coffee pot. She was glad he was there to get her mind off of the doctor's visit.

"We'll need to leave here about 8:30 to get to the doctor's office on time." Newton said as he poured himself a cup of coffee. Leaving at this time would in fact get them there ten minutes early.

"Sounds good to me," Roxie said as she spread butter on the toast sitting at the table.

She picked up some plum jelly and spread it on her buttered toast. She didn't say a word. It seemed she was hungry all of the time lately, but she didn't know why. She didn't give it much more thought. After tidying the kitchen up and waiting for Newton it was time to go.

Once inside the doctor's office it took about five minutes before she heard her name called. She followed the nurse back to the patient room. She was reading a tabloid when Dr. Jung walked through the door.

"Mrs. Prater, how you doing today?" He asked in a friendly voice.

"I'm alright." Roxie just wanted the final verdict.

Dr. Jung pulled out her results and studied them for a minute before he spoke. He took a deep breath and spoke before he lost his courage. "Mrs.

Prater the cancer has spread throughout your body. I feel the best course of treatment would be to begin chemotherapy tomorrow. You'll need to go at least once a week for the treatment." He took a breath.

Roxie saw this opportunity and spoke up. "What if I don't get the treatment?"

"You outlook is not good. I would give you two months."

Roxie was in too much shock to start crying at this moment, but she did notice that her throat was beginning to tighten up. "And if I get the treatments, how long do I have?"

"That could vary Mrs. Prater. It could eradicate the cancer and go into remission, which isn't probable, or you could have a year, maybe."

"Will I be in much pain?"

"The worse part is the treatment. It zaps your energy. You'll probably lose your hair and more weight."

She didn't mind the losing weight part, but losing her hair she didn't like that statement or the being zapped part. She wanted to be able to do some things, like work in her garden. She felt like a bowling ball had hit the pit of her stomach. The doctor seemed to be reading her mind. He had been in many rooms with patients who were full of cancer.

"Mrs. Prater, the hair is simple to fix. You can purchase a wig. They make them now where they look like real hair. As far as the energy goes, we can give you some medicine that will build up your red blood cells."

"How long will I have to do this 'treatment'?" She was beginning to hate that word.

"I want to do it for six weeks, and then we'll run some more tests to see how you're progressing." The doctor handed her a brochure about chemotherapy. "You might want to read this it will answer all the questions that you'll have once you get home and you forgot to ask me."

Roxie just sat there on the table. Her mind was wandering from when her children were little to now when they were all grown up and had children of their own. She wasn't ready to die. She guess no one was ready to die. She wanted to see all of her grandchildren graduate from high school and college. She wanted great-grandchildren. She wanted to make sure everyone was alright. She wanted to work in the garden this spring. There was so much to do and too little time. It wasn't fair. What had she done to deserve this. She was jolted back to reality.

"Mrs. Prater, Mrs. Prater are you alright?"

"Uh-yeah." How could she be alright she might be dead in six months.

"Well if you don't have any more questions, I will see you tomorrow. Go up to the front desk they should have your appointment for you."

"O.K." She got up and went to the front desk in a trance. "I'm supposed to have an appointment tomorrow."

"Your name."

"Mrs. Prater."

"Oh, here you are, you'll need to be here at 9:00 a.m." Roxie took the card. Newton had already gotten up from his seat. He could tell by the look on her face she was in shock. He didn't want to ask her what had happened back in the office. There were two reasons. The first was he couldn't bear to hear bad news, and the second he didn't want to upset Roxie.

They went to the car in silence and drove home in silence. Roxie entered the kitchen and more out of habit made a pot of coffee. Newton stopped to ask Roxie what the doctor said and decided against it. He thought to himself. 'She'll tell me when she's ready too.'

It was 11:00 by now. Roxie sat at the table. Her mind was still racing. How was she going to tell Newton and the rest of the family? Was this chemotherapy going to hurt? Oh, the grandchildren. She got up when the coffee was done and fixed her a cup. She sat back down at the table and drank her coffee in silence. She wished Percy was here. She needed to talk to him before she talked with Newton. She decided to busy herself until Percy came by as he usually did in the afternoon. She pulled the puzzle book out of the kitchen drawer and began working it.

Her mind kept drifting to the treatment. 'Was it going to be painful? How fast would she lose her hair? How was Newton going to react? Stop it.' She told herself. She was worn out. She didn't feel like cooking dinner, but she didn't want to tell Newton that because he would know something was up. She decided to get some vegetables out of the freezer to cook. She placed them in the sink and looked out the kitchen window and saw the barn in the sunset. She remembered Jake, Newton, and Percy building the barn. How they worked on it for a whole summer. In fact, out in the barn Percy and Joe carved their names along with Newton's in the wood in the entrance of the barn. She could see them out their working. Lily was in the kitchen. Roxie was fixing tea. A year later Jake had died. She wondered how he felt when he knew he was going to die. Lily lay back in the bed in the hall and died in their house. She remembered Lily being at peace when she passed on.

    The back door opened and Percy walked in. "Hey, mother. What are you doing?"

    "Oh, I'm just thawing out some vegetables." Roxie took a seat at the table while she waited for Percy to get himself a cup of coffee. Percy sat down and looked at his mother. She looked worn out. He took a sip of his coffee and lit the usual cigarette.

    He took a drag off his cigarette. "Well, how did the doctor's appointment go?"

    Roxie shifted in her chair and looked down at her cup of coffee. "Not, not too good."

    "What do you mean?" Percy asked as his head shot up and looked at Roxie straight in the eyes.

    "The doctor's said the cancer hasn't gotten any better, in fact it has spread, he wants to do chemo." Roxie said this real fast thinking the sooner she got it out the better she would feel.

    Percy's heart sank. He took a deep breath. He hoped by some miracle that his mother's cancer might be gone. When he finally collected his thoughts he asked. "What is the doctor saying you have to do?"

    "I've got to start chemo tomorrow. I've got to have it done at least once a week. They are going to do it for about six weeks, I think, and then run some more tests on me to see if the cancer is shrinking or whatever. If I don't do it I will have about two months." She finally took a breath after the whole explanation.

"Have you told dad?"

Roxie shifted in her chair again, took a sip of her coffee, and looked down at the floor. Percy knew the answer to this question before she answered it. "Well, no, I haven't actually." She shifted again in her chair.

"Do you want me to tell him?" Percy asked then took another drag off his cigarette.

"We-ll, I was kinda of hoping you would like, ah, help me out." She was looking down at the table when she said this, but once she finished she looked up at him with pleading eyes.

"Sure, let me go get him." Percy put out his cigarette and walked back to the den.

Newton looked up at him in the doorway and said. "Percy."

"How you doing dad?"

"I'm fine, fine."

"Can you come into the kitchen so we can talk with you?" Newton got up from his chair and followed Percy into the kitchen. He took his seat at the head of the table. Roxie got up, took his coffee cup, poured him a fresh cup of coffee, set it in front of him, and then sat back down in her usual spot. Percy sat down and lit another cigarette.

He looked at his dad. Newton didn't want Percy to talk because every time Percy talked to him it was usually unpleasant news. "Well, dad, mother's cancer has spread. She's going to have to have chemotherapy beginning tomorrow."

"Tomorrow?" Newton could feel the tears

coming to his eyes. His whole body was flooded with feelings. He pulled out his handkerchief and began wiping his eyes.

"Yes, dad, tomorrow, mother doesn't have any choice. The cancer has spread." He let this sink in a little bit. Streams of tears were flowing down his face now. Newton kept wiping his face. Percy took another drag and continued. "She's going to have to go once a week for six weeks and then they'll run some more tests on her to see if the cancer has shrunk."

"Wh-at, wh-at if she doesn't do it?" Newton didn't know why he asked this, but he felt he needed to ask something. He didn't want this question answered, but then again he did.

"If she doesn't have it done dad then she'll have about two months."

Newton was balling by this time. He blew his nose in the handkerchief and then wiped his eyes again. He wasn't ready to lose Roxie. "What am I going to do, Percy, without Roxie?"

Percy couldn't believe it, but then again he could. His dad was asking what he would do. What about what his mother was going through. She was the one who had cancer. He should be supporting her, but it had always been like this. His dad always thought about how things affected him. Percy wanted to shake his dad and ask 'what about mother?' He knew this wouldn't do any good. He thought of how to answer him.

"You're going to take her to the doctor tomorrow dad."

Roxie had chimed in by now. "Now Newton

you've done got me dead and buried. This treatment is supposed to work. The doctor said it could go into remission. I could be around many more years, don't you go bury me yet. It's just going to be rough for a little while."

With that statement Newton finally dried up a little bit. They all sat at the table for a few minutes, drinking coffee and not talking with each other. Percy finished his cigarette and coffee. "I've got to get going. Now, mother if you need anything just let Linda or me know."

"I will."

Percy walked out the back door. Newton and Roxie ate a silent dinner, cleaned the kitchen together, and had a silent night full of racing thoughts.

CHAPTER 15

Roxie was up the next morning early and quiet nervous. She made coffee, got dressed, and was sitting at the kitchen table before Newton even had gotten up. Newton shuffled into the kitchen, poured himself a cup of coffee, and sat down.

"We'll need to leave in about 30 minutes." Roxie said to Newton then took a sip of coffee.

"Alright," he answered.

Newton finished his coffee and then went to get dressed. He went outside to start the car so it would be warm for them. He came back into the kitchen. "The car's warm, you ready to go?"

"I'm coming." Roxie said as she scurried around the house to gather her purse.

Roxie hurried down the steps, opened the car door, the warm air hit her face and feet, and she climbed into the car. The ride was silent once again. Newton didn't know what to say, 'good luck, everything's going to be alright, or do you want me to come in with you?' so he decided to say nothing.

Roxie was in the same predicament. She really didn't want to talk about her fears of the procedure. She was afraid she would upset Newton, and if he got upset, then she would get upset. She decided it best not to talk at all. She looked out the window as the car was going down Shelbyville Highway. The trees were all bare. The air looked cold and the ground frozen, just like she felt.

They finally arrived at the doctor's office. Newton took his usual seat in the waiting room. Roxie sat beside him. She didn't have long to wait before her name was called. She was escorted back into a room with all kinds of gadgets. She was run through every test conceivable. The nurse finally told her after an hour of tests. "We have to make sure your body can handle the chemotherapy."

"Oh." Roxie didn't know what to say. She was thinking to herself, 'if these are just the tests then I hate to see what the chemo is like.'

"Now you wait here a little bit, until we read these tests, then we'll be back to get you."

Roxie laid on the patient table looking up at the ceiling. She was exhausted and glad the nurse had left. She wasn't lying down ten minutes before Dr. Jung came in to see Roxie.

"How are you feeling today Mrs. Prater?" He asked with genuine concern in his voice.

"I'm alright," was her standard response.

"Good, good, the technicians are getting the chemotherapy ready. You'll be taken down the hall and to the left. You'll be placed on the table. They'll put the medicine in intravenously. The treatment will take about three hours."

"Do you have any questions?"

"Is this going to hurt?"

"No, it shouldn't. The worst part will be laying for three hours without moving too much. Now, I suggest if you need to go to the bathroom, you go now, since you won't be able to move for three hours. Do you need to go to the restroom?"

"Yes, I better go."

"The bathroom is down the hall on the right. Once you're finished you'll need to come back to this room, and the nurse will come and get you."

Roxie was waiting back in the patient room when the nurse came to get her. "Follow me, Mrs. Prater."

Roxie hoisted herself off the bed and followed the nurse. Her stomach was turning. She wanted to run out the exit door. She had a fear run through her body she hadn't experienced before. It was panic. She couldn't do this, but her feet kept keeping pace with the nurse even though her mind was telling her to run. The thoughts were racing by now. 'I'll give it one try and see what happens. I think I'll leave. I want to leave right now. Is this going to hurt? What am I going to do for three hours? What am I going to feel like afterwards? I think I'll go.'

The nurse turned around to face Roxie. "Just go through this door, and Betty will tell you what you need to do."

Roxie's thoughts stopped long enough to comprehend what the nurse said. She replied. "Alright."

The nurse turned and walked back down the hall the way they had come from. Roxie slowly entered the room. It was darker than the others. There was a television bolted to the wall right in front of the bed she assumed she would be laying in. She thought to herself. 'Well, at least I can watch some T.V.'

"Hi, I'm Betty. I will be here with you throughout the day." Roxie turned around to get a look at the face behind the voice. Betty had a nice smile, gleaming white teeth, jet black hair and didn't look a day over 25. Roxie noticed her emerald green eyes, which were set back in her round soft, babish face.

"Oh."

"Yes, now the first thing you'll need to do is to take off your clothes and put this gown on, tie it in the back." Betty said as her hand pointed to another room in the corner that looked like a closet. "I'll be out here waiting for you when you get finished. Just leave your clothes in the room."

Roxie took the gown and went back into the room. 'This is my last chance.' She thought to herself as she got into the closet room. She began taking off her clothes. 'This is it. I'm scared.' She put the gown on and lifted her arms up and tied her gown up the best she could. She slowly opened the door feeling self-conscious.

"Just come on over here and lie down. We'll deaden the spot where the I.V. is going to go. Once that's done you won't feel a thing but a little pressure."

Roxie laid on the table while Betty and another person worked on getting the medicine together. The nurse was right the worst part was the deadening, which really wasn't that bad, just a needle stick in a couple of places.

"Now you need to get comfortable, Mrs. Prater. You're going to be here a while. Is there anything you want to watch on the television?"

"I guess just put it on Channel 2." Roxie replied. She wasn't much on watching soap operas, but if she did happen to watch one it would be on Channel 2. They showed *All My Children* and *General Hospital*. She thought to herself. 'I guess I'll get up-to-date on the soaps.'

"We're going to begin administering the medicine in a few moments. You might feel warm throughout your body, but it will go away after a few seconds. O.K.?"

"Alright."

Roxie laid on the bed while Betty began hanging stuff everywhere all around her. She put a blood pressure cup on her arm, which Betty explained would be taken her blood pressure automatically throughout the procedure. It wasn't five minutes, and Roxie felt her body burn. It jolted her for minute. She had a fleeting thought of running out of the room with everything hooked into her. The hotness turned to warmth and then eventually went away, but it took longer than the nurse said it would Roxie thought to herself.

Roxie laid in the bed for what seemed like an eternity. The first couple of hours went by pretty fast because she watched *All My Children* and then *General Hospital*. There were a couple new characters in each show, but she was able to catch up with Betty filling her in since the last time Roxie had watched the shows. Betty told Roxie that those two shows were the most popular in the room even among the men patients. Considering the slim choices, those two shows were the best of the pick.

The last hour finally ended and all of the needles and contraptions were taken away. Roxie was instructed by Betty to lie still for about fifteen more minutes before she tried to get up. Finally, it was time for her to leave. Roxie swayed a little when she sat up. She collected herself, went into the closet room, put her clothes on and headed down the hall.

"Same time next week, Mrs. Prater." Betty called to her before she went through the exit door.

"See you then." Roxie smiled, waved and was out the door. She was ready to go home. She felt a little weak and queasy, but she figured once she got home, got something to eat these symptoms would go away.

Newton and Roxie took their silent trip home. They had barely pulled in the driveway, and Roxie said. "Stop, the car."

Newton stopped right in the driveway. Roxie proceeded to open the car door and throw up. He waited until she leaned back in the seat and shut the door before he began driving again. They pulled into the garage. Roxie hurriedly got out of the car, ran through the house, and barely made it to the bathroom before she threw up again. She threw up two more times before she began fumbling in her purse for the medicine the doctor gave her to help with upset stomachs. Roxie swallowed two tablets of phenegren with a gulp of water taken from the bathroom sink. She leaned over the sink hoping they would stay down. She looked up into the mirror at herself. She looked so pale, old, and sick. She made it out of the bathroom, put her purse on the hall tree, and fell on the couch in the den . Newton was already in his seat watching the early news.

Roxie laid there thinking. 'I need to get up and start supper. I'm not even hungry. I know Newton's got to be hungry.'

She heard footsteps coming through the house. Percy entered the den followed by Luke. Percy took one look at his mother and felt for her. He knew she had to be feeling rough to be lying on the couch this time of day. She wasn't the lying around type.

"How are you doing?" Percy asked as he looked at his mother lying on the couch with a wash cloth on her head.

She lifted the wash cloth off her forhead and tried to lean up. "I've had better days. I was sick before I even set foot in the door."

"Is there anything I can do for you?"

"No, just make my stomach stop churning."

Luke was looking at his grandmother on the couch. He didn't know what to say to her, so he decided to say nothing. He looked around at all of the pictures on the walls. His great-grandfather and grandmother. His great, great grandfather. Roxie sat up and then began moving towards the bathroom almost running into Luke. Everyone stood around in the den looking at each other and trying not to hear Roxie getting sick. They all felt so powerless.

Roxie stumbled out of the bathroom and made her way back to the couch. Percy waited until his mother got settled back onto the couch.

"Linda made up a little leftover plate for each of you. I've put it on the kitchen table."

Roxie rolled her eyes. "I couldn't eat anything right now. I don't think I could keep it down. I'm sure Newton is hungry though."

Newton had heard Percy mention food and was ready to bolt towards the kitchen to see what Linda had prepared, but didn't want to seem too anxious.

"Newton go on and eat." Roxie said. "Do you want me to make you some coffee or anything?"

"No, no, you just rest." Newton said as he was getting up from his chair and heading back towards the kitchen.

When his dad left Percy sat down in his seat, he looked over at his mother, who was as pale as a ghost. "Mother, how are you really doing?"

"I'm alright other than being sick, and I feel so tired."

"How long will you have to take these treatments, do you know?"

"They said they would give them to me for three weeks and then run some more tests on the fourth week to see if the cancer's shrinking." Roxie paused and shifted her body to get more comfortable. "But I tell you the truth, if it's going to be like this every week, I don't know if I'm going to be able to make it."

"This is just the first day. I bet the first day is worse." Percy said trying to cheer his mother up.

Roxie didn't say anything. The more she talked the worst she felt. She was afraid she might get sick again. Percy picking up that his mother just needed to be left alone said. "I guess we'll be going. I'll come by tomorrow to see how you're doing."

"Alright," Roxie had moved the wash cloth back over her eyes now.

Percy and Luke left the den and moved into the kitchen. Newton was sitting at the head of the table devouring his meal.

"See you later dad. We'll be by tomorrow to see how mother's doing."

"Tell Linda thank you."

"I will."

Roxie threw up a couple of more times and then managed to get her nightgown on. She told Newton she was going to bed. It was only eight o'clock. They said their goodnights. Newton stayed up to watch the ten o'clock news and then retired.

The next morning Roxie still felt queasy. She managed to get down a couple of pieces of toast and a little coffee. Newton ate along with her. She felt like all of the energy was drained out of her. The food wasn't on her stomach for an hour before she proceeded to throw up again. She took some phenegren. This seemed to settle her stomach a little bit. Around one o'clock after laying around on the couch drifting in and out of watching television she decided to try some more toast. This time it stayed down. Newton had the leftovers that Linda had sent over from the night before that Roxie didn't eat.

Roxie lied back on the sofa deciding how she was going to cook dinner for Newton. She didn't even feel like getting off the sofa much less cooking, but she didn't want to ask for help either. If she asked for help that meant she was really sick. Something she didn't want to admit to herself. Maybe Percy will come by with some more food.

Newton paced from the kitchen to the den to the front door. He didn't know what to do. He felt so powerless. What was he going to do without Roxie. He didn't want to think about it. Around four o'clock he could see headlights coming up the driveway. About five minutes later he heard the kitchen door open. It was Percy. He had a loaf of something in his hand wrapped in aluminum foil, a covered plate, and a covered bowl.

Percy had gone home the night before and told Linda how sick his mother was. She proceeded to cook up a storm. Linda had said, "Your mother is no condition to be cooking for your dad. I'll cook up some food, and you need to take it over there tomorrow. This will get them through the next day or two."

Newton walked into the kitchen to get a better look at what Percy had. "Hey, dad. Linda's made you some banana nut bread. This whole plate is full of roast beef." Percy reached inside his oversized coat pocket and pulled out something else wrapped in aluminum foil. "And this is cornbread. She makes flat cakes you know, but I think you'll like it. You've had it before."

Percy laid out all of the food on the kitchen counter. "This is for mother. It's some homemade chicken noodle soup. How is she doing dad? Is she still getting sick?"

Newton stood beside the counter. He began to tear up and pulled out his handkerchief. "Y-es, she's been sick off and on all day. Percy, I just don't know what I'm going to do?" Newton proceeded to burst into tears at this point.

Initially this upset Percy. He thought to himself. 'How can he be thinking about what he was going to do when his mother was the one who was sick and getting the chemo.' But then he thought of how his mother had always babied Newton. If something did happen to his mother, his dad would be in bad shape.

"Now, dad. She's probably going to get better. It's that first treatment making her so sick. Her body's not used to it." He paused and lit a cigarette. "Go ahead and eat. I'm going to take this soup back to mother." He proceeded to open the kitchen drawer and got a spoon out for his mother.

Newton was right behind Percy getting a plate. He was starving. He made himself some coffee and sat at the table. When Percy headed back towards the den Newton was dishing out roast beef and cornbread cakes on his plate.

Roxie was lying on the sofa with a wash cloth on her head.

"Hey, mother."

Roxie didn't budge from her spot. "Hey, Percy, how you doing?"

"I'm fine. What about you?"

"I've been sick off and on all day. I've finally been able to keep some toast down. This is the worst I have ever felt in my entire live. I wouldn't wish this on my worst enemy."

"Linda made you some soup, and she fixed some banana nut bread, roast beef, and cornbread, too."

The soup sounded good to Roxie, but the rest made her stomach churn. She wished she could eat, but knew the consequences. "She didn't have to do that."

"I know that, she knows that, but she wanted to. I've brought the soup back here for you. It's really good. Do you think you might eat some?"

Percy had sat down in the chair next to the couch. Roxie slowly sat up. She didn't move for a few seconds to see if her queasiness had gone away. Percy took the lid off the steaming soup bowl, slowly handed her the soup and spoon. Roxie reached for it and cupped it in her hands. "This smells wonderful."

Roxie took a spoon full of broth with shaky hands and led it to her mouth. She took a few more spoonfuls. This seemed to settle her stomach. In fact, it was the first thing she had eaten that didn't feel like it was going to come back up. She ate a few noodles and a small piece of chicken with the next bite.

"Linda told me she put ginger in the soup, that's supposed to calm the stomach."

"Um." Roxie replied as she continued eating the soup. She ate about half of it, set the bowl on the coffee table and laid back down. "That was good. Tell Linda I said thank-you."

"I will."

Percy lit another cigarette and leaned back in the chair. Roxie finally broke the silence. "Percy, I hope I get to feeling better. If this is how I'm going to be after each treatment, then I'd just soon not get the treatments."

"You'll probably get to feeling better by tomorrow." He didn't know if she would, but he sure hoped she did. He wanted to remain optimistic around his mother. She had enough on her.

CHAPTER 16

The day arrived when Roxie had to go back to get chemotherapy. Dr. Jung came in and asked how she was doing. Roxie spared no details. "Well, before I even got home I threw up. I proceeded to throw up until I went to bed. I'm having to take that phena, whatever, everyday just to keep toast down and soup. I threw up everyday, except yesterday. Oh, yeah, and I'm so weak and tired."

"The tiredness and weakness are part of the side effects of the treatment, some people get sick for a few days afterwards. Let's take two more treatments, we'll run some more tests on you to see if the cancer is shrinking and then go from there. Give me two more weeks."

"Alright, Dr., just two more weeks, but if I'm going to go through this after every treatment it's not worth it."

"That's all I ask." Dr. Jung said as he scribbled something on Roxie's chart.

The next couple of weeks were no better. Roxie was sick to her stomach for the day of and at least five days after the treatment. The family was bringing food to Newton and soup to Roxie. This was all she could eat and hold down. By the fourth week, Newton and Roxie made it to Dr. Jung's office. Tests were run all morning. Roxie was instructed to go to lunch and then come back at 1:00 p.m.

She made it back and was escorted back into a patient room. Dr. Jung came in with the results. He flipped through the chart and then looked up at Roxie. "Mrs. Prater, I hate to tell you this, but the cancer isn't shrinking in fact it's spreading. You've lost twenty-five pounds in a month, and I've determined that you can't take the chemo. You're body can't handle it."

He let this sink in for a moment. Roxie was glad she wouldn't have to be taken any more chemo, but then that meant she didn't have long to live. She wondered if there was another alternative.

"Well, Dr. I'm glad to hear there is no more chemo, but what does, does that mean for me?"

"We can try radiation, but I'm going to be honest. I don't think it will help. The only thing it might do is arrest the growth for awhile, but as for putting the cancer in remission I don't think that will happen."

"We can try can't we. It can't be any worse than what I've been through the last month."
Roxie's voice was elevated with a threat of fear. Her brown eyes were beginning to look like a holocaust victim.

"Yes, we can try. I want to give your body a rest for a week. I'll get my nurse to set you up an appointment a week from today for the radiation. Do you have any more questions?"

"Yeah, uh, if the radiation doesn't work, well, uh, how long do I have?"

"Well, no one can be certain, Mrs. Prater. Miracles have been known to happen, but in your case at the rate the cancer's spreading I'd say two to four months."

This hit her gut like a bomb. This would mean she would be dead in May or July. No more Thanksgivings, no more Christmases, no more birthdays, no more gardens, no more seeing the grandchildren or her children. This couldn't be, it, just couldn't be it. She was trying to hold back the tears. All she could blurt out was, "oh."

"We'll try as hard as we can to extend your life Mrs. Prater."

Roxie was still in shock. How was she going to tell Newton this? She needed to talk with Percy. She wanted to run out of the room. "Can I go now?"

"Just wait here one moment, while I get the nurse to give you your appointment time." Dr. Jung left the room to fetch his nurse.

The nurse came into the room with a slip of paper in her hand. "You'll need to be here next Tuesday at 9:00 a.m. Don't eat or drink anything before you come. Do you need any medications to hold you over till next week?"

"No. I think I'm fine."

Roxie hurried out the door. She was ready to go home. She wondered how she would tell Newton this news. She dreaded it. She would wait until Percy came by later in the afternoon. She made her mind up on the way home that she would give the radiation one try, but if she was sick for days like she was with the chemo then she wasn't doing it. She doubted the radiation would work. The chemo was the stronger of the two, and if the chemo didn't kill the cancer or shrink it why would the radiation. Then she thought of what Dr. Jung said, 'they are just trying to extend her life.' But if her life was going to be constant throwing up then she'd rather be dead.

Newton wondered why the appointment was so short, but didn't ask. He was afraid too. He decided to wait until Roxie told him. The sun was peeking through the clouds, and the temperature had hit 70 degrees. It was a beautiful March day. Roxie didn't want to go home. "Newton, let's drive out to the country like we used to do on Sunday's."

"Alright," Newton checked the gas gauge, and it was sitting a little over a half a tank full. He decided he had enough gas in the car. "Where too?"

"Let's drive towards Deason."

They drove around for about an hour looking at farms that had grown over the years, and ones that had shrunk. Roxie would tell Newton who still lived where. What their kids were doing, and their grandkids, if they had any. Newton decided it was time to get back to the house. He was wanting to stretch his legs. When they pulled into the driveway Roxie saw old blue in front of the barn. She was glad to see his truck.

Newton and Roxie entered through the kitchen. Roxie put away her purse and light coat and headed towards the kitchen to make a fresh pot of coffee. Newton headed towards the den. Roxie had taken out some vegetables before they left to go to the doctor, which were about thawed out in the sink. She began pulling out pots and pans and dumping vegetables into them. She went over to the refrigerator to get some butter to put into the vegetables when Percy walked into the door.

"Hey, mother." Percy said as he waited for his mother to close the refrigerator door since he was on the other side of it and couldn't get through until she did.

"Oh, hey, Percy." She quickly closed the door, scurried over to the stove throwing the butter in by big clumps, and then sprinkling salt and pepper on the food. She turned down the stove. Percy poured himself a cup of coffee and sat at the table. Roxie then poured herself a cup of coffee and sat down at her usual seat.

"Well, how did the doctor's visit go?" Percy asked and then lit himself a cigarette. He took a couple of drags and waited for a response.

"It, it didn't go too well." Roxie said as she looked down at the kitchen table.

"What do you mean?"

Roxie took a deep breath and then proceeded to tell him the news. "Well, I can't get the chemo anymore. I'm sort of I guess allergic to it. I've lost twenty-five pounds, you know."

"What do you mean allergic to it?"

"I was getting sick, throwing up for almost five days after the treatment, and then on the sixth day I'd feel somewhat better. On the seventh day, it was time for the treatment again."

"I see, that's right."

"Yeah, that's not too normal, they say." Then she paused a few minutes before she told him the rest. "And, anyway, they ran the progress tests on me. It seems the cancer wasn't shrinking anyway."

"I hate to hear that, but at least it's not spreading, is it?"

She hesitated again and took a sip of coffee, which had cooled by now, "not exactly."

"You mean it's spreading!" Percy's voice went up an octave.

"Yeah."

"Oh." Percy didn't know what to say. He was in temporary shock for the moment. He didn't have any words of encouragement for his mother. He put his cigarette out and lit another one, took a couple of drags. "Well, what exactly does that mean for you?"

"It's not too good. I can have radiation, which will only, hopefully arrest it for a while, or I can do nothing. I would have two to four months if I do nothing." She finally looked up at Percy for some kind of reaction.

Percy took a couple of more drags off his cigarette and then looked up at his mother. He wanted to break down, but he knew this wasn't the time. He had to be strong for his mother. He shifted in his seat. "Oh, mother. You're going to get the radiation aren't you?"

"I'm going to try it once. I've decided though if I'm sick like I was on the chemo I'm going to stop it."

Percy couldn't much blame her. "I see."

"That's no life being sick to your stomach, not eating, and too weak to even get off the couch."

"You're right."

The room was silent for a while. Percy finished his cigarette and then got up to pour some more coffee. He sat back down in his anointed chair. "Have you told dad?" He knew the answer to this question before he even asked. He was always given the task of telling his dad unpleasant news.

"N-o, no, I thought, well, uh, you could sort of tell him, with me of course."

"Of course," he took another sip of coffee.

"Do you want to tell him now or wait until tomorrow?"

"I guess the sooner the better. There's not going to be really a good time to tell Newton."

Percy got up from his chair and headed towards the den, "hey, dad."

"Hey, Percy," Newton looked up at Percy.

"Can you come in the kitchen with me?" Percy asked in a gentle voice.

Newton got up from his chair and followed Percy into the kitchen. He knew this couldn't be good. Newton took his coffee cup, which was sitting by the coffee pot, and poured himself a cup. He shuffled to the table and sat down at the head of the table. He blew across the top of the cup and took a slight sip of coffee.

Percy lit a cigarette, took a long drag, and exhaled. He felt he just better get it over with. "Dad, mother's not going to have to get the chemo anymore."

"That's good isn't it?" He was hoping it was good. Roxie wouldn't have to get chemo. She would be back to her old self--gardening, cooking, having friends and family over.

"Well, yes in a way. She won't be getting sick like she was." Percy took a couple more drags, inhaled deeply, and then exhaled. "The fact is she can't take the chemo because it was making her sicker, and it wasn't doing any good either." He let this sink in for a minute.

Newton didn't say anything at first. "Any good? What does that mean, Percy?"

He cleared his throat and shifted in his seat. "The cancer's spreading."

Newton bowed his head and began sniffling. He pulled out his handkerchief and wiped his eyes. His life would be over without Roxie. What was he going to do? He kept thinking to himself.

Roxie chimed in at this point. "Now, Newton they're going to try radiation on me next to see if that will at least arrest it or stop it from spreading."

"How long does she have Percy?" Newton acted as if Roxie hadn't said anything or that she wasn't even in the room.

Percy dreaded this part. He waited till Newton had dried his eyes. "Well, if she doesn't get the radiation two to four months. If she does get the radiation, and it works we don't know how long."

All Newton heard was two to four months. She'd be dead before Thanksgiving, before Christmas, possibly before his birthday in June. His mind was racing, and the tears were streaming down his face. "What am I going to do, Percy? What am I going to do?" He was shaking his head and crying. He felt like his life was over.

Percy was trying not to get pissed off at his dad, but he thought he might say something to his mother. He thought about it for awhile and decided Newton couldn't think of life without Roxie. They had been together for over forty years. That's all he knew. That's all she knew. He gathered his thoughts and tried to think of something to say to his dad.

"Right now dad all you can do is be there for mother. You can keep taking her to the doctor's, and try to enjoy the time you have left with her."

Newton had heard enough. He got up from the kitchen table, pushed his coffee cup out of the way, and stumbled out of the kitchen back into the den. He needed to be alone. How could Roxie die on him. He was supposed to go first. He wasn't strong enough to make it on his own. It wasn't fair. He kicked the chair and on the way out the door still crying.

Roxie and Percy sat at the kitchen table in silence for a while. Roxie finally broke the ice. "Well, he took it better than I expected."

"Yeah, he did. Well, I need to go. Do you need me to do anything else for you before I leave?"

"No. I think we've done enough."

Percy got up from the kitchen table, put his coffee cup in the sink after rinsing it out. "Well, I'll see you later. You take care now. Don't do too much."

"I won't."

Percy left and Roxie finished supper. "Newton." She hollered as she was setting the plates out on the kitchen table.

Newton came into the kitchen. Roxie could tell his eyes were swollen from crying, but at least the handkerchief was in his pocket, so maybe they could make it through the meal without him crying. Roxie thought to herself.

The next few days were uneventful. Finally, the day arrived for Roxie to get her radiation. She was nervous as well as Newton. The drive to the doctor's office seemed longer than usual. Finally they arrived. Roxie didn't have long to wait before her name was called. She was lead back into another room and told to strip down and get in the usual gown. The technician explained to Roxie the procedure that would take place. It would take about one hour.

She wasn't ten minutes into the procedure, and she was yelling. "Get me a trash," she proceeded to throw up on the floor, "can." The technician stopped the treatment immediately, but Roxie had enough in her that she threw up for thirty minutes. The technician by this time had given her a trash can because the bed pan wasn't enough to keep up with her throwing up.

After thirty minutes Roxie's stomach began to settle some. She was puking bright green by the end. Dr. Jung entered the room.

"Mrs. Prater." He said to her as he went over to the technician, who was conferring with him what had happened in the room.

She didn't say anything. She was being given medicine to calm her stomach. They felt she could hold it down by now. Another nurse was taking her blood pressure. Once the medicine was taken her temperature was being taken.

Dr. Jung walked over to Roxie with chart in hand. He looked down at her. She was sitting up on the patient table. "Are you feeling any better?"

"A little." She said rubbing her stomach and feeling her head with the back of her hand, which felt cold and sweaty.

"I want you to stay here for about thirty more minutes, so we can monitor you."

"Alright," Roxie felt too weak to get off the table at the moment so she wasn't going to kick up a fuss.

Dr. Jung cleared his throat. "Mrs. Prater, you know we're not going to be able to give you radiation either. Your body can't handle it. I'm sorry."

"It's not your fault."

"Some bodies can't handle the radiation or chemo. I guess yours is one of those."

"I guess." She had lied back down on the table with the back of her arm over her head by now.

"You know this means we can only make you comfortable at this point. You'll come in every week, and we'll give you medicine. But as far as stabilizing or shrinking the cancer we're not going to be able to do that."

Roxie didn't respond. Her eyes were closed by now to stop the room from spinning, but she heard every word the doctor said.

"Do you understand, Mrs. Prater?"

"I understand."

Her skin was beginning to break out in red patches all over. Dr. Jung looked at Roxie. "It looks like you're having an allergic reaction to the radiation. I'm going to give you a steroid and a Benadryl injection along with a prescription to send with you on your way home."

CHAPTER 17

Roxie finally was given the o.k. to go. She dreaded telling Newton this news. She didn't know how he would handle it. She didn't know how she was going to tell him. It wasn't possible she had only two to four months of life left. 'Where did it go? It was over to soon. It wasn't fair. She might see Eliza graduate from high school, but not Luke, Randy, or Amanda. No great grandchildren. No more Thanksgivings or Christmases. She would miss all of them. I've got to pull myself together.' She told herself as she kept walking towards the waiting room. She wiped her eyes and opened the door to the waiting room. 'At least I won't have to get anymore treatments.'

Newton looked up and saw Roxie. It was a shorter wait than he expected. He opened the door for Roxie. The cool spring air hit Roxie's face, buttercups were blooming all up and down the sidewalk that lead to the parking lot. She noticed how vibrant and yellow they were. She thought to herself. 'Here today, gone tomorrow. I'm like a flower to God. I bloom for people's pleasure and then I die. I will be blooming somewhere else before long. I wonder what it will be like in heaven? Will I go straight there or will I be asleep until God calls me?'

Newton could tell Roxie was weak. They had made it to the car. He opened the door for her. She climbed into the seat, put her seatbelt on, while Newton shut the door for her. The sun had warmed the car up to a nice temperature. In fact, it felt cozy to Roxie. Newton lit a cigar, cracked the window, and started the car up.

Roxie's mind raced all the way home. She decided she would tell Newton while Percy was there. She had to talk with him first. There wasn't going to be an easy way to tell Newton any of this. There wasn't going to be an easy way to tell Percy this, but Percy was the strong one in the family. He would know how to handle the situation.

"Newton let's stop at the store and pick up a few things. I'm not going to feel like cooking tonight."

"Alright," Newton wheeled into the local Kroger's. He helped Roxie out of the car. They slowly entered the grocery store.

The aroma of fresh-baked bread hit Roxie's nostrils, along with fresh-baked cookies. She had forgotten this sense about her. She seemed to look at the food in a different light. Everything was so tempting and delicious looking. There were also different kinds of fresh cut flowers. She touched a blooming daffodil. It was so soft and delicate and smelled elegant. The smell of fried chicken caught her nostrils next.

"Newton, let's get some fried chicken. What about some potato salad and coleslaw, too?"

"Sounds good to me," Newton replied as he was pushing the buggy behind Roxie. He was watching her as she stopped throughout the store and picked up certain items, gazed at them, and set them back down.

By the time they had gotten to the end of the line the buggy was full of cookies, chicken, potato salad, cole slaw, milk, coffee, bread, bananas, ice cream, and an assortment of other goodies. The check out was quick, and once out to the car, Newton loaded the trunk full of groceries.

By the time they pulled in the driveway, Percy's truck was parked in front of the barn. Roxie was glad to see it. She knew he would be in before long. Newton brought the groceries in the kitchen for Roxie and then went back to the den. Roxie's appetite was coming back, so she decided to try and eat a banana to see if she could keep it down. She was unloading the groceries eating the banana, finished it, and threw the peeling in the trash can. She tried a cookie next and then wanted some milk. She finally finished putting the groceries away and sat down at the kitchen table with two more cookies and a glass of milk. She enjoyed the taste and texture of the food in her mouth. She was savoring it. She had forgotten how good they tasted.

After she finished the cookies she decided to make some fresh coffee. Once the coffee was finished brewing she poured herself a steaming cup and sat back down at the table to wait for Percy. She didn't have long to wait. She heard the back door open.

"Hey," Percy said as he closed the door behind him. "It was a pretty day today. I took off a little early to work on the barn, some patching up."

"Hey, pour yourself some coffee." Roxie was more chipper than usual Percy noticed. She was glad she didn't have to get any more treatments. She was glad the food had stayed down, and she was glad she wouldn't be throwing up any more. She was going to enjoy her last days--eating what she wanted, cooking what she wanted, and having family over when she felt like it.

"I think I will." He poured himself a cup of coffee, loaded it with sugar and milk, and then sat down at the kitchen table across from his mother. He lit the usual cigarette and took a big drag.

Roxie decided to just tell him and get it over with. "Percy, I've got two to four months left."

Percy almost dropped his cigarette and swallowed his coffee hard, almost choking. "Two to four months!" There was a high pitch in his voice.

"Yep, my body couldn't take the radiation. I wasn't in there an hour, and I was throwing up all over the place. It took another hour to stabilize me. I can't say I won't miss it. Dr. Jung said all they can do now is make me comfortable. I'll still go see him once a week."

Percy was speechless. He didn't know what to say. His mother seemed to be resigned to the fact that she would be dead in two to four months. She didn't seem sad. She seemed indifferent. Percy wasn't quite there yet. His mind was racing. 'How could she be dead in four months. I won't see her anymore. God, I'm going to miss her. I'm going to miss drinking coffee with her almost every day.' And then it hit him. 'What about his dad?' He knew Roxie hadn't told Newton, or he'd be walking around the house crying.

"Are you alright with this?"

"Do I have any choice?"

"I guess not."

"I finally was able to keep some food down this afternoon. First time in I don't know how long I haven't at least felt queasy after eating. Do you want a piece of chicken?"

"No, no, I'm fine."

"I'm not cooking tonight. We stopped at the store and picked up a few things. I'm still weak."

"Have you told dad?"

She did the shifting in the seat and then looked down at her coffee cup. "No, I haven't. I-I haven't told anybody but you."

"I see. Do you want to tell him now or later?"

"I guess, now's as good as time as any."

"What about the rest of the family? Are you going to tell them?"

"Yeah. I was just thinking about that. I was thinking of having a Sunday dinner out here this coming Sunday. You know have everyone bring a little something. I can cook a city ham. Ain't nothing to it just throw it in the oven. Then after we eat I figured I would get all the children around and tell them."

"What do you think?"

By this time it was sinking in, and Percy wanted to do whatever made his mother happy these last months of her life. He wasn't going to lie to himself. It would be nice to have one last get together--the whole family before she got too ill.

"Whatever you want, but don't wear yourself out."

"I won't. It's just something I want to do before you know..."

"Yeah, I know." Percy took another sip of his coffee.

"I guess, we need to, uh, tell, uh, Newton." Roxie said as she was fidgeting in her chair.

"I guess. Do you want me to go back and get him now?"

"I guess you better."

"I'll be back in a minute."

While Percy was gone to get Newton, Roxie said a little prayer to herself. 'Lord, help me here please. Show me how we're to tell Newton. Be with Newton. Amen.'

Percy was back with Newton. Roxie got up and fixed Newton a cup of coffee. She set it down beside him at the table. They came back into the kitchen and sat down. Percy didn't waste any time. "Dad, we've got something to tell you."

Newton's stomach did a flip. He didn't like the sound of this at all. Roxie leaned across the table and laid her hand on top of his. "Newton, I've on-ly got two to four months left."

She let that sink in a bit. She could see the tears welling up in his eyes. "What?" He said almost in a whisper. He withdrew his hand from underneath Roxie's and pulled out his handkerchief.

"My body can't take any of the treatments. They make me too sick. The doctor's given me two to four months to live." She repeated.

"Oh no, it can't be true." The tears were rolling down Newton's face by now. "What am I going to do without you? What am I going to do?" He rubbed his eyes with the handkerchief which was having a hard time keeping up with the tears that were rolling down his face.

"You'll do fine without me." Roxie said as her mind raced to find something to change the subject. "Anyway, Newton let's make the best of it. I'm going to try too. We've all got to die. Am I happy about it? No. But me crying over it the next two to four months ain't going to change anything. In fact, it might make it worse. You never know, either, miracles been known to happen." She didn't figure on a miracle in her case, but she said it just to give Newton a little hope.

Newton cried for a few more minutes, blew his nose and then stuck the handkerchief back in his pocket. He took a sip of coffee. He was at a loss for words.

"I'm planning on having the rest of the family out here on Sunday. I'm going to cook a ham and have everyone else bring something else. I'll tell the rest of the children then. What do you think of it?" Roxie said as she was scooting around in her chair.

"Sounds alright to me." Newton said as he looked down at the table.

"What do you want Linda to bring?" He felt changing the subject and getting on to a future dinner was the best way to get Newton out of his current slump. He was perturbed at his dad for always thinking of himself and not of his mother and what she was going through.

"Have her bring some butter beans. I think I'll have Joy bring macaroni and cheese, Jan sweet potatoes, and Ann some fruit salad. We'll need deserts. Can Linda bring a couple of chess pies?"

"I'm sure she can?"

"I'll get Jan to bring pecan pies, and Ann some cookies. Can Eliza make some of her rolls?"

"I'll get her too." Percy said as he lit another cigarette. "What time are we going to have this dinner?"

"Let's say about one o'clock that'll give everybody time to get back from church."

"Well, I better get going. Linda will be wondering where I'm at. You need anything before I leave?"

"No. You go on. I'm just going to pull the chicken out of the refrigerator and the rest of the stuff. It won't be any problem. You go on now and get home before Linda starts worrying."

Percy couldn't wait to get into the truck. The sun was beginning to set. The sky was streaked with pinks, purples, and yellows. It had been a beautiful spring day. April was just around the corner. Percy started his truck and drove it to the far edge of the field where no one could see him. He turned off the truck and looked out into the field. He watched the sun set and cried because his mother was officially dying. He sat in the field for a good fifteen minutes until he was cried out by then the sky had turned a dark navy blue, and the north star was visible in the sky. He started the truck back up and headed home.

CHAPTER 18

Roxie spent the next few days calling everyone and telling them what to bring. All of them were afraid to ask what the dinner was for. They were just glad that their mother and grandmother were feeling better.

Sunday finally arrived it couldn't have been a more beautiful day. The sky was a cornflower blue with whispy clouds that floated across it. The breeze brought a crispness to the air. The temperature was a lovely 75 degrees. Roxie couldn't have asked for a better day. She had been up since seven putting the ham in the oven, getting the tables ready along with Newton, making iced tea, and walking around the house making sure everything looked o.k.

The cars began pulling down the driveway and parking in front of the wrought-iron fence. Percy, Linda, and Luke were the first to get there followed by Eliza in her Chevy Impala, which were filled with homemade rolls ready for baking.

"Come on in, girls. Hey, Percy, Luke." Roxie said as she eyed the food that Linda and Eliza were bringing in. "Just put those beans on the stove. Eliza I've already heated up the stove. See if you can get two sheets in there at the same time. You know this crew will want to be eating as soon as everybody gets here."

Linda set the pies on the buffet, the beans on the stove, and Eliza got busy with the rolls. The house began filling up and as usual, and the kitchen had the biggest crowd in the room. Percy and Tim were picking pieces off the ham and eating it, while Percy was carving it up for his mother. Everyone had arrived and the last batch of rolls were cooking.

"Let's get started eating, New-ton." Roxie began hollering from the kitchen. Newton finally shuffled into the kitchen. "Tim will you say grace?"

Everyone bowed their heads while Tim said a pray thanking God that Roxie was with them on this special and beautiful day. Everyone said, "Amen" in unison, and the line began forming around the kitchen table. Of course everyone brought more food than Roxie had asked for. There were casseroles, beans, macaroni and cheese, mashed potatoes, sweet potatoes, rolls, and luscious desserts.

Newton began the line between Roxie and the sisters all Newton had to do was hold his plate, while they filled it. Next in line were the kids followed by the mothers and then the rest of the men. Everyone took their places at the tables. The older kids were talking about starting back to school the next day and how they dreaded it because spring break would be over. But they wouldn't have that much more school left before it would be over for the summer break.

The meal was uneventful in conversation, but satisfying to the appetite. Once the kids were finished eating they all went out on the front porch to talk, while the men gathered around the dining room table to talk politics and work. The women began the clean up in the kitchen. Some of the older girls helped.

"Well, mom how you feeling these days?" Ann asked as she was towel drying a casserole dish.

"Oh, alright." Roxie didn't want to say too much until she got her children together to tell them. She had decided she would gather them in the living room.

Ann could tell by the quick response her mother didn't want to elaborate, so she changed the subject. "It won't be long before my kids begin college."

"I know it's hard to believe that Eliza will be graduating from high school this year." Linda said as she stacked up the clean dishes for the others' to take home.

"I guess Michael will keep going to Middle Tennessee State. Tricia will be graduating in a year.

I can't believe it myself." Joy said as she put her stack of dishes and leftover food by the refrigerator.

With six women and Eliza and Tricia the dishes and leftovers were taken care of in no time. Roxie dried her hands on the dish towel. "Well, I'd like all the big kids, which meant her children, in the living room." She said this as she was standing in the doorway that lead from the kitchen to the dining room.

Percy had kept his word and didn't tell a soul, except for Linda of course. None of the other children had a clue. They thought since her mother was having a big Sunday dinner that she was feeling better and actually doing better.

All of the kids and their spouses went into the living room. Roxie sat in her light pink, velveteen-covered ladies chair, and Newton sat next to her. Roxie waited until everyone was seated. Eliza and Tricia hung back in the dining room but were within earshot and could here what was going on.

Roxie cleared her throat, and everyone became quiet. "Well, I don't know how to say this except for to just say it. I'm not going to be getting anymore chemo or radiation. My body can't take it. In a way I'm almost glad because I couldn't eat anything without throwing it up." Roxie paused to catch her breath and to see the reaction of everyone, which seemed to be quiet stillness.

Ann was almost scared to ask the next question. "What does that exactly mean for, for you?"

Roxie made sure everyone was listening, which they were. It was as if everyone stopped breathing for a moment. The children could be heard on the front porch talking about their friends and plans for the upcoming week, oblivious to what was going on inside. "It means I have two to four months to live."

No one said anything for a full minute. The words were vibrating inside their heads. 'Two to four months to live' it couldn't be true, but it was. Tim, who had slipped in with Joy, was the first one to break the silence. "Have you thought about a second opinion? Joy and I will take you down to Vanderbilt. They're the best."

"It wouldn't do any good. The cancer is too far gone." Roxie replied. Newton was sitting next to her crying. He had pulled out his handkerchief and was wiping his eyes.

Ann got up from her chair, walked over to her mother and hugged her. "Is there anything we can do for you?"

"No. Not right now. In fact, I'm feeling better than I have in weeks." She was lying she had been getting more tired as the days wore on. She was exhausted in fact, but she didn't want to let on to anyone in the room. She could stand a couple of more hours and then she would be able to retreat to the couch.

Joy was crying, while Tim was trying to console her. Joe didn't do anything. He just knew he was very uncomfortable. He thought maybe the doctors were wrong that it was a big mistake, but deep down he knew it wasn't. Percy was smoking a cigarette. Ann lit up one too and was standing beside him. Joy walked over to her mother, just held her and cried. Roxie was patting her on the back and telling her it would be alright. Jan was in shock. She didn't know what to do, so she did nothing.

Roxie gathered herself up. "Now everyone there's no use crying about it. Everyone's got to die. My time will be sooner than expected. I just want to enjoy the last days I have, understood. No crying and moping around the house." She couldn't stand to see her girls crying, and Newton too.

Newton gathered up his handkerchief and put it back in his pocket. Roxie had accomplished what she wanted. She had told everyone. "Now ya'll go play cards like you always do. I think I wouldn't mind a game of Rook myself. How about it Newton?"

"Alright." This sounded good to him.

"Who wants to play with us?" Roxie asked.

"I'll play a game with you." Percy spoke up. "Linda do you want to by my partner?"

"Sure."

Joe was ready to start a poker game, anything to get his mind off the news he had just heard. Ann, Joe, Joy, Tim, Tom, Jan, and Randy went into the dining room. Randy, Tom, Tim, Joe, and Ann took seats at the table, while Joy and Jan mixed drinks for everyone. It was somber mood for a while until the effects of the liquor took place.

Percy, Linda, Newton, and Roxie were on their third hand of Rook. The hoopering and hollering was getting louder in the dining room. Ann had just won a load of money from straight poker, nothing wild. It was between her and Joe. Joe showed a pair of Aces, while Ann had three fives.

"Well, I think they all took it pretty well, don't you, Percy?"

"Yeah, I think they did." He noticed his mother was looking extremely tired. She had dark circles under her eyes. He could see her getting weaker by the minute. He decided after this game that he and Linda would leave, and maybe everyone else would follow suit. "I'm getting tired. I got a big day at work tomorrow. I've got to help with the installation of one of those teller machines. That's the new thing you know."

"I've seem them going up around town. I don't trust 'em. I'd rather deal with a real person." Roxie replied. "Wonder if your card gets stuck in one of those things, or it takes your deposit and doesn't give you credit for it? No, I'm dealing with a human being, thank you."

Percy didn't reply. He just listened to his mother. As usual Newton and Roxie were slaughtering them. Percy had already decided they had some kind of code. They could read each other's movements and reactions and know what the other person had. It couldn't be any other way with them playing cards together as long as they had.

"Mom, dad, I'm leaving," said Eliza as she came into the living room. She had heard Roxie tell the news to the 'grownups.' She was ready to cry herself, but didn't want to do it in front of everyone, so she decided she would leave. She needed to smoke a joint in the worst kind of way. Anything to kill the pain she was feeling. Her stomach felt like a hollow hole was in it, and she didn't want to feel it any longer. It was time for her to leave.

"Already leaving." Roxie said as she looked up at her over her glasses at Eliza.

"Yeah, I'm going to meet a friend, Sharon. We're just going to go riding around. I'll be home before dark." Eliza said as she bent down towards her grandmother and gave her a kiss and a hug. Then she went around the table kissing everyone else, hugging them and telling them goodbye. She then left, went immediately to her Chevy Impala, sped out of the driveway and headed towards Sharon's so she could get high and hopefully forget what she heard.

"She'll be graduating this year, won't she?" Roxie said as she laid the Rook on the table.

"Yeah, she sure will." Linda said proudly.

"I hope I can make it to her graduation." Roxie said as she picked up the cards she had just won.

"You'll probably make it." Percy said as he laid out the red one hoping she would make it.

Once again Roxie and Newton won the game. Percy got up from the table and scooted his chair in. Linda took the cue, got up too, went into the front bedroom and got her purse. She went back into the living room and stood beside Percy. "Well, we're going to be going."

"Got to leave so soon?"

"Yeah, I've got a busy day tomorrow."

Newton and Roxie got up from the table. Percy and Linda said their goodbyes to everyone in the dining room and to Newton and Roxie. On the way out they rounded up Luke and got into the car. On the way out the driveway Percy looked at Linda and asked. "How do you think they took it?"

"About like I expected, Ann and Joy cried along with your dad. Joe and Jan didn't react at all but were uncomfortable."

Luke, who was sitting in the backseat asked. "How'd they react to what?"

Percy looked at Linda again. She nodded in the affirmative like it was alright to go ahead and tell him. "Your grandmother isn't going to get any better?"

"I thought she was getting that chemo?"

"It didn't work on her. She had some type of allergic reaction."

"Oh."

"She has about two to four months."

"Two to four months? To what! Live?" He asked loudly.

"Yes." Percy said as he lit a cigarette while on Barfield Road. They were almost to their house.

Luke just sat in the backseat unable to speak. He didn't want his grandmother to die. It was his favorite place to go besides home. Finally the words blurted out of his mouth before he could stop them. "Why does she have to die? It's not fair." He knew everyone had to die. It was part of life, but it didn't make it any easier.

As they pulled into the driveway Percy said, "that's life." He then looked at Linda. "How do you think Eliza is going to take it?"

"I think she already knows, you noticed she was ready to leave, sooner than usual. She looked a little down, too, plus she gave your mother an extra long hug. She was ready to get out of there, but all the same, we'll need to tell her when she gets home tonight."

"You're right."

Eventually everyone left Newton and Roxie's house. Roxie was ready to lay on the couch and take a rest. Newton was waiting for some peace and quiet, too much noise and commotion got on his nerves.

Eliza made it home around 7:00 p.m. higher than a kite. She went into the kitchen. Percy was sitting at the table smoking a cigarette. Linda was making some fresh coffee. Eliza began looking for something sweet. "Mama, do we have anything sweet to eat?"

"Look in that cabinet down there I bought some Oreo's the other day." Eliza found the cookies and tore open the package. Linda was sitting down at the table by now. Eliza got her a glass, went to the refrigerator, got the milk and poured herself some. She was standing at the counter eating cookies and drinking milk. Percy and Linda looked at her. Linda had suspicions she had been smoking marijuana and had given her some brochures about it that was all she could do. Linda couldn't tell if she was high or had been crying. Her eyes were all swollen and most of her makeup had come off. Linda decided she had been crying. Linda then looked at Percy to give him the cue to go ahead and tell her.

Percy cleared his throat. "Honey, we've got something to tell you."

Eliza finished her milk and reached inside her purse, got a cigarette and lit it. "Yeah." She had a feeling what was coming. She couldn't decide whether to tell them she had already heard it at grandmother's or let him tell her and then tell them she had already heard it. She decided on the later.

"You know your grandmother has been getting treatments for cancer."

"Yeah." Eliza replied while she took a big drag off the cigarette and then exhaled.

"She can't get the treatments anymore. She gets too sick, plus it's not helping her cancer any. In fact, it's spreading. She's going to die, honey. The doctor's given her two to four months to live."

Hearing it from her dad made it for certain. She didn't want to hear this. She was ready to go and smoke another joint, but knew she couldn't. They might get suspicious.

"I heard grandmother telling everybody in the living room. Pat and I did. We were in the dining room, where we could hear everything, but you all couldn't see us. That's why I had to leave."

"Oh." Percy said as he took another drag off his cigarette.

Eliza didn't want to talk about it anymore. She thought if she didn't talk about it, it would go away, maybe even disappear. "I'm going upstairs. I'm tired, going to bed."

"Alright honey." Percy said to Eliza.

CHAPTER 19

Roxie woke up the next morning feeling very weak and tired. She barely made it out of bed to go to the bathroom. She immediately went back to the bedroom and had laid down. She didn't have the energy to even go and make coffee.

Newton woke up and got dressed. He went into the kitchen and made some coffee. He stood at the kitchen window, looking outside at the May day. The days were warmer and longer now. The sun had risen in the pale blue sky. The leaves and branches on the maple tree were gently swaying back and forth. It would be a comfortable day Newton determined, not too hot or too cold, just right, a fine day to sit on the front porch.

The coffee had finished percolating. He poured himself a steaming cup and walked back into the bedroom to see if Roxie wanted a cup.

"No, Newton, I don't want any coffee. I'm just going to rest for a little while then I'll get up."

Newton noticed Roxie's face looked a grayish-white. She was paler than usual. He decided he would sit out on the front porch, enjoy the weather, and then he would go back and check on Roxie.

He went back into the kitchen, made himself some toast, lathered it with butter and homemade grape jelly, put it on a paper towel and walked towards the front porch. He sat in the rocking chair closet to the door, sat his toast on the table next to it, took a sip of coffee, then sat the cup down on the table and picked up a piece of toast and began eating it. The breeze was pleasant. It felt good to his skin. He loved days like this. He wished Roxie was out here with him enjoying this beautiful day.

Roxie feel back to sleep and had woken up two hours later. She still felt weak and didn't have the energy to get out of bed. She was thirsty, but didn't know where Newton was at the time. She wanted a glass of water in the worst way. She heard the front door open, hearing Newton's footsteps carry him back into the den, and he appeared in the bedroom.

"You alright Roxie?" Newton said with a little concern in his voice. It wasn't like Roxie to lay in bed until 10'o'clock in the morning.

"I'm just tired." She didn't want to worry him. "But I am thirsty. Could you get me a glass of ice water?"

Newton turned around and went into the kitchen to fix Roxie some water. He went back into the bedroom and handed her the water.

"Thank you." Roxie said as she slowly sat up in bed. She gulped the water and lay back down.

Newton noticed how pale and ashen she looked. "Need anything else."

"No, no. I'm just going to lay here for a little while longer."

"You alright?" He never ever remembered Roxie laying around for a little while longer even when she was sick. She always managed to get up, put some clothes on and make it to the couch, even when she had the chemo, and she was deathly ill.

"I'm just a little weak, that's all."

"I'm going to go back out to the front porch. You need anything just holler for me, o.k.?"

"How long you going to be out there?" She didn't want to tell him she didn't have enough energy to be hollering for him.

"Probably a couple of hours, I guess. I want to enjoy the day outside, it's s-o, s-o nice."

"Yeah, I could tell." Roxie lied. All she could tell was that it was sunny outside, but as far as anything else went she didn't have a clue.

Newton went into the kitchen fixed himself some ice water, walked out to the front porch and took his usual seat. He ended up going to sleep in his chair with his head leaned on the house wall. He came too when he heard a dog barking. The sun was setting in a pale pink sky. He realized he was hungry and wondered why Roxie hadn't called him to supper or come out to join him on the front porch. He got up from his chair and stretched. He then went into the house. It was totally dark inside, not a light was on. He went into the kitchen to see if maybe Roxie had cooked something and left it on the counter. He turned on the light there was nothing on the kitchen counter. It looked like it did when he had last left it. He hurriedly went through the dining room, in the den, and then into the bedroom. There Roxie lay, she looked almost lifeless. He was scared to touch her for fear she could be dead. She had been saying she was tired the last couple of weeks. Maybe her body had just given out.

Newton gently touched Roxie. She didn't respond. Fear shot all through his body. He felt her skin. It was clammy. He put his hand on her chest it was slowly moving up and down. 'She was still alive.' He told himself.

"Roxie, Roxie, wake up."

"U-h-h-h." She said barely audible.

"Roxie, what's wrong?" Newton said almost shouting at her.

"Ge-t, Per-cy." It took all of her energy to get the words out. She then sunk back into her stupor.

Newton hurriedly went into the den, picked up the phone and dialed Percy's number. It rang a couple of times, finally Linda picked up the other end. "Hello."

"Is Percy around?"

"Hey, Mr. Prater how you doing? I think he's in the back with the cows. How's Mrs. Prater?"

"She's not doing too good. I think something's wrong with her."

Linda's tone changed immediately. "Stay right there, I'll go get him."

She ran out the back door and spotted Percy close to the shed. "Percy." She yelled at the top of her lungs.

"Yeah."

"Your dad's on the phone. Something's wrong with your mother."

Percy came running. He picked up the phone. "What's going on dad?" Percy said out of breath.

"It's Roxie, Percy." Newton started tearing up. "She hasn't gotten out of bed all day. Percy she's white as a ghost, and she's not breathing too good. She told me to call you."

"I'll be right there."

Linda looked at him as he hung up the phone. "What's going on?"

"It's mother. She's not doing too good. I'll call you later." Percy said as he sped out the door.

Percy drove down Barfield Road when he got to the field off the road he cut through it, so he wouldn't have to stop at the new stop light they had just installed at the end of Barfield Road, and headed straight for Newton and Roxie's house. He barely got the truck turned off, and put in park before he jumped out of it. He ran up through the garage, up the stairs, and through the house into the back bedroom where Roxie lay.

He was breathing hard when he got to her bed. "Mo-ther." He said through heavy breathing. She responded by barely opening her eyes and trying to smile.

Percy turned around and looked at his dad. "How long has she been like this?"

"Most of the day. Come to think of it I don't even know if she's been up at all. She had me bring her some ice water. She drank it and feel back to sleep. She hasn't eaten anything that I know of."

"Has she said anything else?" He asked as he looked down at his mother who lay helpless on the bed.

"Just that's she's tired."

Percy went into the den, fumbled around in his billfold, found the doctor's number and called it. He told the answering service how his mother was acting. He hung up the phone and lit a cigarette.

"They're putting a message in to Dr. Jung. They said he should call back within thirty minutes."

It wasn't five minutes and the phone rang. Percy picked up the receiver. He told Dr. Jung what was going on with his mother.

"You think you can help me get her out of bed and into the car? We've got to take her to the hospital."

"Sure, Percy."

Percy took her left side and put her arm over his shoulder.

He scooted her body around and told his dad. "You hold her while I put some shoes on her." He found some slip-ons and slid them on her feet.

Percy went back to his spot. "We're probably going to have to carry her into the car because she's so weak."

They lifted Roxie up on the count of three. She was like dead weight. They made it into the dining room and took a break. They then went into the kitchen, got to the back door, and took another break. "Now, dad when we go down these steps I'll go down first. Think you can handle it?"

"Sure."

Percy headed down the steps first. They were trying to be careful not to hurt her as they went down the steps. Percy would have to go down one step, lift his mother's feet to bring down to the next step, and then his dad would come down the next step. They made it to the car and laid her in the back seat. Percy closed the door and told his dad he was driving. Percy got into the car first, started the engine, and then Newton followed suit. Percy put the car in reverse and shot out of the garage.

The trip to the hospital took ten minutes, when it usually took twenty. The traffic was light, and Percy was speeding all the way. He figured by the time the ambulance got to his parents' house he would have had his mother at the hospital, which he was right. Percy wheeled the car into the emergency entrance. Dr. Jung had called ahead, so when Percy went into the admitting room to tell them about his mom and her name, the orderlies were told to go out to the car and get her.

Percy got all the insurance information from his dad and took care of the paperwork, while they had Roxie in the back. Newton took a seat in the waiting room. After Percy finished he went outside to smoke a quick cigarette. He went back into the waiting room and took a seat by his dad. Twenty minutes went by when Dr. Jung came into the waiting room and asked them to come in the back.

  Dr. Jung looked at both of them. "Mrs. Prater isn't doing well at all. The reason she is so weak is because her platelet count is down. We've got to get it back up or it could be fatal. The quickest way is through a transfusion, which is best coming from family." He looked at Percy at this moment. "You'll need to call your siblings and get them all down here, now. We're going to see who is the most compatible with your mother and then we'll do the transfusion."

  Percy shifted his feet and cleared his throat. "How long will this transfusion take?"

  "About eight hours."

  "I'll call them, now."

  "You can use that phone over there." He pointed to a phone at the nurse's station. "Once you're all here let that nurse over there know, and we'll get to testing. The testing will take about twenty minutes. Do you have any questions?"

  Newton who hadn't said anything while the doctor was talking asked. "Can I go in and be with Roxie?"

  "Sure." Dr. Jung pointed to room with the number three above it. "She's in there. She's not coherent. She probably won't even know you're in there, but you're more than welcome to stay in there until we do the transfusion."

Dr. Jung walked off in another direction. Percy headed for the phone.

He picked up the receiver and began making his calls. 'Luckily everyone was home,' he thought to himself. He had told everyone he would be at the emergency room entrance waiting for them. He leaned against the concrete ledge, which was filled with flowers and lit a cigarette. He figured he would be waiting a good while before anyone showed up. Ann was the first to show up, cigarette and colorful purse in hand. She looked like she had just thrown on some clothes. "How is she Percy?"

"She's not doing to good. The doctor said if she doesn't get this transfusion she probably won't make it."

"Oh, no." The tears were welling up in her eyes.

Next came Joy, followed by Joe and Jan. Percy explained to them that they would all get their blood tested and whoever was the most compatible would be the one to do the transfusion. They all agreed. They then followed Percy into the emergency room, through the double doors and into the part of the hospital where Dr. Jung and their mother would be. Percy stood at the nurses' station waiting on the nurse to get off the phone. He told her the Prater family was there to be tested and that Dr. Jung told him to come there when they had all arrived. The nurse paged Dr. Jung. He came over in about five minutes.

"I see you are all here. Are you ready to get started?"

Everyone shook their head in unison in the affirmative.

"This will take about twenty to thirty minutes." He said as he lead them back into a room that looked like a lab. Two people could be done at a time. Percy and Ann went first, followed by Joy and Joe and then Jan. The lab technician called Dr. Jung's name over the intercom. They watched as he went back into the lab room. He came out with a sheet of paper. "Look's like Percy and Joe are the most compatible, which one of you want to do it?" He looked up for a response.

"Between us is there like more of a match?" Percy asked.

"You blood is the most compatible, followed by Joe, but either one of you would be alright, but of course the most compatible the better."

Percy spoke without waiting for a response from his brother or sisters. "Then I guess it will be me."

Dr. Jung looked up at him saying, "I'm going to take your mother to another room where we can do the transfusion. It will take about thirty minutes to get everything ready, so if you need to do anything that needs to be done, now's the time because once you're on the table there won't be any getting off it for about eight hours. When you're finished just go back up to the nurse's station and have me paged."

Percy said o.k. and then went outside to smoke a cigarette first. The rest of the family went out there with him. Everyone was smoking and talking. Percy finished his cigarette. He wasn't hearing anything that his brother or sisters were saying. "I'm going to call Linda."

"Alright, Percy." Ann said as she looked at him strangely.

Percy went to a pay phone and dialed his home number. "Linda. I'm going to be at the hospital for a good while, actually about eight or nine hours."

"For what?" Linda said with concern in her voice.

"Mother needs a blood transfusion to get platelets, and I'm the most compatible out of all the family."

"Oh, no, that doesn't sound too good."

"It's not, if she doesn't get the transfusion it could be fatal."

"Do you want me to come down there?"

"No, no. There's nothing you can do. I'll call you when I get done. I need to go so I can get in there."

"Well, alright, then, take care."

"You too." He hung up the phone and went back outside to smoke another cigarette. He figured he better get his nicotine level up before the procedure. He ended up smoking two more cigarettes and then went inside.

Percy headed towards the nurse's station. "Dr. Jung told me to come up here and get him paged. My mother, Mrs. Prater, is having a blood transfusion, and I'm the one who their taken the blood from."

"Oh, yeah. Dr. Jung told me about you. Your Percy Prater, right?"

"Yeah."

"Let me page him for you." The nurse proceeded to page the doctor.

It wasn't long before Dr. Jung showed up. "Are you ready?"

"Sure." Percy said as he swallowed hard.

Percy followed Dr. Jung into a cold, sterile room. He saw his mother lying on a bed, unconscious. There was an empty bed next to her. She looked so helpless.

"Hi, I'm Darlene. I'll be here through the whole procedure." She said as she bounced on her feet, and her long, blonde hair flowed down her back. She didn't look a day over twenty-five. She didn't seem to breathe much when she talked. "You'll need to get this gown on and tie it in the back. There's a room over there in the corner. Just leave all your clothes in there. When you're ready come on out."

Percy took the gown and went into the dressing room, which was a tight fit. He had to come out of the room to have enough room to tie it in the back. He walked over to the bed.

Darlene turned around. "Now you need to lie on the bed. Do you want covered up?"

"Sure, just with a sheet though."

"Now you need to get comfy because you're going to be here a while."

Percy climbed up on the bed and took a sheet and covered himself up. He shifted the pillow around. He thought to himself , 'I really need two.' "Can I have another pillow?"

"Sure." Darlene said as she went over to a cabinet and pulled out a pillow. She gave him the pillow. Percy stuck it under his head.

"You comfortable now?"

"Uh-um." Percy said as he nodded his head yes.

Darlene began rubbing iodine on his left arm. "Now, you're going to feel a little prick. You're blood is going to go into this." She held up some kind of contraption. "We going to get all of the platelets cells out and shoot them into your mother. Then we'll put the blood back into you."

Percy felt the prick. He was so tired. His mother was safe she was in the hospital. He tried to stay awake, but drifted off to sleep. He woke up about four hours later. It was around midnight. Darlene looked down at him. "Took a little nap did you?"

"Yeah, I guess I dozed off. What time is it, anyway?"

"It's around midnight."

Percy wanted a cigarette in the worst way, but knew he couldn't get up. He looked at his mother. There was no change in her condition. He felt a little disheartened.

Darlene seemed to notice his reaction. "Don't worry Mr. Prater, it takes a good day to see if this is going to help."

"Oh."

"You've got about 3-½ more hours. I would go back to sleep if I was you, get the rest while you can."

Percy didn't need too much convincing. He couldn't do anything else, so he drifted back off to sleep. Percy was awakened by Darlene gently pulling the needle out of his arm. He felt stiff all over. 'Hospital beds have a lot to be desired.' He thought to himself.

"You don't have much longer Mr. Prater. You'll need to lay here about thirty more minutes. Would you like something to drink and eat?"

"Sure." He said as he looked over at his mother. He didn't see any change in her. The rest of the staff was tending to her.

"What would you like? You need something sweet. What about a coke and some brownies?"

"That's fine."

Darlene yelled at one of the orderlies to fetch a cold coke and a couple of brownies. The orderly ran off at her command. "You need to hold your arm up for a minute. Go ahead a sit up. You might feel a little light-headed at first."

Percy sat up, and he had to brace himself as the room spun a little bit. He finally got situated. He was ready for a cigarette, but he only had thirty more minutes to go. The orderly came over with a canned coke and brownies. He handed them to Percy. He popped the top, took a long gulp and then began opening the brownies. He had already finished one when Darlene came back over.

"They're going to take your mother to a room upstairs and monitor her for the rest of the morning. She'll be in Room 202. It'll be about 45 minutes before she'll be up there. We've already notified the rest of the family and to tell them you're fine."

"Thanks." Percy said then he stuffed the rest of the brownie into his mouth, chewed it, swallowed it, and then took a gulp of the coke. He was hungry but didn't realize why until it dawned on him that he hadn't eaten any supper.

"Finish that other brownie and the coke, and you're free to go."

"Alright." Percy was thrilled.

CHAPTER 20

He inhaled the other brownie and gulped the rest of the coke down. He swung his feet over the bed and steadied himself a bit to see if the room would spin. It didn't. He was safe. He went into the dressing room, put on his clothes, left the gown in the room, told everyone bye, said thanks and headed out the door. He was met by his family.

"How is she?" Ann was the first to ask.

"Come on outside. I've got to have a cigarette." Percy said as he headed out the exit door, and everyone followed him out. He leaned up against the stone wall, which had flowers embedded inside it. He lit his cigarette, took a big drag, and exhaled.

"Well?" Ann asked again.

"We won't know anything for a few hours that's what the nurse said. Didn't the doctor come out and talk with you all?" Percy asked as he took another drag.

"Yeah." Joe said as he lit a cigarette. By now everyone had a cigarette lit, and they were smoking in silence.

Ann finally broke the silence. "Well, how are you doing Percy?"

"I'll be alright once I smoke a couple of cigarettes and eat a meal. I guess I'll have to wait until the cafeteria opens to get a meal though. Does anyone know what time it opens?"

"I think around 5:30 in the morning." Joy said as she put out her cigarette.

"Good, I just have about an hour and a half then. I think I'm going to get a candy bar and then call Linda." Percy said as he lit another cigarette. "Are you all going to stay around?"

Everyone nodded their heads in the affirmative.

"Where's dad?"

"He's asleep in the chair out in the waiting room. He finally dozed off around 2:00 not before he cried off and on for an hour and a half." Joy replied rolling her eyes.

"They said mother would be up in the room in about thirty to forty-five minutes. I guess that was about forty-five minutes ago. They said she would be in Room 202." Percy said as he put his cigarette out. "I guess I'm going to go on up there, sit around for a little while until I can get something to eat. I'll call Linda after I eat. I decided I don't won't to wake her up, and after I eat breakfast she should be up."

Percy headed back towards the hospital. He looked for his dad, woke him up, and then headed for the elevator. Percy, Newton, and all the siblings boarded the elevator. Ann pushed number two. They followed the signs which lead to Room 202. There Roxie lay, almost motionless, barely breathing. Percy and Joe sat in the windowsill. Newton took a chair, pulled it beside Roxie, and held her hand, while the sisters took a seat on the cushioned bench behind the door. Everyone was silent. For the next hour no one spoke, they fidgeted, looked at the clock, stood up, and sat back down. Once the nurse came in to check Roxie's IV, but not a question was asked or a word was spoken. Sleep deprivation was taking over the girls and Joe, at least Percy and Newton had slept.

Five-thirty rolled around. Percy had been watching the clock. His stomach was growling, and he was ready for some breakfast. Percy finally broke the silence. "Dad, I'm going down to get me something to eat. Do you want to come with me?"

"No, no. I don't want to leave Roxie."

"There's nothing you can do dad."

"I want to stay."

"Do you want me to bring you something back? A biscuit or something?"

"No, I can't eat."

Joe was ready to leave the room. "I think I'll go down with Percy and get me some coffee. I need to call work, too."

By now the girls had stood up. A cup of coffee sounded good to all of them. Ann said. "I could use a good cup of coffee, myself."

"Me too." Joy said.

"Sounds good to me." Jan joined in.

They all went back down the hall, boarded the elevator, got off the elevator and headed outside to smoke a cigarette. They stood beside the familiar stone hedge. "What do you think Percy? Do you think she's going to pull out of it?" Ann asked, while everyone listened on.

"I hope so. She probably will." Percy replied as he took a drag off his cigarette.

Everyone finished their cigarettes and then headed back into the hospital to the cafeteria. Percy got two eggs, four slices of bacon, two biscuits, gravy, sliced tomatoes, and a large coffee. He also ordered a country ham and biscuit for Newton. He sat down at a table close to the door and didn't wait for his brother or sisters to get seated before he started eating. Joe got two sausage and biscuits and coffee. Ann a bran muffin and coffee. Joy got a biscuit and coffee, while Jan got biscuits and gravy and a coffee. Everyone was glad to have some coffee in them and food.

Percy was scraping his plate by the time Jan sat down. He sipped his coffee, which was loaded with cream and sugar. No one said much to each other. Percy looked at his watch. It was six o'clock. "I'm going to call Linda." Percy announced as he stood up from the table looking around for a pay phone. He couldn't locate one and decided to go to the emergency room hall where he knew one was. He called Linda and told her the news about his mother.

"Has she woken up yet?" Linda asked with concern in her voice.

"No. We're hoping she'll come around in a few hours."

"Do you want me to come down?"

"No, that's alright."

"Do you need anything?"

"No, just prayers. I'm going to go back up there in a few minutes."

"How's your dad?"

"He looks pretty rough. He finally fell asleep in the waiting room last night for a few hours, but other than that he hasn't had any sleep. He hasn't eaten anything since yesterday." Percy answered Linda's question before she had a chance to ask. "I got him a country ham and biscuit to eat. I'm fixing to take it up to him."

"He needs to eat."

"Well, I better get off the phone."

"I guess I'll go on to work, if you need me just call me at work. They won't mind if I have to leave."

"Talk to you later, hon."

"Bye." Linda said as Percy hung up the phone.

Percy walked outside to his usual spot. The sun was coming up in the east. It was a beautiful sunrise filled with pinks, purples, and light yellows. Percy lit a cigarette and enjoyed the sunrise. He finished the cigarette, put it out, and headed back upstairs. He entered the room, and Newton looked up. Percy handed him his biscuit and a cup of coffee. Newton eagerly took the biscuit and had half of it eaten before Percy had pulled up a chair to sit on the other side of his mother's bed. She didn't look any different. He was beginning to think the transfusion didn't take. Newton took the last bite of his biscuit, wiped his hand on his pants, popped the top off the coffee cup, and took a sip. He immediately grabbed Roxie's hand again. He didn't want to let it go for too long.

It wasn't long before the rest of the family came crowding into the room. Percy kept checking his watch for a lack of better things to do. Ann, Joy, and Jan were talking by the window about their kids, and Joe was standing by the door. He kept shifting from his right to left foot. Newton was still holding Roxie's hand. He was full and had almost dozed off when he jolted upright in his chair.

"Percy."

"What dad?" As he got up from his chair.

"Roxie just squeezed my hand."

Percy took a good look at his mother, and he noticed she was trying to open her eyes. It was like she would get just a slit open and then it was like something would close them shut again. Percy ran out to the hall to get a nurse. The nurse came running in after Percy. Everyone cleared a path for her. She took Roxie's vitals. She began leaning over the bed and talking real loud. "Mrs. Prater, Mrs. Prater can you hear me? If you can try to open your eyes."

Everyone hovered over the bed in dead silence waiting for eye movement. Percy was the first to notice. "She did it."

The nurse still leaning into Roxie's face, "yes, she did. I'll call Dr. Jung. Her blood pressure is still a little low, but it is better than it was." She said as she walked out the door.

Everyone began to breathe again. Newton pulled out his handkerchief and began to cry. He blew his nose and stuffed the handkerchief back in his pocket. Ann and Joy looked at each other with disgusting looks after they saw their dad stuff the used handkerchief back in his pocket. Thirty minutes went by, and Dr. Jung made his entrance into the room.

"Hello, everyone, I see we still have a full house."

Everyone exchanged their hellos and waited for Dr. Jung to take a look at Roxie. He checked her chart, took her blood pressure again, stuck a thermometer in her mouth, pulled it out, and read the temperature. About the time he pulled the thermometer out of her mouth Roxie began spitting it out. She rolled her head back and forth, and opened her eyes.

"Well, folks I think she's going to be alright. She'll be weak for a few more hours, probably won't be able to talk too much. I'll be back around noon to check in on her."

Percy exhaled a sigh of relief along with the rest of the family. Newton began crying again. Percy reached down and put his hands on top of hers. "Mom, I'm glad to see you're doing better." She looked up at him but didn't speak. "I'm going outside for a little while. I'll be back in a few minutes."

****

By six o'clock Roxie was sitting up in the bed and talking with her family. She had eaten scrambled eggs and toast for supper, along with some chicken noodle soup. She wanted a cup of coffee, but settled for the juice and milk that was given to her with her dinner tray. Dr. Jung had come back by and told the family she would be able to go home on Thursday. Roxie couldn't wait. She was ready to go back home right then.

Joe was the first to leave, followed by Jan, Joy, and Ann. Percy was the last to leave. "Dad, do you want me to take you home or are you going to stay her tonight?"

"I'm staying here."

Roxie looked at Newton. "You need to go home and get some real rest. You know the nurses will be in and out of here all night long. Hospital's the worst place to try and get some rest. I'm fine. There's enough people looking after me here Newton. Let Percy take you home. I'm sure he'll drop you off here in the morning on his way to work." Roxie didn't want the family to stop living their lives due to her and that included Newton.

Newton looked down at the floor and said, "alright." He got up from his chair, squeezed Roxie's hand. She squeezed his back. He followed Percy out the door.

Percy turned around when he got to the door. "You need me to bring anything tomorrow?"

Roxie got a grin on her face. "Yeah, do you think Linda could make me a loaf of banana nut bread?"

"I'm sure she can."

"See you tomorrow then with the bread, and tell Linda I said thanks."

"See you later," Percy headed out the door with his dad.

By eight o'clock the next morning Newton and Percy walked through the door which led to Roxie's room. Percy had the banana nut loaf in hand. Newton looked a little more rested to Roxie than he had when he left. Percy looked at his mother and could tell she was feeling better. She had more color in her face than when they left. She was eagerly eyeing the loaf that Percy handed to her.

Roxie took it from his hand and unwrapped the foil that surrounded it. It had already been cut into slices for her. "Tell Linda I said thanks."

"I already did. She said it wasn't any problem."

Roxie took a piece, took a small bite, and enjoyed the delicious flavor. "Um, this is delicious." She said as she finished that piece and started on another. "I wish I had a cold glass of milk."

No sooner than when she said that the nurse came in with the breakfast tray, which was full of toast, scrambled eggs, bacon and a carton of milk. "Well, I see you've already started on breakfast." The nurse said as she winked at Roxie. She put the tray in front of Roxie and left.

Roxie tore into the carton of milk and took two big gulps. She took a couple of bites of egg and left the rest. She was happy to have the banana nut bread. She looked up at Percy and Newton. "Well how's everything at the house?"

"Fine, fine," Newton said. He was glad to see Roxie back to her old self. He was ready for her to come home so they could sit on the front porch and watch the traffic go by on Shelbyville Highway. He wanted to have some of her fresh iced tea and homemade cornbread, and he wanted to spend the last of her days together at the house they raised their family in.

"How about the cows, Percy?" Roxie looked up at him for a response.

"They're all accounted for. We'll be having some calves before long."

"I can't wait to get out of this room and get back home." Roxie finally said breaking the lull in the conversation.

"It won't be long. You just have one more day. I'd take advantage of the rest if I was you." Percy said. He knew once his mother got out of the hospital she'd go straight home and cook a meal big enough to feed six people like she had always done.

"It's going to be a long day though. Could you get me some circle puzzles?"

"I'll get Linda to pick you some up?"

"Thanks."

"Well, I need to get to work. I'll see you later." Percy said as he headed out the door. "I'll come back after I get off work to check on ya'll."

"See you later."

The rest of the family came and kept Roxie company throughout the day. Linda brought her a couple of circle puzzle books as she walked through the door. Newton was almost asleep when Linda came in. Roxie was bored and was twiddling her thumbs.

"Hey, Mrs. Prater," Linda said smiling as she handed the puzzles to Roxie. "You doing alright?"

"Yeah, I'm doing pretty good. Thank you so much for the banana nut bread and the puzzles. I'm about to go crazy in here."

"I'd enjoy it. Let somebody wait on you hand and foot for a while, you deserve it."

Roxie thought about the statement for a minute. She realized she didn't know how to do it, and that was why she was so uncomfortable being in the hospital and being sick. She was used to waiting on others, being the strong one. She didn't know what to say so she just responded. "You probably right."

"Is there anything else I can get for you?"

"No, this ought to hold me over till tomorrow."

The door opened and Percy came walking through. "Hey, hon," He said as he saw Linda. He walked over and kissed her on the cheek. "How you doing mother?"

"I'm better since I've got something to keep me busy."

"Dad, you want me to take you home now or come back and get you. Linda and I will probably go and get something to eat. You can either go with us, or I'll come back after we get finished eating."

"I'll just stay here." Newton replied rubbing his tired eyes.

"Newton, why don't you go eat with them. You're not going to get any good food here. I'm alright."

Newton thought about it for a minute.

Percy interrupted before he could finish his thought. "Come on dad, why don't you go with us?"

"Well, alright."

Percy thought for a moment and realized his mother might want something besides hospital food after eating it for a couple of days. "Mother do you want us to bring you something back?"

She thought he would never ask. She blurted out, "yes" before she even thought about it.

"What would you like?"

"Where you going?"

"We'll probably go to Don's." It was a local family diner in which Percy and Linda went to frequently.

"Let's see." Roxie put her finger on her chin and thought for a moment and then it came to her. "I know. I'll have some vegetables. I probably shouldn't get something too spicy. What about some mashed potatoes, green beans, corn, and squash."

"Do you want rolls or cornbread?" He knew the answer before he even asked.

"Cornbread."

"We'll be back in about 45 minutes to an hour then." Percy headed for the door followed by Linda and Newton.

"See you then."

Roxie busied herself with the puzzles Linda had brought to her. Mr. And Mrs. Coleman, old-time friends, had come by to see her for a few minutes. Roxie was getting hungrier by the minute. The nurse came in to take the dinner order. "I've got someone bringing me something to eat, thank you." The nurse left not blaming her for wanting food other than the hospital's. The Coleman's left, and Roxie picked up her puzzle book back up. She had almost finished one page when Percy and Newton came through the door. The aroma filled the room. Percy sat the to go container in front of Roxie on her tray. Roxie said the obligatory thank you and proceeded to inhale her food. She took time for a few gulps of sweet tea that Percy had brought for her too. Newton and Percy just sat there while Roxie ate.

She finally finished and burped under her breath. "That's just what I needed. Boy, that was good."

Percy saved the best for last. I brought you something else. Roxie just looked at him quizzically. Percy pulled from behind his back another container, but it was quite small.

"What is it?" Roxie asked anxious to see what was in the container.

"It's your favorite, blackberry cobbler." Percy said grinning at her as he handed her the other container.

She wasn't expecting this and was quite thrilled. She eagerly opened the container like it was a Christmas present. She savored every bite. "Thank you so much. I bet I sleep tonight. I'm as full as a tick."

Percy and Newton hung around for another hour until Roxie told Newton and Percy. "You better get going. It's getting late, and Percy I know you have things to do around the farm. Now, Newton you don't need to stay here with me. I'm fine. You go on home and get some rest. I'll be coming home tomorrow, and I can't wait. I hope I don't have to sit here all day and wait on the doctor to release me."

"You probably won't." Percy said as he took his mother's hand, squeezed it, and winked at her. He then began for the door.

Newton got up from his chair, bent down and kissed Roxie on the cheek. "I'll see you tomorrow." He followed Percy to the door.

"We'll be here around seven o'clock." Percy said as he opened the door.

"Alright, see you then." Roxie said as she grabbed her puzzle book and pen.

CHAPTER 21

Roxie was ready to leave the hospital at five in the morning. She was dressed and sitting on the bed when Dr. Jung walked into the room.

He looked over his glasses at her as he walked towards her. "I see you're ready to go. Let me have a look at your charts. Everything looks fine to me. Now you know you don't need to be overdoing it, or you'll end up right back in here. Do you promise?" He had already figured out that Roxie pushed herself to the limit.

"I won't. I promise." Roxie said as she was planning what she would be cooking for dinner. "Does this mean I get to go home?"

"Yes, I'm signing the release papers right now. You're free to go." Dr. Jung said as he handed her some papers. "You'll need to take these down to billing on your way out. Do you have someone to pick you up. You probably shouldn't be driving for a few days to get those red blood cells good and built back up."

"Alright. I won't drive. Thanks." She had been too scared to drive since she began the chemo. She was afraid she would have a wreck, so she hadn't been driving and wasn't planning on it in the near future.

Dr. Jung left the room. Roxie was eyeing the clock. It was 6:45. She just had fifteen minutes to go before Percy would be bringing Newton to take her home. Newton had left his car in the hospital parking lot the entire time Roxie had stayed in the hospital. She looked at the clock again it was 6:47. The door opened it was Newton and Percy.

Percy looked at his mother. "I see you're ready to go. Has the doctor been by here yet."

"He's already come and gone. I'm ready to go. I just have to stop by billing before we go."

"I guess I'll get off to work. Now, mother when you get home don't you overdo it." Percy said as he was standing by the doorway.

"I won't. Dr. Jung told me the same thing you know."

"I'll see ya'll later." Percy said as he walked out the door.

"Come on, Newton, let's get this billing taken care of."

Newton followed her as she happily walked out the door. They rode the elevator down to the first floor, took care of the billing, and then were out the door. The first thing that Roxie noticed was all of the irises that were blooming up and down the sidewalk.

"Look Newton, aren't they beautiful. I wonder if our irises are blooming." She looked down at the sidewalk. There were deep purple ones and bright yellow irises. She reached down and picked one of each.

They made it to the car. Newton opened the door for her, and Roxie climbed in shutting the door. Newton started the car. Driving down the road on the way home Roxie looked at the leaves in full bloom, the light breeze swaying the trees back and forth, and the gorgeous irises. They finally pulled up in the driveway. Roxie was anxiously waiting to see if their irises were blooming.

"Look, look, Newton. Aren't they beautiful?" She asked as the car passed the wrought-iron fence, and she could see the irises.

"I see." Newton said between the cigar he had in between his teeth. Newton pulled the car into the garage.

Roxie didn't even wait for Newton to cut off the ignition before she was out the door and in the kitchen. She first made a strong pot of coffee. While she was waiting for the coffee to perk, she went into the dining room and pulled out three huge vases out of the china hutch. She went back into the kitchen gleeful as a little girl. She opened a drawer and found the scissors. She took a cup out of the counter and poured herself a cup of fresh-brewed coffee.

Newton was standing in the kitchen just watching her. He decided he would have a cup of coffee too, so he got himself a cup. Roxie poured each of them a cup of coffee. "Let's sit at the table." She said to him.

They both sat down in their appointed seats. "I'm so glad to be home, Newton. As soon as I get finished enjoying this cup of coffee I'm going to go outside and cut some irises."

"Uh-hum." Newton said in between his sip of coffee. "Don't you overdo it. You here?"

"I won't."

"I'm glad you're home too, gets lonely around here without you."

Roxie almost dropped her cup of coffee. She wasn't used to Newton actually saying how he really felt, and that he really missed her. It made her feel a little special. She gave him a broad smile and reached over and squeezed his hand. He squeezed hers back.

They finished their coffee. Newton went outside to sit on the front porch. Roxie followed him and went straight down the sidewalk towards the irises. She began clipping the irises. The deep burgundy ones were her favorites. Next, she went to the deep purple ones and then the yellow ones and then the light purple ones with yellow centers. It wasn't long before she had two handfuls. She went through the house into the kitchen and laid the flowers on the kitchen table. She looked out the kitchen window and noticed the irises blooming in the flower bed in the back yard, which used to be a concrete watering trough for the cows but had since been filled with dirt and Roxie's irises.

She went out back and cut the solid yellow irises and the white ones. She went back into the house rinsed out the three vases. She stuffed the irises into the vases and filled them with water. She took a quick sniff. "These smell heavenly."

She put one vase on the kitchen table, one on the dining room table, and the other on the coffee table in the den. She went back into the kitchen and onto the back porch, opened the deep freezer and pulled out corn, butter beans, and squash. She filled the kitchen sink with water and put the containers in there to thaw out.

She went back out to the front porch where Newton had dozed off. When the door opened he startled. "I didn't mean to scare you."

"I must of dozed off."

Roxie took her seat next to him. She took a deep breath through her nose. "Isn't this weather just wonderful?"

"Uh-hum."

She sat outside enjoying the gentle breeze hitting her skin. It felt so good to be home. The sun was a pale yellow against the baby blue sky. White fluffy clouds floated across the sky. Roxie sat looking up at the clouds. She made out dinosaurs, cows, and an elephant. She stretched. "Newton, I think I'm going to go in for a while a lay down on the couch. If I happen to still be asleep at four get me up, alright?"

"Alright."

Roxie laid down on the couch. She had no sooner put her head on the pillow when she had drifted off to sleep. Hours later she was being awakened by Newton tapping her on the shoulder. "W-h-at?"

"You told me to get you up."

"Wh-at time is it?"

"It's four."

"Already?"

"Yep."

Roxie roused herself up from the couch. She went straight to the kitchen took the containers out of the sink, pulled out pots from the cabinets, and dumped the contents into the pots. She was going to the refrigerator when the back door opened.

"Hey, mother." Percy said smiling. He was glad to see her moving around. He knew she was the most happy when she was doing something.

"Hey, Percy, have a seat." Roxie said as she took the pots one by one to the stove threw in a slab of butter in each and turned the stove on. "I'm just getting supper ready. I'm starving."

Percy poured himself a cup of coffee and took a seat at the kitchen table. He lit himself a cigarette and took a drag. He looked at the irises sitting on the kitchen table. "I see you've been picking some flowers."

"Aren't they beautiful? I've got some on the dining room table and the coffee table too."

"You haven't been doing too much have you?"

"No. I just got up from a nap. I didn't realize I was so tired. I hope I'll be able to go to sleep tonight."

"You probably will."

She knew he was right. She didn't want to get up and cook supper because she was still tired, but hunger took over. Roxie pulled a bowl out of the cabinet and began throwing stuff in it to make cornbread. She didn't have to use any kind of measuring cups. She had made cornbread so much that she could eye it. She stuck the iron skillet with oil in it in the oven to get it good and hot, while she mixed the cornbread.

"Percy, I want you to do something for me."

"What's that?"

"I want you to get some type of papers drawn up for me and Newton. You know, if I get so sick I'm not in my right mind, I don't want to be put on life support. Just let me go." She figured the quicker she said it the quicker it would be over, but she had been thinking about it while she was in the hospital.

Percy shifted in his seat and took the last drag off his cigarette. "I can talk to Matt and see what he can do, but you know that both you and dad will have to go to his office and sign the papers?"

"Yeah, I know." Roxie took the iron skillet out of the oven and poured the mixture into it. It sizzled as soon as it hit the oil. She took a seat at the table and sighed. "I figured we could get a draft out here and let Newton and me go over them, sort of prepare him. Then will go in and sign them. You know how we have to handle him. He has to have it in piecemeal. There's no hurry, though. You know in the next two to three weeks would be fine."

"What exactly do you want in the papers? Percy asked as he lit another cigarette and took a drag.

"The usual, I guess, like I don't want to be put on life support. I want Newton to have all assets, and if something happens to him I want you and Ann to be the executors. I want my jewelry dispersed among the kids. That's about it."

She got up from the table and began setting the table. She hurriedly set out the plates and silverware then she began talking and stirring the vegetables. "Percy, me lying in that hospital bed gave me a lot of time to think. I don't want to be some vegetable. And I don't want to be a burden on you all. If I get so sick that I can't take care of myself I want to be put in a nursing home. I don't want ya'll wearing yourselves out taking care of me. I remember when Newton's mother lived with us, and her dying in the house. It about wore me out. I swore to myself then I wouldn't be a burden to any of my kids, but things were different back then. You had to take care of your own. Nursing home were far and few between and expensive, plus we couldn't do that to Mama Lelia. I wouldn't have it." She was out of breath and looked tired and worn out after the long speech.

Percy took another drag off his cigarette, took a sip of coffee and swallowed hard. "I'll talk to Matt in the next couple of days."

"Thank you, Percy, you don't know how much I appreciate this." Roxie said as she opened the oven to check on the cornbread.

"It's no problem." Percy put his cigarette out and got up from the table. "I need to be getting home. Linda's probably waiting on me."

"I'll see you later." Percy went out the back door and got into his truck. He went through the field to check on the cows. Once the cows were all accounted for he went to the very edge of the field, turned off the truck, lit a cigarette, before he could take a drag off it, the tears started coming down his face. He sat there with memories flooding his mind of his mother that he couldn't stop. The more the memories hit the more the tears came down his face. He didn't like the responsibility he was carrying. He had to be so strong for his mother and his father and the rest of the family. It didn't seem quite fair. The sun was setting in the west. Percy noticed it was a pale pink and deep yellow, the color of mums. He turned the ignition, put the truck in drive, wiped his swollen eyes on his shirt sleeves and drove home.

"Newton, you about ready to go? I don't want us to wear our welcome out." This wasn't the truth at all. She had become very tired. She just wanted to lie down and rest.

Newton, who had just taken a puff off his cigar, said. "Sure."

Percy and Linda escorted them to the back door. The pleasantries were said and then Newton and Roxie were gone. Linda made sure they were good and gone. "Oh, hon. She's gone so downhill. Her skin is even losing its color. She's looking grayish. This isn't good, isn't good at all. And the weight she's lost. I'd bet she's lost fifty pounds."

Percy was sitting at the kitchen table now lighting a cigarette as Linda was standing by the sink.

He took a drag. "I know. She wants me to draw up some papers for her and dad."

"What kind of papers?"

He proceeded to tell her that his mother didn't want to be a vegetable; she wanted her jewelry divided; and she wanted the rest to go to Newton with Ann and him as executors. "I'm meeting Matt tomorrow during lunch."

"Oh. She must know it's not going to be much longer then."

"That's what I'm thinking, too."

Newton and Roxie pulled into the driveway. Roxie looked at the sky it was almost a purplish, blue with streaks of pink. It was beautiful. She admired God's work. Her mind drifted to what it would be like in heaven. Would the streets really be made of gold? They were in the garage and Newton shut his door which jolted Roxie back into reality. She got out of the car, headed up the stairs, and into the house. She headed straight back to the bedroom where she took off her clothes, and put on her nightgown. "Newton, I'm going to go ahead and go to bed. I'm exhausted." Her body ached all over, but she wasn't going to tell anyone.

"Alright," he said as he turned on the television and took his seat in the den. He took a look at her when her back was too him. She looked so frail he thought to himself. He didn't want to think about it too long, or he would start crying so he turned his attention to a baseball game.

Roxie laid on the bed and in no time was fast asleep. The next morning she didn't wake up until around nine. She slowly got dressed because her body was still achy. She went into the kitchen where Newton had already made a pot of coffee. She poured herself a cup and found the prescription of pain pills she was looking for. She popped a couple of pills and washed them down with a gulp of coffee. The pain was becoming increasingly worse as each day went on, but she didn't want to say anything to anyone, especially Newton. He would just cry, worry, and really couldn't do anything for her. 'Really no one could do anything for her.' She thought to herself. This was her cross to bear and alone. No one could help her die. All anyone could do was be there when she died, and she didn't even know if she wanted anyone there or not. It was a trip she would have to take by herself, just like being born.

She went out to the front porch where Newton was sitting and took her seat beside him. The day was going to prove to be another hot one. Roxie grabbed the newspaper on the wicker table and began fanning herself. "Did you eat anything for breakfast?"

"Some buttered toast." Newton said. He had become used to fixing his own breakfast now that Roxie wasn't getting up till about nine each morning. He was beginning to learn to fix his own lunch by now too, since Roxie really didn't have the energy to fix lunch or have the appetite to eat. His lunch usually was a ham sandwich. "Have you eaten?"

"No, not really too hungry. Maybe I'll eat something after while." This was the same conversation they had every morning. Roxie would try to eat some toast around ten, but usually could only eat one piece. The only real meal she ate was supper.

She opened the newspaper and began reading the obituaries, which had become a daily habit. She wondered what hers would say. She figured the family would figure out what to say about her. She then turned the page to see what the high today was going to be. "Looks like it's going to get up to 98 degrees with a heat index of 105 degrees."

"Um-um." Newton replied lighting his cigar.

Roxie finished reading the paper, set it down, got up, and headed towards the house. "Do you want some ice water?"

"No, I'm fine." Newton replied as he was chewing on the stub of his cigar.

Roxie went into the kitchen, looking at the clock. It was already noon. She began filling her glass with ice when the phone rang. She went over to the phone and picked it up. "Hello." She said wondering who might be on the other line.

"Mother." Percy said. "I'm glad you answered the phone. I just met with Matt we've drawn up a rough draft of the papers you wanted. Do you want me to come by later on tonight with them?"

"Sure, that'll be fine."

"Well, I'll be around about five then, o.k.?"

"Alright." Roxie said. "See you later then." '

She hung up the phone her stomach tightening up a little bit in anticipation of dreading telling Newton. She decided she would wait until Percy got there so she would have back up. She filled her glass of ice with water and drank it down. The pain pills were wearing off, and her body began to ache again. She took two more pain pills and decided she would lie down. She put the glass in the sink and walked out to the front porch.

"Newton, I'm going to lie down for a while. I'm a little tired wake me up around four, if I'm not up, will you?"

"Sure will." Newton said as he was relighting his cigar and was taking a puff on it to stoke it.

Roxie took a blanket from the closet, laid down on the couch in the comfort of the cool air-conditioned room and covered up with her blanket. She dreamt of the past when she was younger and what it would be like when she would die. She was peaceful, floating, and surrounded by love she hadn't ever experienced. She was beginning to step onto the street of gold and was roused by Newton shaking her on the shoulder.

"Roxie, Roxie, wake up." Newton said as he was bending over her saying it almost in a whisper.

Roxie sat up startled. "What, what time is it? Is it already four?" She asked in a haze not believing it was already four o'clock. It just seemed like she had laid down. She rubbed her eyes and stretched. "I guess I better get something cooking." She had no idea what that would be and to be honest she didn't even feel like cooking much less eating, but Newton needed to be fed.

She got up from the couch and headed into the kitchen. Newton had made a fresh pot of coffee. She poured herself a cup and sat at the table drinking it trying to wake up and get her bearings about her. She got up and looked in the refrigerator hoping there would be something simple in there to cook, but there was nothing. She walked past the sink and noticed three containers sitting in there. It looked like fried corn, squash and field peas. Newton must have taken them out for her. She thought how sweet that was and proceeded to dump the thawed vegetables into their pots. She turned the stove and oven on at the same time. She put the iron skillet with grease in it in the oven then went about mixing her cornbread. She then seasoned the vegetables adding plenty of butter. The oven light went off, and she poured the batter into the skillet listening to it sizzle.

Supper would be ready in about ten minutes. She was already exhausted and in pain, but she didn't want to take any more pain medicine until bedtime. She set the table, filled the glasses with ice, poured tea into them, and set them on the table. She sat down to take a break. Newton came into the kitchen and took his seat at the table.

Roxie got up from the table and began setting the pots on the table. The cornbread was ready. She pulled the skillet out of the oven, turned over the cornbread onto a plate and sliced it into eight pieces. 'This will give Newton something to snack on tomorrow.' She thought to herself. She brought the plate to the table and sat it down.

Newton began filling his plate to the rim with food and the biggest piece of cornbread slathering it with butter. Roxie put minute portions of food on her plate. Newton noticed but didn't say anything. She ate slowly trying to hide that she was in pain. She could feel it in her body the cancer taking over. Newton was just finishing the food on his plate when the back door opened.

"Hey, ya'll." Percy said as he went straight for the coffee pot, filling his Styrofoam cup up with some fresh coffee. He took some milk out of the refrigerator adding it to his coffee along with some sugar. He took a seat at the table and began nibbling on a piece of cornbread. He laid the manila folder beside him on the table.

Newton eyed the folder for a second and finished his last bite of cornbread. Roxie began shifting in her seat knowing the inevitable had arrived. They would have to tell Newton, and the time had arrived. Roxie stirred her food and finally took a bite of the fried corn.

Percy took a couple of more puffs off his cigarette and then put the cigarette out. Roxie took her plate and set it beside the sink. She went over to

Newton. "You finished?" He nodded his head in the affirmative.

"Do you want a cup of coffee?" Roxie asked Newton.

"Sure." He had a funny feeling in his stomach, and it had to do with the manila folder.

Roxie brought him his coffee and then took her seat back at the table with her own cup of coffee. She cleared her throat. "Um, um." She figured she just better spit it on out. "Now, Newton, Percy went to see Matt today. You know Matt, the attorney. I got him to draw up some papers for us. Well, basically the papers say if something happens to me. You know where I'm unconscious or something." She hesitated again and gulped hard. "I don't want to be put on life support."

CHAPTER 22

Newton and Roxie were rocking on the front porch when Percy pulled up in old blue. It was late afternoon. The day had been hot and humid with a temperature of 95 degrees. The haze was lying in the sky, but Newton and Roxie wanted to sit on the porch with a glass of ice water each. The irises had died down. Summer had arrived the first week of June. It had finally cooled off enough for them to sit on the front porch. Roxie was trying to think of something for supper. Newton was worried about Roxie. He had just woken her up from her daily nap. He knew in his heart she was getting worse, but wasn't ready to fully concede to it.

Percy parked the truck in front of the wrought iron fence, got out, slammed the door shut and began walking up the sidewalk towards the steps. "Hot enough for ya'll today." He said as he made it up the last step and pulled a rocker up next to his mother.

Roxie was fanning herself with a newspaper. Newton was just rocking back and forth trying to get a breeze going. "Just a little bit." Roxie said as she took a sip of ice water. "Do you know what the temperature got up to today?"

"They said on the radio it got up to 95 degrees with a heat index of 101." Percy replied.

"Lord," was all Roxie could say.

"What are you all going to do for supper?" Percy asked while he was lighting a cigarette.

"I don't know. I'd kind of like something cool to eat myself." Roxie said.

"Well, Linda's got some fried chicken that's been chilling, potato salad, and coleslaw at the house. She wanted to know if you all wanted to come over and eat."

"Sounds good to me, what about you Newton?" Roxie asked as she stopped fanning long enough for Newton to answer.

"Sounds fine," was Newton's short response.

"What time?" Roxie asked as she proceeded to start fanning herself again.

"Anytime, why don't ya'll just come on over now?" Percy asked out loud to his mother and father.

"Does she need me to bring anything?" Roxie asked.

"No." Percy said as he got up and put his cigarette out in the ashtray his dad used for his cigar butts. "I'm going to get. I need to check the cows then I'll be on over there."

"See you later," Roxie said to Percy as he headed back towards old blue, what he liked to call his faithful beat up half ton truck.

Newton and Roxie sat out on the front porch for about thirty more minutes. "Well, I guess we better get going." Roxie said as she stood up with her newspaper and glass of ice water. Newton followed suit. He held the screen door open for Roxie as she headed towards the kitchen.

They got into their car. Newton was chewing on his cigar stub as he backed out of the garage. "It'll be nice not to have to cook."

Newton didn't respond. He just kept driving. He was getting hungry.

They pulled into Percy and Linda's driveway.

Everyone's car was there--Linda's cutlass, Percy's old blue and Eliza's tank the Chevy Impala. Newton squeezed their car beside Eliza's. They walked into the house. The aroma of the food hit Roxie's nostrils. She was beginning to get hungry herself.

Eliza was in the breakfast room setting the table. Luke came in the house when he saw his grandparent's car. Linda was busy setting food out on the kitchen table. It would be buffet style she had decided. Percy had a little niche at the kitchen table with an ashtray and a cup of coffee. He was sitting there smoking a cigarette.

"Hey, Percy, Linda," Roxie said as she looked at all of the food on the table. "You've outdone yourself Linda, everything looks delicious."

"Oh, it's nothing. I fixed too much of course. I thought it would be nice for ya'll to come over." She said knowing the real reason was to give her mother-in-law a break. She told Percy she could see her going down as each day went by. She had lost over fifty pounds by now. Roxie's skin was even looking "ashish" as Linda called it.

"You know you're dad can't cook a thing besides toast and coffee. You can't live on toast. You know that. We all, meaning the whole family, need to start pitching in helping your mother out. You know she feels obligated to cook your dad supper every night. Let's have them over tomorrow. You need to talk with your brother and sisters about it."

Percy knew he needed too. He decided he would talk with them over the weekend. Percy told her it was fine with him. "Hey, mother, dad." Percy said as he took a big drag off his cigarette. "I hope ya'll are hungry. As you can see, Linda fixed enough to feed an army."

"You need me to do anything Linda?" Roxie asked Linda as she stood in the kitchen watching Linda hurriedly get everything ready.

"No. Eliza's helping me. You all just go and sit in the breakfast room." She said as she found a spot for the coleslaw. "Eliza, you got the table set in there." She hollered from the kitchen.

"Yeah, everything's set, mama." Eliza said as she was walking from the breakfast room to the kitchen. "What do you need me to do now?"

"Ask everybody what they want to drink."

Eliza took everyone's order and proceeded to fix the drinks. She set them on the table where Roxie, Newton, and Percy had moved to by now. Percy had cracked the door to let some of the smoke out. Roxie took a look at Eliza. "Eliza, you're going to melt away if you lose any more weight."

By now Eliza had graduated from pot, to speed, and now to LSD. She was eating speed everyday so she could be skinny. She thought she looked good. Everyone else thought she looked bad. "I think I need to lose about five more pounds."

"Five more pounds, where. The jeans you have on right now are about to fall off." Linda had said as she entered the breakfast room. Luke came in behind her and took a seat by his grandmother.

"Hey, Luke, how was school this year?" She asked him as he sat down.

"It's great. I'll probably graduate a year early."

"Really, that's good."

"Well, everybody, the food's ready. Just go into the kitchen, get you a plate and then come on in back here. It's going to be buffet style."

Newton and Roxie were the first in line. Newton filled his plate till it wouldn't hold anymore. Roxie took a little of everything, but she took small portions because she couldn't eat much without feeling sick to her stomach.

When the meal was over Eliza began taking everyone's plate and putting them in the kitchen sink. She couldn't bear to look at her grandmother. She looked so sick. She would be glad when this was over. She was ready to go smoke a joint with her friend and ride around. She thought to herself it wasn't fair. She wanted her grandmother to live forever, but knew that wasn't possible. She felt like a part of her was dying. She went back into the breakfast room to get another load of dishes.

"Linda, everything was so good, thank you." Roxie said as she took her last bite of food off her plate.

"Are you finished grandmother?" Eliza asked.

"Sure honey, here you go." She said as she handed the plate to Eliza. Eliza bent down to get the plate and then gave her a kiss on her cheek. The whole room got quiet. Eliza hurriedly left the room before she began to cry. The family she came from showed their love through providing shelter, food and clothes, but open affection was a rarity.

Eliza was in the kitchen rinsing off the plates and putting them in the dishwasher when her mother came in. "Eliza, will you help me get the dessert?"

"Sure, mama." Eliza said as she finished putting the plates in the dishwasher.

Linda scooped out the warm blackberry cobbler putting it into the bowls. Eliza followed by putting a huge clump of vanilla bean ice cream. Linda was lucky to find the blackberries. They usually didn't come into season in Tennessee until the first week of July, but a man happened to come by her office selling quarts of blackberries which she bought knowing this was Percy and Roxie's favorite dessert. Linda and Eliza each took three bowls a piece into the breakfast room.

When Roxie saw that it was blackberry cobbler she was beside herself. "Ooh, homemade blackberry cobbler." She took a bite and savored it. "Um-um this is melt-in-your-mouth. How'd you come across these blackberries, Linda?"

Linda told the story of the man coming by her office selling blackberries and how she bought a whole quart. "I made two blackberry cobblers. One for us tonight and the other one you can take home."

"You didn't have to do that."

"I know I didn't, but I wanted too."

Roxie looked at Eliza. "Have you decided what you'll be studying in college?"

"No, not really. I'm going to be staying in a dorm with Sharon, though."

"That'll be fun." Roxie said as she reminisced when she went to Middle Tennessee State University when it was a two-year college, and how much fun she had with her friends. "You've got plenty of time to decide about what you want to do with your life."

Everyone finished their cobbler and coffee.

Eliza began cleaning the table off again. She was ready to get out of the house for awhile at least long enough to smoke a joint. Eliza crammed the dishwasher as full as she could, started it, and went back into the breakfast room.

"Well, I need to go. I told Sharon I would meet her in town at six-thirty. The dishwasher is packed full. I couldn't get anything else in there. I went ahead and started it, too. I'll see ya'll later." She said as she bent down and gave both her grandmother and grandfather a hug.

"See you later, honey." Roxie said as Eliza walked out of the breakfast room. Eliza ran out to the car, fumbled around in her glove box, and found her stash of pot. She opened the bag retrieving an already rolled up joint. She backed out of the driveway. Speeding down Barfield Road she lit her joint, took a drag, held it in her lungs for as long as she could and then exhaled. She felt much better now. The world wasn't so harsh anymore. Reality was drifting away in a distant fog.

Roxie offered to help Linda with the rest of the dishes, but she wouldn't hear of it. She told Roxie to just sit there and relax. Luke went out to the den to watch some television leaving the adults in the breakfast room drinking coffee. It wasn't long before Linda joined them. They talked for about thirty more minutes.

"Newton, you about ready to go? I don't want us to wear our welcome out." This wasn't the truth at all. She had become very tired. She just wanted to lie down and rest.

Newton, who had just taken a puff off his

cigar, said. "Sure."

Percy and Linda escorted them to the back door. The pleasantries were said and then Newton and Roxie were gone. Linda made sure they were good and gone. "Oh, hon. She's gone so downhill. Her skin is even losing its color. She's looking grayish. This isn't good, isn't good at all. And the weight she's lost. I'd bet she's lost fifty pounds."

Percy was sitting at the kitchen table now lighting a cigarette as Linda was standing by the sink. He took a drag. "I know. She wants me to draw up some papers for her and dad."

"What kind of papers?"

He proceeded to tell her that his mother didn't want to be a vegetable; she wanted her jewelry divided; and she wanted the rest to go to Newton with Ann and him as executors. "I'm meeting Matt tomorrow during lunch."

"Oh. She must know it's not going to be much longer then."

"That's what I'm thinking, too."

Newton and Roxie pulled into the driveway. Roxie looked at the sky it was almost a purplish, blue with streaks of pink. It was beautiful. She admired God's work. Her mind drifted to what it would be like in heaven. Would the streets really be made of gold? They were in the garage and Newton shut his door which jolted Roxie back into reality. She got out of the car, headed up the stairs, and into the house. She headed straight back to the bedroom where she took off her clothes, and put on her nightgown. "Newton, I'm going to go ahead and go to bed. I'm exhausted." Her body ached all over, but she wasn't going to tell anyone.

"Alright," he said as he turned on the television and took his seat in the den. He took a look at her when her back was too him. She looked so frail he thought to himself. He didn't want to think about it too long, or he would start crying so he turned his attention to a baseball game.

Roxie laid on the bed and in no time was fast asleep. The next morning she didn't wake up until around nine. She slowly got dressed because her body was still achy. She went into the kitchen where Newton had already made a pot of coffee. She poured herself a cup and found the prescription of pain pills she was looking for. She popped a couple of pills and washed them down with a gulp of coffee. The pain was becoming increasingly worse as each day went on, but she didn't want to say anything to anyone, especially Newton. He would just cry, worry, and really couldn't do anything for her. 'Really no one could do anything for her.' She thought to herself. This was her cross to bear and alone. No one could help her die. All anyone could do was be there when she died, and she didn't even know if she wanted anyone there or not. It was a trip she would have to take by herself, just like being born.

She went out to the front porch where Newton was sitting and took her seat beside him. The day was going to prove to be another hot one. Roxie grabbed the newspaper on the wicker table and began fanning herself. "Did you eat anything for breakfast?"

"Some buttered toast." Newton said. He had

become used to fixing his own breakfast now that Roxie wasn't getting up till about nine each morning. He was beginning to learn to fix his own lunch by now too, since Roxie really didn't have the energy to fix lunch or have the appetite to eat. His lunch usually was a ham sandwich. "Have you eaten?"

"No, not really too hungry. Maybe I'll eat something after while." This was the same conversation they had every morning. Roxie would try to eat some toast around ten, but usually could only eat one piece. The only real meal she ate was supper.

She opened the newspaper and began reading the obituaries, which had become a daily habit. She wondered what hers would say. She figured the family would figure out what to say about her. She then turned the page to see what the high today was going to be. "Looks like it's going to get up to 98 degrees with a heat index of 105 degrees."

"Um-um." Newton replied lighting his cigar.

Roxie finished reading the paper, set it down, got up, and headed towards the house. "Do you want some ice water?"

"No, I'm fine." Newton replied as he was chewing on the stub of his cigar.

Roxie went into the kitchen, looking at the clock. It was already noon. She began filling her glass with ice when the phone rang. She went over to the phone and picked it up. "Hello." She said wondering who might be on the other line.

"Mother." Percy said. "I'm glad you answered the phone. I just met with Matt we've drawn up a rough draft of the papers you wanted. Do you want me to come by later on tonight with them?"

"Sure, that'll be fine."

"Well, I'll be around about five then, o.k.?"

"Alright." Roxie said. "See you later then." '

She hung up the phone her stomach tightening up a little bit in anticipation of dreading telling Newton. She decided she would wait until Percy got there so she would have back up. She filled her glass of ice with water and drank it down. The pain pills were wearing off, and her body began to ache again. She took two more pain pills and decided she would lie down. She put the glass in the sink and walked out to the front porch.

"Newton, I'm going to lie down for a while. I'm a little tired wake me up around four, if I'm not up, will you?"

"Sure will." Newton said as he was relighting his cigar and was taking a puff on it to stoke it.

Roxie took a blanket from the closet, laid down on the couch in the comfort of the cool air-conditioned room and covered up with her blanket. She dreamt of the past when she was younger and what it would be like when she would die. She was peaceful, floating, and surrounded by love she hadn't ever experienced. She was beginning to step onto the street of gold and was roused by Newton shaking her on the shoulder.

"Roxie, Roxie, wake up." Newton said as he was bending over her saying it almost in a whisper.

Roxie sat up startled. "What, what time is it? Is it already four?" She asked in a haze not believing it was already four o'clock. It just seemed like she had laid down. She rubbed her eyes and stretched. "I guess I better get something cooking." She had no idea what that would be and to be honest she didn't even feel like cooking much less eating, but Newton needed to be fed.

She got up from the couch and headed into the kitchen. Newton had made a fresh pot of coffee. She poured herself a cup and sat at the table drinking it trying to wake up and get her bearings about her. She got up and looked in the refrigerator hoping there would be something simple in there to cook, but there was nothing. She walked past the sink and noticed three containers sitting in there. It looked like fried corn, squash and field peas. Newton must have taken them out for her. She thought how sweet that was and proceeded to dump the thawed vegetables into their pots. She turned the stove and oven on at the same time. She put the iron skillet with grease in it in the oven then went about mixing her cornbread. She then seasoned the vegetables adding plenty of butter. The oven light went off, and she poured the batter into the skillet listening to it sizzle.

Supper would be ready in about ten minutes. She was already exhausted and in pain, but she didn't want to take any more pain medicine until bedtime. She set the table, filled the glasses with ice, poured tea into them, and set them on the table. She sat down to take a break. Newton came into the kitchen and took his seat at the table.

Roxie got up from the table and began setting the pots on the table. The cornbread was ready. She pulled the skillet out of the oven, turned over the cornbread onto a plate and sliced it into eight pieces. 'This will give Newton something to snack on tomorrow.' She thought to herself. She brought the plate to the table and sat it down.

Newton began filling his plate to the rim with food and the biggest piece of cornbread slathering it with butter. Roxie put minute portions of food on her plate. Newton noticed but didn't say anything. She ate slowly trying to hide that she was in pain. She could feel it in her body the cancer taking over. Newton was just finishing the food on his plate when the back door opened.

"Hey, ya'll." Percy said as he went straight for the coffee pot, filling his Styrofoam cup up with some fresh coffee. He took some milk out of the refrigerator adding it to his coffee along with some sugar. He took a seat at the table and began nibbling on a piece of cornbread. He laid the manila folder beside him on the table.

Newton eyed the folder for a second and finished his last bite of cornbread. Roxie began shifting in her seat knowing the inevitable had arrived. They would have to tell Newton, and the time had arrived. Roxie stirred her food and finally took a bite of the fried corn.

Percy took a couple of more puffs off his cigarette and then put the cigarette out. Roxie took her plate and set it beside the sink. She went over to Newton. "You finished?" He nodded his head in the affirmative.

"Do you want a cup of coffee?" Roxie asked Newton.

"Sure." He had a funny feeling in his stomach, and it had to do with the manila folder.

Roxie brought him his coffee and then took

her seat back at the table with her own cup of coffee. She cleared her throat. "Um, um." She figured she just better spit it on out. "Now, Newton, Percy went to see Matt today. You know Matt, the attorney. I got him to draw up some papers for us. Well, basically the papers say if something happens to me. You know where I'm unconscious or something." She hesitated again and gulped hard. "I don't want to be put on life support."

  She let this sink in for awhile. The rest of it would be easy. Newton pulled out his handkerchief. The tears were rolling down his face. "But, I-I don't want you to die." By now the tears were streaming down his face.

  "Newton, I don't want to die either, but I have no choice. If it's my time, it's my time."

  "I-I just thought I'd go before you. I don't know what I'll do without you."

  "You'll be alright. You've got family."

  "Newton, I don't want to be kept alive for everyone to come by and just gawk at me and say 'poor Roxie.' There's another thing I want; my jewelry divided. I want you to receive everything else I have, which you have anyway, and I think it's a good idea for Ann and Percy to be executors."

  She let this sit in for a few minutes. She looked at Percy. He lit another cigarette and took a big drag and blew it out. "Dad, the papers are in here." He pointed to the manila folder. "It's just a rough draft. Why don't you and mother look over the papers tomorrow. Matt can make any changes that need to be made. I've made an appointment for you both to go in to Matt's office to sign the papers because they have to be notarized. The appointment is the day after tomorrow. But if there are any changes, you just let me know tomorrow, or if you want to change the appointment let me know."

Percy got up from the table. "I'll see you tomorrow." He went to the door.

"See you later, Percy." Roxie said.

Newton said nothing. He stuffed the handkerchief back in his pocket. He got up from the table, went to the sink, began running the water and squeezing dishwashing detergent into it. Roxie took the cue and went to the sink. She put the dishes in the sink, began scrubbing and handing them to Newton to rinse off and dry. Not a word was spoken. Roxie's body ached all over, but she wasn't going to tell anyone. She just couldn't wait to get finished with the dishes.

Once the dishes were finished she took two pain pills and went to the bedroom to get her nightgown on. She washed her face and took her dentures out to let them soak overnight. She told Newton she was going to bed. It wasn't even dark, but Roxie didn't care. All she wanted to do was lie down. She hadn't been in the bed five minutes, and she was fast asleep.

Newton turned the television on and dozed off and on in the chair until the ten o'clock news came on. He watched the news and then got in the bed. He looked at Roxie's frail body, almost began to cry, but he was so tired that sleep took over.

CHAPTER 23

The sun hit Roxie in the face. She had no idea was time it was. Her mouth was dry, and she wanted something to drink. She rolled to the edge of the bed, put her feet to the floor, and then she heaved herself out of the bed. She walked into the bathroom rinsed out her mouth and put her dentures in. She slowly walked into the kitchen where Newton was sitting reading the last page of the papers that Matt had drawn up. He had already made coffee. Roxie walked over to coffee pot, poured herself a cup of coffee, and sat down at the kitchen table.

Newton finished the last page, took out his handkerchief, wiped his eyes, blew his nose and stuck it back in his pocket. He fixed himself a glass of ice water and began walking out of the kitchen.

"Well, how does it look?" Roxie asked.

"Sounds fine to me," Newton said as he continued to walk out of the kitchen. He didn't want to talk about it. He didn't even want to discuss it because if he did he knew he would start crying. He didn't want to face the fact that his beloved Roxie was dying.

Roxie took the papers. She got up from the table, went over to the buffet, and pulled out a pair of reading glasses. She walked back over to where her pain pills were, took a couple out, put them in her mouth and swallowed hard. She went back over to the table, took a sip of coffee, and the pills finally went down. She gathered the papers up, put her reading glasses on, and began reading them.

When she got finished she was quite depressed. Reality was setting in. She was going to die before she or anybody else wanted her too. But she wasn't dead today, so she was going to try and enjoy the rest of the day even though her whole body ached. She felt like going back to bed, but that would mean Newton would know she didn't feel good and then the whole family would know too. She didn't know how much longer she was going to be able to put up the front. She looked at the clock, and it read ten. She thought to herself, 'What time did I get up? How long have I been here reading this?'

She got up from the table and fixed herself a big glass of ice water. She walked out to the front porch where Newton was sitting. She took her seat. "Look's like everything's in order doesn't it?" Roxie asked.

"Yep." He didn't want to talk about it because he knew he would start crying. He wanted to try and be strong for Roxie.

Roxie took the paper and read the obituaries. When the sun began beaming down on her she couldn't take the heat any longer. "Newton, I've got to go in. It's getting too hot out here for me."

She went into the house, into the kitchen, and opened the refrigerator door. She stood there looking until she spotted the ham. This sounded good to her for a change--a ham sandwich on white bread smothered with mayonnaise and mustard. She decided while she was at it she would make Newton a sandwich. About the time she got finished he came into the kitchen. They both sat down at the table about the same time.

"Just what I wanted a cool ham sandwich and a tall glass of iced tea," Roxie said before she took a big bite.

"Um-hm," Newton replied because his mouth was already full.

"It was nice of Linda to bring it by for us, wasn't it?" Roxie asked Newton with her mouth full of ham sandwich.

"Sure was." Newton said with his mouth also full grateful he didn't have to make his lunch for a change.

The sandwiches were finished in five minutes. Newton took the paper towels and threw them in the trash. It was getting too hot for him to go back outside himself. It was already 100 degrees and promised to get up to 105 with a heat index of 110. He decided he would go to the den and watch some television even though it would be slim on choices, mostly soap operas.

Roxie went back with him and lay on the couch. She was out in ten minutes. She drifted in and out of sleep. Around three o'clock she was laid on the couch with her eyes barely open. She was slowly waking up. She rolled over to see the television and pulled the covers up to her neck. She lied on the couch for about another thirty minutes, laying there trying to decide what she was going to fix for supper. She really didn't want to get up. She was so comfortable, but in the end she heaved herself up from the couch.

Newton was still sitting in his chair, but he was dozing with his chin bent down to his chest. Roxie quietly walked out of the den through the house into the kitchen. She made a pot of coffee. She took a seat at the kitchen table. She was still groggy. She waited for the coffee to perk when it was finished she went over to it and poured herself a cup. She stood there for a minute waiting for it to cool.

She then took a couple of sips and waited for the caffeine to take effect. She opened the refrigerator door and looked inside hoping there might be by some magic a meal that had appeared. There was nothing.

She went back to the kitchen table and sat down. She was drinking her coffee when the phone rang. She went over to pick up the receiver. "Hello."

"Hey, mother, what cha' doing?"

"I just got up from a nap and was trying to think of something to cook for supper."

"You don't have to think about it anymore. Linda's cooking two sausage casseroles, one for us and one for you all."

"She doesn't have to do that." She was just saying this to be nice. She didn't want Percy to know how grateful she really was for the unexpected meal because she didn't feel like cooking.

"She always cooks too much anyway. I'll bring it by around five, but I'm not going to be able to stay too long."

"That's fine."

"Did you and dad read the papers that Matt prepared?" Percy asked

"Yeah, everything looks fine. What time is our appointment?"

"It's at 10:30 tomorrow. I'll meet you all there." Percy said.

"Alright, we'll be there," Roxie replied.

"I've got to get back to work and finish up something."

"See you in about an hour." Roxie said as she hung up the phone. She sat back down at the table and finished her coffee. She was so worn out. She wanted to lie back down, but she had to stay up at least long enough for Percy to get there, eat supper, and clean the kitchen. She had to get her rest because she would have to get out and about. She was worn out thinking about it. She got up and pulled out a circle word puzzle book from the drawer. She sat back down and began working on the puzzles. She had finished three by the time the back door opened.

Percy walked in with the sausage casserole in a disposable aluminum pan. "Hey, mother." He said as he sat the pan on the table. He walked over to the coffee pot, poured himself a cup, and then sat back down.

Roxie got up from her seat and began setting the table.

Percy took a good look at his mother. She looked so frail and tired. "How you feeling?" He asked as he lit a cigarette.

"I'm getting worse each day. I can feel it. My whole body aches. I'm weak. I keep about half my food down. I think I could have stayed in bed all day today."

Percy didn't know how to respond. He wasn't used to his mother really telling how she felt. She was always the strong one, but now she was weak. He took a drag off his cigarette and exhaled. "Oh, I about forgot Linda put rolls wrapped in aluminum foil on top of the casserole."

"Tell her I said thanks for doing this. She didn't have to you know.."

"She knows that but she wanted too. Is there anything I can do for you?" He was getting back to how she was feeling, and the only thing he knew to do was to ask if she needed any help. He figured she would say there was nothing he could do for her, and he was right.

"No. I can't think of anything, but--" She was answering him and then Newton walked in, so she changed the subject.

"Look what Percy brought us." She showed him the lay out. The room was filled with the aroma of the casserole by now.

"Um-hum," Newton responded as he took his seat at the table.

"How you doing dad?" Percy asked as he stood up and scooted his chair in.

"Fair, fair. Hot enough for you?" He asked Percy.

"Yeah, it is dad, well, I need to get going." Percy responded as he put his cigarette out.

The door closed, and Newton began putting food on his plate, while Roxie waited her turn. The meal was eaten in silence. The dishes were cleaned. Roxie was ready to put on her gown, take out her teeth, and get to bed. She went back through the den to go into the bedroom. "Newton, make sure and get me up around nine in the morning because we got an appointment at ten-thirty."

"Alright." Newton said as he was watching the evening news wishing the appointment wasn't tomorrow. Wishing none of this was going on.
****

Roxie was awakened the next morning by Newton tapping her on the shoulder. "Roxie, Roxie, it's time to get up."

Roxie opened her eyes in a fog, laid there a minute and then realized that they were to go to Matt's office and sign the papers. She rolled out of the bed, went to the bathroom, took her teeth out of the glass they were sitting in, and put them in her mouth. She went back into the bedroom and slowly got dressed. Her body and joints ached. She went into the kitchen where coffee was waiting for her. Newton had poured her a cup. She went over to the medicine took two pills, went back over to the kitchen table with her cup of coffee, and took her medicine. She looked at the clock it was nine-thirty.

"I guess we need to be leaving here around ten. Don't we?" She asked in an attempt to make some casual conversation.

"Yeah," Newton replied, half pouting, and half dreading the meeting.

Ten o'clock rolled around. They piled into the car. Roxie hadn't been outside since she had been to Percy and Linda's house. She was trying to remember how long ago that had been, but couldn't. She gave up on the effort. The sky was filled with haze from the hot, sticky humidity in the air. 'Thank, God, they had air-conditioning in the car.' She thought to herself as they made their way down Shelbyville Highway, which turned into Church Street. Matt's office was on Church before it crossed over to Broad. It didn't take them fifteen minutes to get there, but both believed in getting to place on time. It was disrespectful to show up late, anywhere.

Newton pulled the Chevy into the parking lot, where they saw Percy standing outside smoking a cigarette waiting on them. The car stopped, and

Roxie got out. The heat almost took her breath away as she stood up out of the car.

"Hot enough for you?" Percy asked as he noticed his mother taking a big breath. He walked over to her to make sure she was alright and wasn't going to fall or pass out. Newton had just gotten out, shut the door, and was oblivious to the whole scene.

Percy kept close to his mother, while they walked into the office. The cool air hit their faces. Roxie breathed a sigh of relief. Newton and Roxie sat down in the cushy leather chairs, while Percy went up to the receptionist to let her know that the Praters' were there to see Matt. Percy then took a seat beside his mother.

It wasn't too long before Matt came out to greet them. Roxie had gone to school with his grandmother and grandfather. She noticed how much he looked like his grandfather when he was younger. Matt was a mere thirty years old but was doing well for himself as an estate attorney. He was not over five feet eight inches tall. His hair was the color of mahogany with eyes to match. His features made him quiet handsome. He led them back to his office. He pulled up another chair that was against the wall to go with the other two, which were sitting in front of his desk. He took a seat behind his long walnut desk, which sort of swallowed him.

When everyone settled and said their pleasantries Matt got down to business. "Well, I see you're here to get your papers signed. Is that right?"

"Yes, it is." Roxie said as she shifted in her chair and looked up at one of the paintings hanging on the wall behind him.

"Now, these are the same papers which Percy here brought to you the other day to read over. I didn't make any changes. He said you all read them and were fine with the contents."

Newton and Roxie both shook their heads in unison.

"All I need you to do is to read over them again and sign on the two back pages." He slid a shiny new pen to each of them.

Roxie went first. She glanced through the contents of the papers, sort of hitting the high points, and couldn't detect any type of changes. She took her pen and signed her name to both pages, and then slid the stack of papers to Newton.

Newton just sat there for a moment. He then picked up the papers and flipped through the pages. He laid the papers down, put the pen in his hand, and began crying. Percy was the first to notice. He looked at Matt, who then looked at Newton. Percy had warned him in advance that this might happen. Matt was used to this. He had many a family in here from all walks of life, and crying wasn't unusual under these circumstances.

Matt leaned forward towards Newton. "Mr. Prater, it's alright, just take your time."

"I don't want to do this." He blurted out between tears. He was wiping his face with his handkerchief by now.

Roxie jumped in by now. "Newton, you know we talked about this before. This is for your protection and mine. You know I don't want to be some kind of vegetable for people to come by and gawk at. You don't want me just to be alive on machines or something so you'll just have me around and won't have to be lonely do you?"

Newton stiffened up a bit. He did want to keep her alive as long as possible even if it meant her being a vegetable. Having some of her in his mind was better than having none of her. He felt a twinge of guilt at being so selfish and not thinking about Roxie and how she felt about it. He put himself in her shoes for a minute and decided he wouldn't want to die that way either. He took a deep breath, swallowed hard, stuck the wet handkerchief back in his pocket, and signed the papers before he could think about it any further. Everyone else in the room held their breath until he put the pen down because they knew another breakdown could be coming.

Matt got his notary stamp out and went to business legalizing everything. He kept a file at his office and gave one to Newton. "Just give it to Percy." Newton said as Matt tried to hand him the papers in the envelope. Newton treated it as a necessary evil. He didn't ever want to see those papers again. He wanted to forget about the whole day. He was ready to leave. He put his hat on and stood up.

Roxie and Percy took the hint and both of them stood up at the same time. Roxie told Matt not to forget to tell his grandparents 'hello' from them, meaning Newton and her. Matt shook everyone's hand and led them out to the reception area.

Percy shook Matt's hand one more time and thanked him. They promised to get together for lunch, which both of them knew would never happen. Percy walked his mother and father to their car, told them he would stop by later on.

Back home, Roxie took off her nice clothes and put on some stretch pants and a sleeveless shirt. She was exhausted and in almost unbearable pain. She went into the kitchen, fixed her a glass of ice water, took two pain pills and retreated into the den. The heat drained what little energy she had left. She lay on the couch and was out in ten minutes.

The next few weeks entailed Roxie deteriorating quickly. She was in bed more than she was out of it. She was in constant pain. She took the pain medication religiously every four hours, but it was just making the pain bearable. The family was bringing over cooked casseroles that had to just be heated up. They decided a microwave was in order, so one was purchased. Percy showed Newton how to use it so he could heat up his food, and if Roxie happened to want anything he could heat her something up too. She usually just took a couple of bites and was done with her meal. When Roxie was in bed Newton would go in there and just sit and cry, saying. "What am I going to do, what am I going to do." His head in his hands, and him bent over.

About noon, Percy walked in on this and it ran all over him. He thought how could his dad be so selfish. He collected himself before he spoke. He thought this was all his dad knew was life with Roxie and calmed down a bit. "Dad." Percy said. Newton jolted in upright position and he turned to look at Percy. "We need to talk."

Newton followed Percy into the kitchen where they sat down at the kitchen table. Percy made the decision on the way into the kitchen to not mince words. He lit a cigarette and took a deep drag. Newton lit his cigar and did the same.

"Dad, we're going to have to get some type of home health care out here for mother. You can't do it alone, and she needs the care."

Nothing was said for a few moments then Newton asked. "How much will it cost?"

"I've been checking around. It'll cost around $100 a day, and that includes bathing, feeding, and caring for her. Now, insurance won't cover it." He took another drag off his cigarette, got up and refilled his Styrofoam cup with coffee.

"I can't afford it." Newton said looking down at the table with his cigar hanging out of his mouth.

Percy sat back down ready to strangle his dad. The thoughts racing through his mind. 'What do you mean you can't afford it. Do you want her here or at a nursing home?'

"Dad, it's either here or a nursing home."

"Will the insurance cover the nursing home?"

"Probably, yes."

Newton started to cry. He pulled his sopping wet handkerchief out of his shirt pocket, began wiping his eyes, blew his nose, and just sat at the table shaking his head in the negative. Percy sat there finishing his cigarette waiting on his dad for some response. "W-ell," in between tears, "I guess, we'll get the ho-me heal-th care." He finally got it out. "I want her he-re as lo-ng as poss-ible."

"O.K. dad, I understand. If you let me, I'll call and have them out her tomorrow."

"Alright." Newton put the handkerchief back in his pocket.

Percy got up from the kitchen table and called his sister, Ann, who happened to be the accountant for the largest nursing home in Murfreesboro. They had already been talking about home health care for their mother. By the time Percy got off the phone they already had someone coming out in the morning at seven o'clock. Percy told his dad the news. This required another bout of crying and blowing of the nose. Percy reassured his dad this was the best thing for his mother. When Newton finally calmed down Percy went back to see his mother before he left.

He went back to the bedroom, slipped his hand on top of hers. She slowly opened her weak eyes and looked up at Percy as if to say, 'I'm dying.' "Hey, Percy." She said slowly and almost in a whisper.

"Hey, mother." He didn't want to ask how she was doing. One look at her could tell him everything, but he did want to tell her about home health coming out to the house. "I just wanted to let you know that Ann and I got someone from home health coming out here from seven in the morning to seven at night, every day. They can help you. You know make you more comfortable and help with the cooking and cleaning."

He could see a relief on her face. One he hadn't seen in a long time. "They'll cook. Oh, good. I won't have to worry about Newton anymore." She said lightly and slowly. She then squeezed Percy's hand as if to thank him, and she closed her eyes.
****

Newton was up at six in the morning waiting on the person from home health. Promptly at seven

Newton could hear the knock on the front door. He went to answer it. "Are you Mr. Prater?"

"Yep," Newton said as he was eyeing the lady. She looked to be in her forties, dyed black hair, sharp features, which made her look mean, jet black eyes and a round body.

"I'm Janice Weaver. You can just call me Janice. I'm from home health. Well, I guess I better get to cooking breakfast."

Newton immediately opened the door for her. 'A fresh breakfast,' he thought to himself. He tried to remember the last time that he had had a good breakfast. Newton showed Janice the way into the kitchen. She took a look around, found the refrigerator, and opened the door. She stood there for a moment looking to see what was available to cook. Ann had gone grocery shopping the night before for them. She pulled out eggs, bacon, butter, jelly, and asked Newton where the bread was. He showed her where the pots and pans, silverware and plates were. He stayed in the kitchen watching her cook. 'This isn't a bad deal after all.' He thought to himself again.

Roxie was laying in the bedroom drifting in and out of sleep. She rolled over and opened her eyes when she felt someone in the bedroom. She looked up and saw Janice's black eyes looking back at her.

"Hi, I'm Janice Weaver, you know from home health." She was grinning from ear to ear, her pearly whites showing. She was holding a tray full of food. She set the tray on the floor went over to Roxie and began to help her set up. "We need to get some food in you. I made some fresh eggs, bacon, and toast.

Now try to eat as much as you can. Here is your medicine to take once you get something on your stomach."

Roxie was still in a fog looking at the food wondering how she was going to eat all of it. "Where's Newton?"

"He's in the kitchen eating."

"Good." Roxie said as she breathed a sigh of relief.

"Thank you, it looks so delicious."

"Don't thank me. It's part of my job. I'll be back in here in a few minutes to check on you. Do you need anything else from me?"

"No, no, thanks."

Janice went back into the kitchen to clean up the dishes. Newton had already cleaned his plate and was walking out when she entered. "Did everything set well with you?"

"Sure did." Newton was holding a tall glass of ice water and went out to the front porch to enjoy the weather before it got too hot. The heat and humidity wasn't letting up this summer.

Janice finished cleaning the kitchen. She went back to the bedroom to gather Roxie's plate. She was still sitting up in bed. Janice notice she had eaten about a third of the food, which was pretty good for someone in her stage of cancer.

Janice asked, "Was everything alright?"

"Um-hum."

"Good, I'll take this from you now." Janice bent down to get the tray. "I'll be back after I clean up this plate. Would you like to take a bath? I'll help you."

Roxie wondered if she stunk. She couldn't remember the last time she actually got in the tub and took a good bath. She was actually afraid to because she was scared once in the tub she wouldn't be able to get herself out. She really didn't care too much for Janice seeing her naked, but she wanted to feel clean. The cleanliness won over. Roxie figured she did this for a living and had seen much worse, which she had.

"Uh-hum," Roxie nodded her headed in the affirmative.

It wasn't too long afterward and Janice was back. She helped Roxie out of the bed and into the bathroom. Roxie felt so weak, and Janice felt so strong. 'What happened to her all of energy and strength.' She thought to herself as Janice was leading her into the bathroom. Janice started up the bath water and helped Roxie undress. Roxie held onto Janice's arm while she got into the tub and then sat down. The warm water felt so good to Roxie's aching body.

"Do you need any help washing yourself?" Janice asked standing over the tub.

"No."

"Well, I think, if you don't mind, that I'll strip the bed and wash the sheets. There's nothing like getting into a good clean bed after a bath."

Roxie thought the same thing, there was nothing better. "I don't mind."

"I'll be back in here in about, say, twenty minutes to check on you."

"Alright."

Janice left the bathroom, went into the bedroom, stripped the sheets and threw them in the washing machine. She could tell they hadn't been washed in a while. Good to her word, she was back in the bathroom in twenty minutes.

"You about ready to get out of the tub? I brought you a fresh nightgown."

"Yeah, I'm ready." Roxie thoroughly enjoyed her bath. She hadn't felt this clean in a month. She wished the water would have stayed warm so she could have stayed in the tub for hours.

Janice bent down to help Roxie out of the tub. Roxie grabbed her arm and put what little weight she had and leaned on her while she heaved herself out of the tub. Janice was pulling her up at the same time. Janice helped her get dressed and led her back into the den and laid her on the couch where a pillow and blanket awaited her.

Roxie lay down on the couch, got comfortable, and drifted off to sleep. She was awakened by Janice, who had brought a tray of food into her. She set it on the coffee table and helped Roxie sit up. The tray had a bowl of chicken noodle soup, a grilled cheese sandwich, glass of orange juice, and a cup of chocolate pudding. Roxie sipped on the soup, took a couple of drinks of the orange juice, took a bite out of sandwich and ate all of the chocolate pudding. Newton came in about the time Roxie had finished up.

"What do you think of Janice?" Roxie asked anxiously to see his reaction.

He sat in his chair and said. "She's alright." He didn't want to sound too grateful, but he was glad she was there. She had only been there for the day, but she was cooking all the meals, enough for both of them. He was glad to have her there to look after Roxie and to enjoy a good hot meal fresh-made from the kitchen. He didn't like the price, but he would think about that later.

"I think she's great." Roxie said as she popped her two pills that were sitting on the tray. She swallowed hard. "I've had a bath. I've had some hot food, and I know you're taking care of."

Roxie pushed the tray away and lay back down on the couch. Janice came in and took the tray. "How you doing? You need anything else before I get back to the kitchen. The sheets are about dry. I'll get them on the bed for you."

"No. I'm fine, thank you." Roxie said as Janice was walking off. "Hey, I really appreciate you being here."

"It's nothing." She said as she walked off.

Roxie drifted off to sleep and was awakened again by Janice. "It's time for dinner."

Roxie slowly opened her eyes. Janice leaned down and helped her up. Roxie held on to her arm. Janice looked into her weak eyes and asked. "Do you want to eat in the kitchen?"

"Sure," Janice lead her into the kitchen.

She took her seat around the kitchen table. The table was filled with mashed potatoes, green beans, fried corn and chicken patties. Janice sat down wear Percy usually sat. Newton already had his plate filled with food. Roxie got a little of everything. She especially wanted some fried chicken patties. She hadn't had any of those in so long. Finally, Janice filled her plate. Everyone was quite while eating and then Roxie broke the silence.

Her voice was getting weaker by the day. She was running out of energy daily. "How long have you been doing this?"

"Oh, about ten years," Janice said as she put a spoonful of mashed potatoes into her mouth. She swallowed. "I love it, helping people. It's what I do best."

"I can tell. This sure is a lovely meal you cooked." Roxie said as she stared at the table. She wished she could eat all of the food on the plate. This was one thing she didn't like about the cancer not being able to enjoy her food like she used too. She cut a piece of chicken patty and put it in her mouth. She chewed and was actually able to savor the taste. "This is delicious. I don't know the last time I've had chicken patties."

"Thank you."

Dinner was over. Janice gave Roxie her pills to take. "Are you ready to lay back down, Mrs. Prater?"

"Call me Roxie."

"Alright, well, are you?" Janice asked as she was standing beside Roxie at the table.

"I think so. The meal made me tired."

Janice helped Roxie up from her chair. She led her back into the bedroom. She laid her in the bed. Roxie could smell the fresh scent of clean sheets. "Oh, it's so nice to get into a clean bed." Roxie grabbed Janice's hand. "Thank you so much for being here. I worry about Newton you know. I at least know he's getting a good meal now."

"It's no problem. Well, I'm going to clean the kitchen and then be off. Do you need anything before

I leave?"

"No, I'm fine."

"I'll see you tomorrow then. I'll be back around seven in the morning."

Janice and Newton cleaned the kitchen. Janice walked back to check on Roxie before she left. Roxie was sound asleep. Newton was in his chair watching television. "I'll see you tomorrow, Mr. Prater."

"See you later." Newton said not moving his eyes from the television set.

The next few weeks Roxie began growing weaker and weaker. She rarely got out of bed. Janice came by every day. She called Dr. Jung by the fourth week and told him her prognosis. "I'm giving her pain medication every three to four hours. She doesn't even have the energy to get out of the bed. I try to set her up but that lasts only about five minutes before she's lying back down. I think she needs constant care. She probably could use more medication because she does tell me she's in pain. She barely talks in a whisper, and poor Mr. Prater he just sits in there and cries, which that's not helping thing."

June. Janice told Percy she had called Dr. Jung and what she had told him. She was very animated with her hands flailing around in the air. She was trying to talk low in the living room, but Newton could hear her in the den. When Janice was finished Percy asked. "Do you think she needs to go to the Middle Tennessee Medical Center and put in the part for chronic patients?"

"Yes, Percy, I think she needs round the clock

care. Her last days shouldn't be full of suffering." Janice finally consented.

"Does Dr. Jung think the same thing?" He asked as he pulled out a cigarette out of his shirt pocket and then lit it.

"Yes."

Newton heard it all. He sat in his chair in the den and began crying again. 'What am I going to do? What am I going to do?' He asked himself with his head in his hands.

Percy heard his dad in the den. He told Janice thanks, left her standing in the living room and then went back into the den to check on his dad. Janice followed him. "What's wrong dad?"

"I-I-I heard ya'll talking."

"Oh," Percy said as he took a drag off his cigarette and blew the smoke out. "Dad, it's for the best you know."

"I don't want her to leave me, Percy. What will I do?"

"You'll be alright dad. Mother needs constant care right now. She needs to be comfortable. You know she's going to have to go someday, dad. I know you don't want to hear this, but mother is going to pass on and pretty soon. Let's make her journey to the next world a comfortable one. We don't want her to suffer. I'm sure they'll let you stay in there with her."

Janice chimed in at this point. "Oh yes, Mr. Prater, they sure will. They'll let you stay in there with her."

"They will?" Newton said calming down by the second.

"Yes, dad, they will. I'm going to set it up for her to go day after tomorrow. Alright, dad?" Percy was going to talk with the other siblings, but he knew once he told them the situation they would all agree. He just needed the nod of his dad's head.

Newton dried his eyes, sniffed and said, "alright," nodding in the affirmative.

CHAPTER 24

 Percy made all the necessary calls to his siblings. It was agreed Roxie would be going to the Middle Tennessee Medical Center chronic care. It was a go between a hospital and nursing home. She would have her own room. Working at the post office had given her good insurance, so the family got the best for her. She would have round the clock care. It was decided she would go on Wednesday.

 Janice insisted on being there to get Roxie out to the car. She was there promptly at seven in the morning waiting on Percy. When Percy arrived Newton was crying, so Janice and Percy heaved Roxie out of the bed. It wasn't too much trouble because she was so light. Percy hadn't realized how much weight she had lost in the last few weeks. He had picked up calves heavier than her. Percy quickly pulled himself together. Roxie tried to help, but was too weak to keep her arms around their shoulders, which kept falling down Janice's and Percy's back. Newton held the car door open for them. They strapped her in the backseat. Percy decided to drive not trusting his dad from breaking down emotionally on the way.

 Linda had planned to pick Percy up from the center and take him to work. She told him she could be late for work. She would be there around nine. Janice followed in her car, which was an older Ford. The trip to the center was uneventful. Roxie was feeling nauseous so she slumped down in the back seat and put her arm over her eyes. The sun was hurting her eyes. Every bump in the road made her whole body shudder from the jolting pain running through it.

They arrived at the center. Percy went in and was followed out by a nurse with a wheelchair. The nurse, Janice and Percy managed to get Roxie out of the car without causing her too much pain. She was ready to lie back down in a bed and not be touched. She was wheeled into her room, which looked like a hospital room but a little more homier. Roxie noticed the flowers on the nightstand beside her bed. A vase full of yellow, peach and white roses stuffed with baby's breath. She took a shallow breath to get a scent of the roses, smiled and with a shaking hand took the card.

"They're from the girls that was nice." Roxie said almost in a whisper.

Janice, Roxie and Percy got her into the bed. Roxie looked to her left and saw more flowers. The vase was full of carnations, daylilies and other types of summer flowers. "It's beautiful."

Janice handed her the card. It read from Percy, Linda, Elizabeth and Lance. She looked up at Percy. "Ya'll didn't have too."

"I know, but we wanted too."

Roxie looked up at Janice while the nurse was getting the needle into her vein. "Thank you for all you've done, Janice. You don't know how much you helped Newton and me. I probably won't see you again." She was almost whispering, and Janice had to bend down to hear her.

"You'll see me again. I'm going to come by to see you, don't you worry about that." Janice said almost insulted that she would think Roxie would forget about her.

Roxie was hooked up to IV's that dispersed all her medications. Roxie was grateful because it was getting harder and harder for her swallow all the pills she had to take on a daily basis, almost every three hours. The medicine hit her bloodstream, and she began to fell a floating sensation. All pain was gone for the moment. She closed her eyes and was fast asleep.

Newton pulled up a chair and sat right beside Roxie determined not to leave her side. Percy went outside to smoke a cigarette. He wasn't out there too long before he saw Ann drive by, park and begin walking up the sidewalk. She stopped when she got to Percy, fumbled around in her purse, withdrew a cigarette and lit it. She took a long drag off of it.

"How is she Percy?" She asked as she blew the smoke out of her mouth.

"It's just a matter of time." Percy said trying to hold his emotions back. "They're just making her comfortable. She's out like a light right now."

"I'm going to stay up here most of the day." Ann said as she was fidgeting back and forth on her feet.

"Linda's going to pick me up so I can go to work. I'll be back later this afternoon and see if I can get dad to go home. He'll rest better there. At least I think he will."

"Good luck with that, you know dad."

They finished their cigarettes and went back into the center. Percy led the way since Ann didn't know where she was going. They entered the room, and Newton was sitting in his chair crying. He didn't even look up when they entered.

"Hey, dad." Ann said.

Newton shot up, startled by her voice. "Hey, hey, Ann."

Ann was trying to hold back her tears. 'My mother looks awful.' She thought to herself. She would be better off dead than like this.

Newton dabbed his eyes and stuck his wet handkerchief back into his pocket. Ann's eyes were full of tears finally they began rolling down her face. She spotted a box of Kleenex, took a few and wiped her eyes. She went to the corner of the room with her back to everyone. The room was full of silence. Percy and Newton staring at Roxie in the bed oblivious to anything going on when Linda entered the room.

Percy was the first to turn around. "Hey, hon."

"Hey, Percy. How's everything going?" She noticed Ann by this point standing in the corner who had turned around.

"How you doing Linda?" Ann asked more as a obligatory question.

"I'm alright and you?"

"Can't complain."

"Hey, Mr. Prater." Linda said as she looked at Roxie for the first time full of tubes running out of her arms.

"Linda."

Percy filled the rest of the conversation. "We've got her settled in." He looked at his dad. "Dad, we're going to get going. I'll be back after I get off work to see if you need a ride home. If not, Linda can take me back to my truck."

"Alright." Newton said not even looking up.

"We're going to get." Percy said as Linda followed him out of the room.

They got into the car, which wasn't parked too far from the center. They both got in the car, shut the doors, and Linda was the first to break the silence. "Oh, Percy. I didn't realize she had deteriorated so fast since the last time I've seen her."

"I don't give her more than a month if that long." Percy said as he lit a cigarette as he was trying to hold back tears. Linda was driving the car and noticed Percy's eyes filling with tears.

"You o.k. hon?"

"Yeah, I'll be alright. It's going to be a rough couple of weeks ahead of us. I'm afraid."

"You think your dad will be o.k?"

"I just don't know. That's whom I'm worried about the most."

"I know what you mean."

"Mother's alright. She knows she's in her last days. To be honest I think she's ready to go. I would be. I wouldn't want to have to live like that it's not living." He took a drag off his cigarette.

Linda pulled up beside the bank and dropped Percy off. She told him if he needed to go back there to just call her, and she would come pick him up. Percy tried to stay busy at work, but his mother's image lying in the bed kept clouding his brain. He met Linda for lunch which brought a little relief, but then back to work where he sat at his drafting table drawing the plans for a new branch couldn't bring any solace to his troubled mind.

He drifted from memories of his childhood to adolescence to adulthood. He thought of the big snow when school was let out and everyone managed to get out to his house. They had snowball fights, built snowmen and played in the snow. His mother fed the crew, bitching and moaning, but loving every minute of it. He remembered his mother planting one of the biggest gardens by hand in Rutherford County and dragging Newton out there to help harvest the vegetables--it was her pride and joy. He remembered when his mother was one of the first women in Tennessee to go to the Republican

Convention. She was so excited and proud. She was a tough person surrounded by softness, but the cancer she couldn't beat. It was beating her. Tears were rolling down Percy's eyes, and they hit the bottom of the drafting paper before he realized he was crying. He stood up, lit a cigarette, looked at his watch. It was four o'clock where had the time gone? Linda would be here any minute. He turned off the lights to his office, told Sue, his secretary, bye, and headed out the door.

    Percy didn't even wait a full minute before Linda pulled up. They drove to the center Linda chatting about work trying to keep his mind off his mother and father. They parked and went inside. Roxie was still drugged up, but awake.

    "Hey, Mrs. Prater." Linda said as she walked up to Roxie and took her hand.

    "Linda, thank you for the flowers, they're beautiful." Linda had to bend down to hear her. She was trying to hold back the tears.

    "Oh, it was nothing." She said and squeezed her hand lightly.

    "Hey, mother."

    "Hey, Percy." She motioned for him to come closer. Percy bent his ear almost to her mouth. "Try to get Newton to go home." She took a shallow breath. "He needs to rest. He might as well get used to me being gone." She took another breath and then rested again.

Percy squeezed her hand, looked her in the eyes, and said. "I'll see what I can do." He lifted up, turned around and walked towards Newton.

"Dad, why don't you come on home with me?" Ann had come in by this time and was listening for the response.

"Don't want too."

The babying began. "Now, dad you won't rest good here. We'll go out to eat before we take you home. Want we Linda?"

"Sure, Mr. Prater, we'll go to City Café or Shoney's or anywhere you want to go."

Newton began tearing up again. He pulled out his handkerchief. "I-I don't wa-nt to leave her, Percy."

"I know dad, but there's nothing you can do for her. The doctor's and nurse's will take real good care of her."

Newton looked over at Roxie. She moved her head motioning for Newton to go with Percy and Linda. "Go on Newton. I'll be alright." She whispered.

Percy interjected. "They'll call if something happens."

Linda chimed in by this time. "Mr. Prater why don't you come on and go with us. You'll sleep so much better in your bed."

Newton slowly got up from his chair, bent down squeezed Roxie's hand, kissed her on the cheek. "I'll see you tomorrow." He said in between the tears that were dropping on Roxie's face.

Roxie was trying not to cry herself. She would miss Newton more than he would ever know. She didn't want to leave him all alone, it wasn't fair, but had life ever been fair? She asked herself. She kissed him with what energy she could muster on his cheek. Newton moved away, wiped his eyes, blew his nose and stumbled across the room towards Percy and Linda.

Percy and Linda said their good-byes. Percy promised to be back tomorrow with Newton and himself. Before they left he talked with the head nurse, while Linda kept Newton busy talking about Elizabeth and Lance. Percy asked the nurse to call if Roxie took a turn for the worse. She promised she would call him first and not Newton.

The next two weeks Percy picked up Newton every morning, went to work and then picked him up to go home. Even on the weekends Percy went by in the morning and got Newton and took him to the center. Percy would go back and work at the farm until dark and then pick Newton up. Percy and Linda took him out to eat almost every night. Newton picked at his food. Linda tried to encourage Newton to eat more but to no avail.

Roxie was getting weaker and weaker. She had a glazed look over her eyes. She was slowly succumbing to death. Roxie was tired of laying in the bed and not being able to move. She was tired of being drugged up just to bear the pain. She was tired of sleeping. She was ready to meet her maker. All of the relatives and close friends had come by to see her for the last time, except Elizabeth. Percy and Linda knew this. They decided they would talk to her when she got home.

Elizabeth pulled into the graveled driveway spewing dust all over the place. She had been riding around with her friend smoking pot. The high was almost gone, but Elizabeth was starving. She walked into the kitchen. Her dad was sitting in his usual seat facing the window that looked out to the hills. Her mother was fixing a pot of coffee. Elizabeth said the usual hello and went straight for the refrigerator. She took out the package of hot dogs, put one in her mouth, while with another one she put on a piece of white bread. She ate the one in her mouth.

Percy cleared his throat and lit a cigarette. He figured he would get straight to the point. "Elizabeth, honey, you know you need to go see your grandmother."

Elizabeth was relieved in a way they weren't going to talk to her about the possibility that she might be smoking pot. She knew her mother knew because she had gotten her a bunch of brochures, but Elizabeth denied that she was smoking pot and promised to read the brochures, which she did and then threw them in the trash. Her father never said a word.

"I know, but do I have too?" Elizabeth didn't want to see her grandmother that way. She wanted to remember her the way she was when she was alive. She didn't want to have to face death.

"Yes, Elizabeth, you really need too. It's the right thing to do." Linda said as she poured Percy a cup of coffee and then one for herself. "You just go by there, say hi, and then you can go. This will probably be the last time you'll see her, and I know she wants to see you."

That's exactly what Elizabeth didn't want to hear that this would probably be the last time she would see her. She thought maybe if she didn't go see her she wouldn't die or maybe make a miraculous recovery.

"You'll need to go tomorrow." Percy said before he took a sip of his coffee.

"I'll go tomorrow afternoon. I'll see if Sharon will go with me or at least ride with me."

"That's fine." Percy said as he put out his cigarette.

Elizabeth finished her hot dog, lit a cigarette and stayed down in the kitchen with her parents until she finished it and then went upstairs. Elizabeth took the phone off the receiver and dialed Sharon's number. She lit another cigarette, took the ashtray by the phone, put it on the floor and sat on the floor.

"Is Sharon there?" She waited until she got on the other line.

"Sharon?" Elizabeth took a drag off her cigarette. "I got to ask you a favor." The lump was in her throat.

"Yeah, what is it?"

"Well, you know my grandmother is at the uh-Murfreesboro Medical Center. My parents uh-want me to go and see her before, be-fore she, you know dies." Elizabeth was trying to hold back the tears, but they were coming down her face anyway. "I want to know if you'll uh go with me tomorrow." She then began talking real fast. "You don't have to go in with me, you know just ride with me."

"Sure, I'll go." Sharon could tell Elizabeth was upset, so she took control of the conversation. "What time were you thinking about going?"

"Around two." The tears were pouring down Elizabeth's face by now.

"Do you want me to pick you up or do you want to come by and get me?"

Elizabeth put her cigarette out, wiped her face and took a deep breath. "I'll come by and get you. I need to go. Thanks for going with me."

"No problem."

Elizabeth hung up the phone, went into the bathroom, unrolled the toilet paper, took the wad in her room and then laid on her bed and proceeded to cry. She wished she had another joint to smoke, so she didn't have to feel these feelings. She didn't have any pot on her at the moment. She thought about leaving to get some more pot for a moment, but then feel asleep.

The next day was a bright, sunny, hot and typical humid day in Tennessee. Elizabeth roused herself out of the bed and then realized that she was going to see her grandmother. She fell back into the bed for a moment, reached for her cigarettes, found the pack and proceeded to light one. She took a deep, long drag and blew a smoke ring. She sat up on the edge of the bed, feet dangling off of it. She touched her feet to the floor, opened her door, and went downstairs to get a drink of iced tea. Her mother and dad had already left for work. She didn't know where her brother was. He had probably gone with some friends. She looked at the clock, which read ten.

    She decided she would call Sharon to see if she could pick her up at noon. She knew Sharon had some pot on her. They could ride around for a couple of hours getting high before she went to see her grandmother. 'That would take the edge off,' she thought to herself. She went into the den and called Sharon, who had just gotten up herself. They made their plans. Elizabeth would be by to pick her up at noon.

    Elizabeth opened the back door and stepped outside with a freshly lit cigarette. She had to have at least three cigarettes and a glass of iced tea before she could get going in the morning. She wanted to check the weather out so she would know what to wear. It was hot and sticky. The air hung in the air and didn't seem to move at all. It would be shorts and a sleeveless top today.

    Elizabeth was ready and got into her Chevy Impala. She turned the car on which always blew out hot air. She rolled down every window in the car. Her radio didn't work, so she had a portable stuck in the front seat next to her. She wondered why she put on any makeup because she hadn't even pulled out of the driveway, and she was already sweating. She needed to get the car moving to get some air circulating.

By the time she pulled up into Sharon's parents driveway, Elizabeth's face was dripping with sweat. She hoped they would go in Sharon's car because at least she had air conditioning, plus she didn't know what kind of shape she would be in to drive to the center or how she would be once she got out of it. She decided she would offer to give Sharon some gas money that always worked. Elizabeth didn't like to drive stoned anyway.

Elizabeth went into Sharon's house. Her parents were gone, so they decided to roll up a few joints at the house.

Sharon was licking the papers, looked up at Elizabeth and said. "You don't look too good."

"I need to get high. I'm not looking forward to this, but my parents would be pissed if I didn't go see grandmother." Elizabeth said as she filled up another paper with Columbian Gold pot. "They say I'll be glad I went when I get older. I just want to remember her like she was. The last time I saw her she didn't even look like my grandmamma."

The joints were rolled. "I guess we better get rolling." Sharon said as she stood up. "Let's go in my car. It's got air-conditioning."

"I'll give you some gas money." Elizabeth was relieved she didn't have to drive.

"That's alright." Sharon said as she closed the back door. She knew Elizabeth was uptight. She wanted to do something nice for her. She knew Elizabeth would do the same for her.

The rode around on the back country roads listening to Led Zeppelin, Jethro Tull and Rush. They had finished their second joint. Elizabeth was feeling a little better. She felt like she could face her grandmother now. She still didn't know what she was going to say. 'How's it feel to be dying?'

Sharon looked at her watch. "Hey, it's about 1:30. I guess we better head towards the center. What do you say?"

"I guess." The lump returned to her chest. She felt the heaviness return.

Sharon pulled the car into the parking lot across the street from the center. She turned off the car, looked at Elizabeth. "Do you want me to go in with you?"

"Do you mind?"

"No."

They got out of the car and headed towards the side door of the center. With each step Elizabeth's feet seemed to get heavier. She didn't know what she would have done if Sharon hadn't agreed to go. Elizabeth had known Sharon all through high school. Sharon was a little heavy set, had thick blond, curly hair and pale blue eyes. Her skin was flawless. She had a natural beauty to her. She didn't have to wear makeup, and she was pretty.

Elizabeth's chest felt like a two-ton brick was sitting on it. She took a deep breath and opened the door. The smell of anteseptic hit her nostrils. Sharon was behind her. Elizabeth looked at each passing door and the old, shriveled up, people in their beds waiting to die. 'What a way to spend your last days.' Elizabeth thought to herself. As she got closer to the door, her feet seemed to slow down. She told herself to get going and get it over with.

She got to her grandmother's door, turned around at Sharon. "Will you wait in the hall?" She thought she'd be better off going in there alone even though her brain was telling her to make a run for it.

"Sure." Sharon said as she patted her on the shoulder and gave her a little push.

Elizabeth opened the door. She wondered why her grandmother's door was closed, but only for a moment. Her grandmother was sitting up in the bed. Her eyes seemed to bug out of her head because her face was sunken in with all of the weight she had lost. Elizabeth made eye contact with her.

"Elizabeth." Roxie said in a low voice, almost a whisper.

"Hey, grandmamma. I thought I'd come by and see ya."

"I'm glad you did." Roxie said slowly.

Elizabeth took a good look at her grandmother hooked up to the machines. She didn't even look like she remembered her. She was a bone. She could see bones sticking out all over her with loose skin covering them. Her hair was thin and gray.

She had stopped the chemo, so her hair was growing back in it's natural color and in patches. Elizabeth always remembered her grandmother with the chocolate brown hair. She had it colored at least once a month whether it needed it or not and lightly teased. She looked so weak and helpless in that bed. Elizabeth wanted to scream and run out of the room, but she knew she couldn't so she took a deep breath and stood her ground. She was fighting back the tears. She didn't want to cry in front of her grandmother. She needed to be strong she told herself for her grandmother.

She moved out from in front of the bed she was standing five feet away from it like she was going to catch the cancer. "Sharon and I were riding around, and I told Sharon I needed to come and see you."

"Where's she at?"

"She out in the waiting area."

"Oh, well, how have you been doing?"

"Alright. I've been just taking a break this summer before I start college."

"Do you know what you're going to major in?" Roxie was getting weaker talking to Elizabeth, but she didn't want to show it. She was the last grandchild to come and see her. She knew why. Elizabeth was the most sensitive of the grandchildren and would take this the hardest. She could see Elizabeth struggling to be there, much less talk. Roxie was just struggling to talk. She knew this would be the last time.

Elizabeth was shifting from foot to foot. She was wanting to run out of the room. "Oh, I don't know. I'll have to take a bunch of basic courses first anyway. Maybe by the time I get through those I'll know what I want to major in."

Elizabeth looked at her grandmamma. She was getting droopy-eyed. She used this for her out. "Well, grandmamma you look like you're getting tired. I think I'll go so you can get some rest." It sounded good to Elizabeth. She hoped it sounded good to her grandmother. The reality of the situation she was ready to get out of there. The smell of the place was getting to her. Looking at her grandmother was beginning to be too much for her. She was ready to break down and start crying.

"Yeah, honey. You go on. I'll see you later." Roxie knew she wouldn't be seeing her later. Maybe in heaven, but not on this earth.

Elizabeth went over to her, bent down, and hugged her frail body. She was nothing but bone. She kissed her lightly on her cheek. She was fighting back the tears. She whispered in her grandmother's ear. "See you later. Take care. I love you."

Roxie lightly hugged her back. She didn't have any strength left in her. "Love you too honey."

Elizabeth turned around and headed for the door. She turned back and looked at her grandmother. Her brown eyes, which looked twice as big, since her face was shrunken in by the weight loss, was filled with tears. Elizabeth opened the door, stood in the hallway and took a deep breath.

She felt like she hadn't been breathing while she was in there. She hurried to the waiting area and found Sharon.

Elizabeth ran her fingers through her thick, curly hair. "Let's get out of here."

Sharon followed Elizabeth out of the medical center. They got into the car, shut the doors. The words came pouring out of Elizabeth's mouth. It was like they had been pinned up in her for ages. "Oh, Sharon, you should see my grandmother. She looks awful. She's not going to make it much longer. I don't ever want to see her again, unless by some miracle she gets better. I want to remember her the way she was." She finally took a breath. Sharon was rolling a joint listening to her and nodding every now and then.

"God, I need a joint." Elizabeth said wiping her face like that was going to clear the stress off of it.

Sharon started the car, turned on the air-conditioner, handed the joint to Elizabeth, and put the car in reverse. Elizabeth took the joint, lit it and took a huge drag. She held it for at least 20 seconds and then exhaled. "I needed that."

CHAPTER 25

The next couple of days were filled with Newton sitting by Roxie's side saying. "What am I going to do? What am I going to do?" His face lay in his hands and the tears fell to the floor. The handkerchief stayed out at all times for tear wiping. Newton refused to leave Roxie's side. Percy tried to talk his dad into going home, but to no avail.

Roxie was deteriorating day by day. The weekend came, and Percy had Air National Guard duty. He decided to go by and see his mother before he went to Nashville. He just had a gut feeling. He couldn't explain it. He went into the room. Roxie was sitting up in the bed like she hadn't been sick at all.

"Hey, Percy."

"Hey, mother. I see you're feeling better."

"I feel pretty good today."

"You look like you do. I just thought I'd come by and see you before I went to Guard."

"I'm glad you did. You better go on so as you won't be late."

Percy leaned down, kissed his mother on the cheek, and gave her a hug. "I'll see you later on. I'll come back by when I get through with Guard."

Percy left, got in ole blue and headed down Interstate 24. He knew his mother was going to die. She had what the old people used to call "the feel good's" before you die. It's like you know God is taking you home, and he gives you a taste of what it will be like before you leave this earth. It happens right before people die.

Percy pulled his truck into the Tennessee Air National Guard and parked. He went into his office. The phone rang. He was told that his mother had just died by the nurse at Middle Tennessee Medical Center. He wondered what his dad was doing and how he was acting. His mind began to race. He needed to call Ann, Joy, Jan, and Joe. He needed to call Linda. He needed to get back for his dad. What about the funeral?

He sat down, pulled his cigarettes out of his shirt pocket, and lit one. He took a deep drag and exhaled. He decided to make all his phone calls before he left. He would then tell his next in command what had happened. They knew his mother had been ill.

He picked up the phone, dialed his home number and waited for someone to pickup. Linda picked up the other line. "Hello."

"Hey, Linda."

"Yeah, what's wrong, hon ?" She knew it wasn't like him to call her while he was at Guard.

"She's gone. They just called me."

"Oh, hon, I'm so sorry. Is there anything I can do?"

He took another drag off his cigarette, exhaled and put it out. "No, I think we should wait until I get home to tell the kids. I'm leaving as soon as I call the rest of the family."

"I'll be here. Do you think I should go to the center to be with your dad?"

"No, I'll get Ann to go down there. Just stay there until I get home and try not to let the kids hear about it till I get home."

"Alright, hon." Linda answered as she took a seat at the chair at the desk.

"I need to go."

"I'll see you later."

Percy then called his sisters and his brother last. They all decided to meet at the medical center. Ann went over there right away as soon as she hung up the phone. Percy found his commander told him about his mother. Condolences were offered, and Percy left. He tried to drive the speed limit, but it was useless.

Percy arrived at the medical center, parked ole blue, and almost ran into the medical center. Newton and the rest of the family were still in the room that his mother once occupied. A funny feeling ran through his stomach, but he ignored it. He was full of adrenaline. His eyes shot around the room. Newton was hovered in a corner sobbing like a baby. He looked up at Percy and said his famous line. "What am I going to do, Percy?"

Percy didn't know how to answer him. His

mind was racing. All of his sisters were crying, and Joe was standing in a corner looking uncomfortable. Percy went over to Ann. "When did they come and get her?"

Her blue eyes were blood shot from crying. "By the time I got here she was gone. They made dad leave and go to another room, while they took her out. I would have liked to seen her one more time before, you know, before she's in a casket."

"Don't you think we ought to leave? I don't think being here is good for dad."

"Yeah, you're probably right."

Percy was trying to think of a place they could all go. He thought it best to go out to his dad's house. He thought to himself not to do it right now because of his dad, but then again his dad was going to have to go out there sometime, mise well get it over with now. They would all go out there and be a support to his dad.

Percy cleared his throat. "I think we better leave." He looked at Ann for some kind of affirmation.

"Yeah, dad, come on, let's go, we can't do anything here, now." She went over to her dad and took his arm. He shuffled along the floor with her.

They got outside, but not before Percy stopped by to thank the staff for caring for his mother. As soon as he was outside he lit a cigarette and took a deep inhale, and slowly exhaled. "Dad, do you want to ride with me out to your house?"

"I guess."

Ann had taken the time to tell the rest of the family they were going out to their dad's. Joy and

Jan decided to stop and get something to eat at the grocery store. Newton had already lost twenty pounds himself. He was looking thin and frail. The girls worried that Newton wouldn't be far behind their mother.

Percy helped his dad into ole' blue and shut the door. He then got in the truck, started it up, and pulled out of the parking lot. Newton pulled out his handkerchief and rubbed his eyes. "I just can't believe she's gone Percy."

Percy didn't know what to say. He decided not to say anything, but to keep on driving. He knew this was going to be hard on his dad. He didn't think his dad would make it long without his mother, but he had in his mind taking on the role of making sure his dad would be alright until it was his time to go. It was the southern thing to do. His dad and him were never close, but he knew in his mind that his dad had done the best he could. He always made sure he had a roof over his head, clothes to wear, and food to eat, as for affection shown that was out of the question.

Newton blew his nose, which made Percy come back into the present moment. He made a mental note to call Woodfin's Funeral Home when they got out to the house. They had to decide what day to bury his mother on. The rest of the funeral plans were pretty much made.

Percy wheeled into the driveway. He helped his dad out of the truck and followed him through the garage and up the steps. Newton was stumbling from time to time, and Percy had to catch him from falling. Newton sat at his usual spot at the kitchen table, and Percy at his. Newton began crying uncontrollably.

Percy got up to make some coffee to keep himself busy. Newton was just crying and not saying anything. Percy let him cry hoping it would get it out of his system. With the coffee percolating Percy lit a cigarette and smoked it, looking out the kitchen window, while listening to his dad cry for Roxie. Percy felt so powerless.

The girls arrived with lunch meat, bread, mustard, mayonnaise, chips, pickles, cold drinks, cookies, and paper plates. They began emptying the bags of groceries on the kitchen table. Ann began making Newton a sandwich and filled the rest of his plate up with chips. Everyone else began making their own sandwiches. Joe walked in, said he wasn't hungry, but had him a beer in hand. They all ate what they could, which was only about half of what was on their plates. Joy picked up the paper plates and cleared off the kitchen table. It seemed like everyone lit a cigarette about the same time.

Percy cleared his throat and tried to decide how best to begin the subject of the funeral. "Well, what day do you think we should have the service?" He looked around at everyone, hoping for some type of response. Instead he got his dad crying again.

Ann took a long drag, exhaled and spoke. "What about on Tuesday?"

Percy looked around at everyone at the table waiting for someone else to speak up. Finally, Joy nodded in agreement. Newton was still crying and had his handkerchief out by now. Jan and Joe didn't say anything.

"If anyone doesn't object I think Tuesday would be enough time to get the preparations done."

Percy said and then put his cigarette out. "I guess I need to call Woodfin's to see if they have an opening on Tuesday. Ann can you look up the telephone number?"

Ann got up from the table, retrieved the phone book and found the number. "Here's the number Percy."

He took it and went over to the phone that hung on the wall with an extension cord on it that was long enough to walk the whole kitchen. He dialed the number, went back over to his seat and sat down. Buddy Woodfin answered the phone. Percy went to school with him, and Buddy's dad went to school with Roxie and Newton. Woodfin's would get all of the Prater's funeral business.

"Hey, Buddy." Percy said.

"Hey, Percy, what can I do for you?"

"Mama, passed this morning."

"Oh, I'm so sorry to hear that Percy. How's Newton doing?"

"He's holding up." He looked at his dad, who by now had his head buried in his hands hoping this was just a bad dream.

"And you and the rest of your family?"

"We're doing alright for right now." There was a moment of silence then Percy broke it. "I'm calling to see if we can have the funeral at your place on Tuesday."

"Let me get my calendar." There was silence on the phone while Buddy went and got his calendar book. "Look's like Tuesday will be fine, just fine. What time are you thinking about having it?"

"Well, I don't know. What time would you

suggest?"

"I would suggest around lunch time, maybe 11:00 or 12:00. It wouldn't be too early, people could come during their lunch hour, and it would be before it got too scorching hot."

"That sounds reasonable." Percy took the phone away from his mouth, looked at everyone around the table. "Buddy, said 11:00 or 12:00 would be a good time. What time do you all want it?"

Newton raised his head and looked at Percy with tears streaming down his face. "We'll have it at 12:00." He wanted to have some say in the final arrangements.

"We'll have it at noon, Buddy. Can we come by tomorrow say around 2:00 to iron out the details?"

"Sure, I'll mark my book. I'll see you all at 2:00, and once again, I'm so sorry. If there's anything I can do for your family you just let me know? You know we go way back."

"Yeah, I'll see you tomorrow." Percy hung up the phone and went back to his seat at the table, lit a cigarette and took a huge drag.

He looked at Newton. "Dad, we've got to go tomorrow and see Buddy around 2:00, alright."

Newton just nodded his head in the positive. He couldn't talk. It felt like a big lump was in his throat.

"If anyone else wants to come we'll just meet at Woodfin's at 2:00."

No one said anything. It was like they were waiting for Percy for direction. The rest of the family was numb. They couldn't believe there mother was actually gone from this earth. It was slowly sinking in. Percy stayed busy to keep his mind from wandering on the morbid thought about his mother, but he knew she was better off now. At least she wasn't in anymore agonizing pain.

Percy looked at Ann, who looked like she was the most capable of the bunch, to respond. "Do you want to work on the obituary now? Do you think it's a good idea?"

"I guess. Let me see if I can find a piece of paper." She got up and went to the hutch. She began rumbling through the drawer looking for pen and paper. She finally found a couple of pieces of paper and a pen. She went back to her seat. "We'll have it ready for Buddy by tomorrow so he can get it in the paper."

They put the normal information that belonged in an obituary--where she was born, where she worked, who she was survived by and the like. Newton gave his nod of approval. Ann put the paper in her purse. Percy reminded his dad to bring his checkbook when he picked him up in the morning. Joe offered to stay with his dad that night, and Newton took him up on it.

Everyone said their good-byes. Percy got in ole'blue, started her up and pulled out of the driveway. Tears were welling up in his eyes. He had one hand on the wheel and the other he tried to wipe his cheeks, while driving. He had to tell Eliza and Luke. His mind was racing. 'How would they take it? Eliza would take it hard. Luke he didn't know, but he would accept it before Eliza would. The family wouldn't be the same with mother gone. What about Christmas and Thanksgiving? How would his dad hold up? How would he tell the kids?'

Before he knew it he was pulling into his driveway. Eliza's Chevy Impala was in the drive. Linda was home and so was Luke. He took a deep breath. There was no way to avoid this. He got out of the truck and headed towards the house. He opened the back door, walked through the den and into the kitchen. He took his seat at the kitchen table, lit a cigarette, and took a deep drag. Linda was standing in front of the counter waiting on the coffee to finish perking.

She turned around. "Hi, hon, how you doing?"

"I'm fine, is the coffee almost ready?"

"Just about, you look worn out."

"I am. We're going to Woodfin's tomorrow. We're supposed to be there around 2:00. We're going to have the funeral at noon on Tuesday. We wrote the obituary. I just don't know about dad. How he's going to hold up. Where are the kids?"

Linda began pouring the fresh, hot coffee into cups. She drank hers black and filled Percy's with honey and milk. She went over to the table and sat across from Percy. "The kids are upstairs in their rooms. Do you want me to get them for you?"

"No, not just yet, let me sit here for a minute and take it all in before I tell them. How do you think they'll do when I tell them?"

"You know Eliza how sensitive she is. She'll take it hard. Luke probably will too. This is the first real death they have had to accept and deal with." Linda replied and then took a sip of her coffee.

"At least mother's not suffering anymore.

You know she was in a lot of pain. I knew it was going to happen. I went to see her this morning, and she was in one of the best moods I had seen her in a long time. She had the feel-goods. You know how people get before they die. Like a taste of heaven on earth."

Percy and Linda had about fifteen minutes of silence between them. Percy's mind was racing. Linda was just waiting on Percy to talk. When Percy heard the kid's coming down the steps. He took a cigarette out of his shirt pocket and lit it with a match. He looked at Linda. His face looked like it had aged ten years. "We'll here we go."

Eliza was the first to hit the kitchen. She had the munchies. Luke was right behind her. His appetite was due to the growth spurt he had gone through the past year. Eliza took out some sliced ham out of the refrigerator, rolled it up, leaned up against the kitchen counter next to her mom and began to eat it. Luke was rummaging through the refrigerator. He came upon some left over fried chicken in the refrigerator and pulled it out.

Eliza eyed it. "Let me have a piece of that Luke."

Luke took him a piece and then handed the bucket to his sister. Percy waited on them to finish eating, which didn't take too long. Eliza lit her a cigarette and took a drag.

Percy took this as an opportunity to speak up. "I've got something to tell you kids."

"What is it daddy?" Eliza asked, but afraid to at the same time.

"It's about your grandmother."

Eliza's stomach did a flip. Luke began fidgeting.

Percy continued in between taking a drag off the cigarette. "She passed away this morning."

Eliza's eyes began to well up with tears. Her mind began to race. 'The family won't be the same again. No more Christmas dinners, no more Thanksgiving's, no more Easter's, and no more going over to grandmamma's on Sunday's. It wouldn't be the same. The family wouldn't be the same. The person who held it together was gone now. Who was going to hold the family together now?' She wanted to run out of the room.

Luke had many of the same thoughts, but he wasn't going to cry at least not in front of anyone. He had learned that a good southern gentlemen doesn't cry in front of others. His stomach was flipping and flopping.

Percy went on. "We are going to have the funeral on Tuesday at noon. There will be a private viewing an hour before for the immediate family members."

Eliza began fumbling for another cigarette, lit it, and took a drag. Her face was wet from the tears streaming down it. She took a big drag and then exhaled. She felt a tad better, but not much. She was trying to think of something to say, but it was like all the words were stuck in her throat. Nothing would come out.

Eliza yearned to see her grandmother one more time alive, but knew that wasn't going to happen. "Is, is the casket going to be open?"

Percy thought that was an unusual question

considering all funerals had open caskets, except if the person wasn't recognizable. "Yeah, hon, it is."

"I just wanted to see her one more time, you know, before they bury her."

"Oh." Percy said realizing why she had asked the question.

Luke finally spoke up. "At least she's not hurting anymore." It took all he had to say it without breaking down.

"You're right." Linda said. "She's in a better place now."

Eliza was ready to get in her car, roll a joint, smoke it and listen to Jethro Tull. Maybe that would ease her mind. She doubted it, but she was going to give it one hell of a try.

"Listen mama, daddy, I'm going to go ride around for a couple of hours. I'll be back after while." Eliza grabbed her purse and cigarettes and headed out the door, slinging snot from her face. She had to have her pot fix.

Luke went up to his room and was in deep thought. He laid on the bed and the tears started coming. He couldn't stop them. It was a silent cry.

Eliza got in her car and rolled the biggest joint she could manage out in the driveway. She was balling now. It was a gut-wrenching cry. She lit the joint and took a deep inhale, held it for as long as she could and then exhaled. She could feel her nerves calming down. She didn't want to crawl out of her skin as bad. She headed down Barfield-Cresent Road towards Christiana. She was going out to the country. She needed to think.

Percy looked at Linda. "How do you think

that went?"

"Eliza's probably out smoking that marijuana that she doesn't think we know anything about. Luke is probably up in his room crying. Considering, I guess it went as well as could be expected." She poured him another cup of coffee.

Tuesday got here too quick for Eliza. She laid in bed dreading the day ahead. She would have to go to Woodfin's and look at her dead, cold grandmother in a casket and stone-cold sober. No joint to get her through this. She thought she would at least have enough respect not to get high at the funeral, but afterwards would be a different story, besides if she did smoke a joint she would be coughing her head off. People might get suspicious.

Luke was already ready when Eliza passed him in the hallway. Percy was downstairs drinking a cup of coffee with Linda. Percy was ready. He was going to get to the funeral home early. Linda downed her cup of coffee. "I guess I better get upstairs and get ready. I'll meet you there hon."

"Alright," Percy got up and gathered his keys and cigarettes along with his billfold and put them in the appropriate places. Eliza met him in the kitchen went straight to the refrigerator, pulled out the pitcher of iced tea, got a glass and poured her some. She sat down at the table, lit and cigarette, and drank her tea without any ice.

Percy looked down at her. "You going to ride with your mama, right?" This was his way of telling her she was going to ride with her.

"Yeah, I guess, so." Eliza said wondering why she couldn't just meet her mother at the funeral home. "Can't I just meet her there. I won't be late."

"Yeah, yeah, that's fine. I just want you to ride with us in the line to the burial grounds."

"Oh, o.k."

"I'll see you later, hon."

"See ya daddy."

Eliza finished her cigarette and took her tea upstairs with her while she got ready. It took her fifteen minutes to decide what to wear and finally decided on a navy cotton dress, trimmed in white. She would wear her navy stackers. Not too flashy.

She followed her mother and brother out to the funeral home. The closer she got to the funeral home the more her stomach tightened. When they parked their cars Luke opened the door, stood up, and became weak in the knees. He was dreading seeing his grandmother in the casket.

They walked in and signed the book that was sitting on the oak podium. The smell of the funeral home hit Eliza's nostrils. It smelt like preserving death. You know how certain places have certain smells, nursing homes smell like poo-poo, hospitals smell antiseptic, and then there's the dreaded funeral homes. The carpet was plush red, and the furniture was dark and dreary along with the rest of the room which had lighting that made the walls have an eery yellow halo effect to them.

The family was gathered around the casket. Eliza happened to get up front. She didn't know how, and she really didn't want to be there but did at the same time. She looked at her grandmother, who looked so pale and frail in the casket not anything like she did when she was alive. The tears started to flow down her face. She heard Mark behind her crying and a few other sniffles and tears, but couldn't distinguish whose they were. She just knew she wanted to scream at the top of her lungs but couldn't because everyone would think she was crazy. She thought to herself. 'Why do people have to die? It's not fair. Why couldn't someone else have died instead.? Why did she have to get cancer anyway?'

Percy was the first to leave the room. He went outside to smoke a cigarette. The rest of the smokers followed shortly afterwards. No one said anything. They just stood outside in the hot, humid, and sultry day. Perspiration beading up on Percy's face. There wasn't even a breeze to lighten the heavy air. The weight of the air was about as heavy as everyone's heart, mind, and soul. The matriarch was gone. It didn't seem real, but she was inside lying in a coffin.

Percy threw his cigarette in the ashtray, opened the door, and was hit by the cool, refreshing air. He took a look around at all the flowers that had arrived for his mother. He read each card carefully. He remembered people from long ago that he had forgotten about--the Bradley's, the Pope's, the Jenning's and so on. He wondered if they would be at the funeral.

Linda walked up beside Percy. "How you doing, hon?"

"I was just looking at all these flowers. I don't think I've ever seen so many at one place." He looked at the flowers encircling the whole room. It was quite a sight.

People began pouring in offering their

condolences to the family. Newton stayed right beside Roxie. It was like he didn't want to leave her. He didn't want her to leave him either. He cried and one could hear him blowing his nose every so often. It was a pitiful sight.

The family was instructed by Buddy to sit off to the side. The family would be separated by a partition in which the other funeral goers couldn't see the family, but they sure would be about to hear them. Everyone took their places with Kleenex and handkerchiefs in hand.

The reverend began the eulogy. He went on about her being a mother, wife, grandmother, friend, and so on. He talked about her being a rural route carrier for the Postal Service. Most of the family was in full tears by now. Eliza didn't even get past the reverend saying grandmother, neither did Mark. Newton never had stopped crying. Even Percy was getting wet eyed. Joy and Ann were crying hard.

The eulogy was finished and the family was then instructed to get into their cars to go to the grave site. Percy, Linda, Eliza and Luke piled into the Cutlass. Percy and Eliza immediately lit a cigarette and took a big drag. They both needed it. Eliza was dreading when they put their grandmother in the ground. She would be gone. A part of her life would be gone. Her whole being ached all over.

The ride was maybe a quarter of a mile. The immediate family sat under the tent that was set up. The casket was brought to the hole that was dug. The preacher said a few more short words and then the casket was lowered into the ground. It was a pitiful site. Tears and snot were slinging everywhere.

Newton was crying uncontrollably as well as three quarters of the family. The pall was set aside to put on top of the dirt. It was full of yellow roses-- Roxie's favorite. All of the grandchildren removed a rose. Eliza swore to herself she would keep her rose until she died.

Food was waiting out at Newton's house. After the funeral everyone went out there. It was somber and not much food was eaten. Newton was overtaken by so much grief he couldn't eat. He just wanted to die to be with Roxie. He didn't know what to do with himself. He kept walking around the house muttering to himself. "I just want to die. I want to be with Roxie. I don't know what I'm going to do Percy. I don't know what I'm going to do Joe."

Whoever would listen Newton would say the same thing over and over. Percy was worried about leaving his dad at home alone that night. "Dad, why don't you come over and stay with us tonight?"

"No. I want to be here." He said in an almost adamant tone. The fact was he wanted to be close to Roxie. Her presence was still in the house.

Around six everyone began leaving the house. Percy was the last to leave. "Now, dad, if you need us just call me. I'll be right over. You know the number right?"

"Yeah, I know the number." Newton wanted to be left alone, but then again he didn't want to be left alone. Exhaustion was overcoming him.

Percy finally left the house. The day was still hot and humid. He started ole' blue up and drove around the field to check the cows. He figured he give his dad a few minutes of alone time but also the opportunity to give him a yell in the field if he needed him.

Newton closed the door. He walked around the house like he was looking for Roxie, but she was no where to be found. He went to each room. The memories of her flooding his brain like a wave crashing ashore. He went into the living room and sat down by the window next to the piano. He remembered when she had the thing moved into the house. He cried. "I sure miss you Roxie."

He got up and went into the den and turned the television on so there would be noise in the house. Maybe it would drown out his thoughts. He looked into the bedroom hoping to see Roxie in the bed. She wasn't there. The tears wouldn't stop. He didn't know if he would be able to sleep in there or not. He decided to go into the kitchen maybe that would change his feelings.

He sat at the kitchen table in his usual spot. He saw Roxie sitting next to him. He remembered her. He already missed her tremendously. He wanted to feel her, to touch her, to hear her laugh, to taste her good cooking, to have her back in his life. He wanted the house filled like it used to be with kids and Roxie. He was alone at the kitchen table, but not for long.

ABOUT THE AUTHOR

Elizabeth C. Jenkins has a degree in Journalism and is certified teach History. She has published a trade article and several news releases. This is her first novel.

www.ingramcontent.com/pod-product-compliance
Lightning Source LLC
Chambersburg PA
CBHW061631040426
42446CB00010B/1360